OECD Studies on SMEs and Entrepreneurship

Understanding Firm Growth

HELPING SMES SCALE UP

OECD
BETTER POLICIES FOR BETTER LIVES

Please cite this publication as:
OECD (2021), *Understanding Firm Growth: Helping SMEs Scale Up*, OECD Studies on SMEs and Entrepreneurship, OECD Publishing, Paris, *https://doi.org/10.1787/fc60b04c-en*.

ISBN 978-92-64-93345-3 (print)
ISBN 978-92-64-37479-9 (pdf)
ISBN 978-92-64-45379-1 (HTML)
ISBN 978-92-64-57876-0 (epub)

OECD Studies on SMEs and Entrepreneurship
ISSN 2078-0982 (print)
ISSN 2078-0990 (online)

Photo credits: Cover ©Getty images / merovingian

Corrigenda to publications may be found on line at: *www.oecd.org/about/publishing/corrigenda.htm*.

Foreword

Few small and medium-sized enterprises (SMEs) scale up but these few firms are the major driver of new jobs added to OECD economies. In the aftermath of the global COVID-19 crisis, scalers can play a key role in getting growth back on track. In contrast to the 2007-08 global crisis, the potential of scalers seems to be strong as countries rolled out unprecedented policy responses to support viable firms facing extraordinary – but temporary – challenges. However, firms, and particularly SMEs that aim to scale up, still face barriers in unleashing their growth potential such as finding workers with the right skills, making the most of new digital tools or integrating into global value chains.

A better understanding of the characteristics of scalers and of the transformation process that they undertake is essential for effective policy design to address growth barriers. This report highlights the wide and varied range of firms with scaling-up potential, pointing towards the need for equally varied policy support. Often, policy packages target only a small share of potential scalers, such as recent start-ups, firms in high-technology sectors or prospective (ever-elusive) unicorns, i.e. privately held companies with a capital-based valuation of USD 1 billion or more. But there are opportunities to unlock growth and job creation in many other types of firms. With the right policy mix in place, scalers can play a key role in transforming new opportunities into jobs and economic growth. However, without detailed knowledge of the characteristics of scalers, policy makers might target their efforts at only a fraction of firms with scaling-up potential or support them with the wrong tools.

This report provides new evidence on scalers based on analysis of detailed firm-level data from a pilot project implemented in Finland, Italy, Portugal, the Slovak Republic and Spain. The project serves as proof of concept of the value of opening up the wealth of data locked in the vaults of OECD member countries. Different authorities in the five pilot countries agreed to work with the OECD to facilitate access to their confidential microdata sources. In-depth analysis is possible as national statistical offices and other authorities in the participating countries have made significant efforts to link a wide range of data sources that allow for a much better understanding of the firms that are or will become scalers. A harmonised approach in defining scalers, analysing their performance and exploring their characteristics allows for direct comparison of the results between the five countries.

Being a pilot project, the report illustrates the powerful potential of leveraging on microdata, and, in turn, what is possible in many (if not all) OECD member countries by better capitalising on existing data within countries. In that sense, through the provision of powerful new policy messages and indicators - without increasing response burdens and without breaching confidentiality - the project is also intended to provide motivation and momentum for other countries to engage with the OECD in developing similar analyses for their country, and to better exploit the rich, and often untapped, potential of their microdata.

This report builds on work carried out by the OECD Committee on SMEs and Entrepreneurship (CSMEE) in the pilot project "Unleashing SME potential to scale up: Framework and proof of concept for new evidence and policies for SME growth" with further results on support policies published in a separate report. The work was carried out between 2019 and 2021 and this report was approved by the CSMEE by written procedure on 9 November 2021 [CFE/SME(2021)26].

Acknowledgements

This report was produced by the OECD Centre for Entrepreneurship, SMEs, Regions and Cities (CFE) led by Lamia Kamal-Chaoui, Director. It is part of the Programme of Work of the OECD's Committee on SMEs and Entrepreneurship (CSMEE).

The report summarises the findings of the first part of an OECD project on "Unleashing SME potential to scale up", co-funded by the European Commission (EC). It provides new evidence on scalers based on a novel analysis of detailed firm-level data in a pilot implemented in Finland, Italy, Portugal, the Slovak Republic and Spain. A forthcoming report complements the analytical work by mapping selected policy initiatives relevant for scalers across OECD countries.

The OECD Secretariat would like to thank Ludger Odenthal, Markus Hell and Borut Ložar of the EC Directorate-General for Internal Market, Industry, Entrepreneurship and SMEs (DG GROW) for their input and support throughout the project. The analysis in this report would not have been possible without the help of national experts (Pontus Lindroos, Statistics Finland; Antonio Accetturo and Andrea Linarello, Bank of Italy; Vladimir Peciar, Ministry of Finance, Slovak Republic; Aitor Lacuesta and Eduardo Gutierrez, Bank of Spain) to whom the OECD Secretariat extends its thanks for providing advice and data on scale-up dynamics in their country. Advice and comments at different stages of the project were also received from delegates of the CSMEE, Participants of the European Commission's Working Group on Policy-relevant Research on Entrepreneurship and SME and the European Union SME Envoys, Alex Coad (Waseda University), Mercedes Teruel (Universitat Rovira i Virgili), as well as from OECD (and former OECD) colleagues, in particular Nadim Ahmad, Mattia Corbetta, Lucia Cusmano, Andres Fuentes Hutfilter, Shayne Maclachlan, Bruno de Menna, Joaquim Oliveira Martins, Andrew Paterson, Lora Pissareva, Alessandra Proto, Paolo Veneri and Alison Weingarden.

The project was co-ordinated by Alexander C. Lembcke and Sandrine Kergroach, Heads of Unit in CFE, under the supervision of Rudiger Ahrend, Head of Division, Economic Analysis, Data and Statistics, and Celine Kauffman, Head of Division, Entrepreneurship, SMEs and Tourism in CFE. The report was prepared by Carlo Menon and Lenka Wildnerova with significant inputs by Julian Emmler, Hoang Thanh (Mai) Nguyen and Maria Reis.

Thanks are also due to Pilar Philip for editorial support and Eleonore Morena for formatting the manuscript.

Table of contents

Tables

Figures

Boxes

Executive summary

Scalers are firms that undergo a period of high growth in employment or turnover by transforming the way they operate. OECD countries routinely collect and disseminate information on high-growth firms but little is known about the factors that support high growth, the transformations that accompany high growth, and the ability of firms to sustain their new scale. One key challenge is that aggregate data, even when broken down by sector and size, struggles to capture the full diversity of scalers and in particular the factors driving or acting as barriers to their transformation and success. This report shows how to achieve substantial progress in filling knowledge gaps by leveraging on confidential firm-level microdata that combines firms' balance sheets with information on imports and exports and detailed information on workers. By using microdata, it is possible to respond to a range of questions that cannot be answered by aggregate data currently disseminated by national statistical offices.

Scalers make an important contribution to job creation and economic growth. In the 5 pilot countries, Finland, Italy, Portugal, the Slovak Republic and Spain, 13%-15% of SMEs with 10 to 249 employees (non-micro SMEs) scale up (measured on an employment basis, i.e. growing at an annual average rate of 10% or more over 3 years). Between 2015 and 2017, these scalers accounted for 47% to 69% of all jobs added by non-micro SMEs. The fastest growing scalers with annual average employment growth of 20% over 3 years make a particulary important contribution. They account for about one-third of all scalers but over half of the jobs created by scalers. In Portugal, for example, over the 2015-17 period around 2 000 of these high-growth scalers created 78 000 jobs.

Firms from all types of places can scale up. Across large (TL2) regions, the share of scalers in employment in all non-micro SMEs ranges from 10% to 17% in Italy; 8% to 13% in Spain, 8% to 14% in Portugal, and 14% to 17% in the Slovak Republic. Importantly, scalers are not limited to the most economically developed parts of a country. Regions such as Andalucia and Murcia in Spain or Apulia and Campania in Italy, with per capita gross domestic product (GDP) below the national average, are also among the regions with the highest shares of scalers.

Young and knowledge-intensive SMEs are more likely to scale up, but the typical scaler is a mature SME in less-knowledge-intensive or low-tech sectors. Young firms, less than 6 years old, are about 2-3 times more likely to scale up than older firms. Firms in knowledge-intensive sectors are 70% more likely to scale up in employment and 20% more likely to scale up in turnover than firms in the low- and medium-low tech manufacturing sector, the sector with the lowest share of scalers. However, only one-fifth of non-micro SMEs is young, and only around 15% of non-micro SMEs operate in knowledge-intensive services.

About 60% of employment scalers continue to grow or maintain their new scale in the 3 years following their initial scaling up. Whilst there is some variability across sectors, even in construction, with the lowest shares, around 50% of scalers continue to operate at their new scale or grow further. Some employment scalers in the 5 pilot countries even enter a second high-growth phase – varying from 11% (Spain) to 29% (Portugal) for young firms and from 10% (Spain) to 20% (Portugal) in older firms. Whilst other firms will shrink or exit the market, related job losses are more than compensated by those that continue to grow, i.e. support provided to scalers continues to "pay off" even after the scale-up phase.

Turnover scalers are less likely to scale up again in turnover but many do subsequently scale up in employment. Scaling up in turnover often anticipates scaling up in employment: between 14% (Spain) and 33% (Portugal) of turnover scalers become employment scalers in the following 3-year period. The opposite dynamics – from scalers in employment to scalers in turnover – is however less frequent. Even when firms do not enter a second high-growth period, there are other changes that transform the way the firm operates that accompany scaling up. Some of these changes relate to investments in innovation, physical or human capital undertaken in anticipation of scaling up, others to transformations that continue after the high-growth period.

Scaling up appears to be a strategic choice, as scalers' transformation begins before their high-growth phase materialises. The transformation is not confined to the years in which scaling up takes place. For many dynamic factors, such as labour productivity, integration in foreign markets or access to credit, scalers differ from their non-scaling peers in the 2 years that precede their high-growth phase. For instance, employment scalers in Finland, Italy, Portugal and Spain are 5-15% more productive than their peers before scaling up. Scalers also appear to prepare their expansion through different investments, e.g. by increasing the share of their workforce dedicated to research and development (R&D) by 15% to 40% compared to their peers. The investment focus is also evident on the financial side as scalers have higher ratios of debt than their peers. Overall, the evidence points to scaling up being predominantly driven by a firm's strategic investment in disruptive innovations in the way the firm operates or in the products and services that it sells.

1 The knowledge gap on scalers

This chapter summarises findings from various strands of academic and policy literature on scalers and highlights important knowledge gaps that may limit effective policy design. As the recovery from the COVID-19 crisis opens a window for scalers to transform new market opportunities into jobs and economic value, an open question remains on how the different responses to the current crisis will affect future scaling-up dynamics.

In Brief

Fast-growing small- and medium-sized enterprises (SMEs) – "scalers" – play a crucial role in job creation and economic growth but little is known about them

A small number of "scalers" create the majority of new jobs. Evidence from Scandinavian and other OECD countries, such as the United Kingdom (UK), shows that only about 5% of high-growth non-micro SMEs contribute more than half of new jobs created in the economy by those firms. Newly created and slow-growing firms contribute the remainder of new jobs. The majority of SMEs, however, do not grow at all over the course of a year. Understanding what makes some firms scale up and how this process can be supported can therefore make an outsized contribution to overall job creation.

What makes a scaler is less well understood than general determinants of firm growth. Research has shown that firm growth depends on a variety of factors, some of them are internal to the firm, e.g. disruptive innovation. Others are external to the firm, e.g. market regulation. Much less is known about scaling up, defined here as rapid growth in employment or turnover within a short period of time. One area where research sheds light is the role of the entrepreneur in scaling up. The ambition to grow and the motivation to be an entrepreneur play an important role but remain hard to assess for policy and research purposes alike. A second known factor is that the growth potential of a firm is uncertain even for the entrepreneur or management themselves until the firm enters a market or introduces a product or service. For young firms in particular, this implies a bifurcation of trajectories: some will (rapidly) grow as the firm finds its niche while others will turn out to be less viable than anticipated and cease operating.

The currently available evidence on scalers raises more questions than it provides answers for policy making (Figure 1.1). There is a limited number of findings on which available evidence is unanimous. Beyond the "average" scaler – i.e. a mature firm operating in less knowledge-intensive services that experiences fast growth only once in its lifetime – there are a variety of other models, e.g. the stereotype of young start-ups in high-technology (high-tech) manufacturing or information and communication technology (ICT) that grow repeatedly over time exists as well. However, as there are fewer young firms than mature firms, the counterintuitive result is that there are fewer young scalers than mature ones but the likelihood of a young firm scaling up is higher than it is for a mature firm. There is also some variation in the incidence of scaling up across countries, which points to a potentially important role for national policies; however, there is little evidence available on "what works".

A lack of substantiated knowledge limits effective policy design and responses. Policies require data and tools to identify and understand the needs of different types of SMEs and entrepreneurs. Available statistics and country-specific studies provide only limited information about scalers. Policy makers may look for scalers in the wrong place and support them with the wrong tools, based on assumptions on their characteristics – e.g. that they are young, high-tech firms operating in the manufacturing sector – that do not correspond to reality.

The COVID-19 pandemic and associated policy response are unprecedented, alleviating concerns about future scalers. Firm entry and exit dynamics in 2020 differ from those of previous recessions. Entry rates of new firms increased or declined only slightly, while bankruptcies in many OECD countries were fewer than in pre-crisis times. The rapid introduction of public financial support played a key role as the contrast with the prior global financial crisis shows. Following the 2007-08 crisis, the number of firms that were in a high-growth phase between 2008 and 2011 dropped by up to 65% compared with the number of scalers in the preceding 3-year period (2005-08) in the 7 OECD countries with available data. Even in 2013, the number of firms that had scaled over the 2010-13 period was still below pre-crisis levels in most countries. This is partially attributable to the exit of high-potential but credit-constrained businesses and to fewer new businesses entering the market.

The crisis opened opportunities for scaling up that can be leveraged during recovery. The enhanced uptake of digital tools by firms and households opens new markets and creates room for new products and services, as well as cost-saving measures. The diffusion of e-commerce has improved access to viable markets without the need for large investments in marketing and distribution. Demand for online services and goods during the crisis opened up opportunities for existing firms and new entrepreneurs. Cheaper access to shared information technology (IT) resources in the "cloud" and the potential of continued homeworking promise productivity gains or cost savings (e.g. as less office space is required). There are clear opportunities for scaling up created by the crisis but whether they will materialise and translate into jobs and economic growth will also depend on how extraordinary support is wound down and how SMEs will be supported during the recovery. Lack of skills or adequate digital infrastructure may represent binding constraints that are more difficult to tackle than access to financial resources.

The crisis makes it urgent to address the divide between SMEs that can benefit from digitalisation and those that lag behind. The health crisis exposed a divide across SMEs in their ability to use digital technologies such as remote working, online sales and remote communications with suppliers and customers. Such a divide exists also for other digital technologies – such as the Internet of Things, cloud computing and data analytics – that are revolutionising firms' potential capacity for simulation, prototyping, decision making and automation. These digital technologies are creating unprecedented opportunities for SMEs (OECD, 2021[1]). However, a significant share of SMEs lag in the adoption of digital tools and employing IT specialists that could help implement the digital transition. Cross-firm divides were already growing before the crisis (OECD, 2021[2]). For example, 28% of firms in France with 20-49 employees used cloud storage services in 2018, compared to 70% of firms with 250 to 499 employees (Nevoux et al., 2019[3]). It is still unclear whether the divide has widened or narrowed during the crisis but the new digital impetus has certainly further weakened the position of SMEs lagging behind.

Figure 1.1. What is known about scalers?

The share of scalers differs across countries and sectors

- National policies play a role in explaining cross-country differences.
- The typical scaler is not a high-tech firm.

Young firms are more likely to scale up but the majority of scalers are mature businesses

- The share of scalers is highest among young firms (less than five years old) but young firms represent a small share of all firms; therefore, most scalers are not young.

For many scalers, high growth is an isolated episode in their lifetime

- Consecutive high-growth phases are rare.
- Scalers may scale up again later during their lifetime.

Scalers are not necessarily small

- Firms of different sizes have similar propensity to scale in most countries.

High-growth firms attract a lot of policy attention but there is little evidence of "what works"

- There is little available evidence to help policy makers design more effective policies.

Scalers are important because they drive aggregate growth

A small share of high-growth firms plays an outsized role in job creation. SMEs are a very large and diverse group of firms. They account for more than 99% of all firms in the business sector and for over half of all employment and value-added in most OECD economies (Box 1.1). They also play an important role for growth with remarkably consistent facts that are evident across OECD countries: i) most SMEs have stable employment over time; and ii) among the small share of companies that grow, a few grow very fast and they account for most new jobs in the economy.[1] These firms are known as "high-growth firms" or "scalers". There is a range of similar definitions for these concepts. The most common definition of scalers includes companies that grow in employment or turnover at an average rate of 10% or 20% per year over a 3-year period (Box 1.2). In the following of the chapter, "scalers" are firms that meet the 10% yearly growth requirement, while firms that grow at 20% or more per annum over a triennium are defined as high-growth firms or high-growth scalers. However, the next chapters of the report provide new evidence that points to scaling up being more than "just" a period of rapid growth. Rather, it is the expression of a transformative process that a firm undergoes, which includes aspects such as changes in the managerial structure or a firm's engagement in new activities, e.g. research or export.

Previous research found that around 5% of high-growth firms account for at least 50% of all "net jobs" (i.e. the difference between the jobs created by expanding business and the jobs destroyed by contracting businesses). For example, in the UK, high-growth firms (about 6% of the total number of firms based on the 20% growth threshold) generated 54% of net jobs between 2005 and 2008 within the group of firms with 10 and more employees (NESTA, 2009[4]). Nordic countries and Canada have similar shares of net jobs generated by high-growth firms (Box 1.3). Between 2003 and 2006, Finland's 5% share of high-growth firms generated 89% of the total number of net jobs (Deschryvere, 2008[5]). Canada had 1.24% of high-growth firms in all firms (including micro firms with less than 10 employees) between 2009 and 2013, which accounted for 63% of total net employment growth (Rivard, 2020[6]). Analyses for emerging or developing countries also reach similar findings (Grover Goswami, Medvedev and Olafsen, 2019[7]). The concentration of growth in few firms is similarly high if it is measured in turnover (or sales) rather than in employment (Box 1.4).

The economic literature provides only a partial explanation of why growth is strongly concentrated in a few firms. An area that attracted attention is the motivations and objectives of the entrepreneurs. In contrast with well-known examples of dynamic and ambitious entrepreneurs, representative survey data show that most business owners report having no desire to grow big and no desire to innovate along observable dimensions. For example, for over 50% of new businesses founded in the US, the owners reported that non-pecuniary benefits such as "wanting flexibility over schedule" or "to be your own boss" were the primary reason why they started their business (Hurst and Pugsley, 2012[8]). Recent results from a survey in the 27 countries of the European Union (EU) are broadly aligned: 51% of companies do not plan to grow over the following 3 years and only 6% of them plan to grow more than 20% per year (EC/Kantar, 2020[9]).

Uncertainty about future growth matters for scaling up. Differences in ambitions and motivations are only a part of the story: even growth-oriented firms led by ambitious entrepreneurs show a wide difference in growth between the top and bottom performers. Another reason is the uncertainty that entrants face about their profitability and the learning and selection that follows (Jovanovic, 1982[10]). Uncertainty implies that firms enter small, as entrepreneurs are unsure whether their business idea will prove successful in the market. Those that learn that they are highly productive grow rapidly, as they need to reach the minimum efficient scale. Conversely, those that learn that they are an unsuccessful contract and potentially exit. Across OECD countries, only 3% of new firms entering the market with less than 10 employees have more than 10 employees after 5 years (Calvino, Criscuolo and Menon, 2018[11]).

Box 1.1. SMEs represent a diverse group of firms across OECD countries

SMEs represent almost the entire population of firms in most of the OECD countries, which implies a large heterogeneity under one label. Statistics can help identify some factors of heterogeneity across countries and sectors. One of these is the large variation in the shares of SMEs of different size classes across OECD countries (Figure 1.2, upper chart). SMEs are on average around twice as big in Germany, Japan, New Zealand and the United States (US) as in the majority of the other European countries; these differences still hold when the country sectoral composition is taken into account. Cross-country differences in the share of value-added accounted for by SMEs of different sizes are even more sizeable, with micro SMEs with less than 10 employees accounting for 27% of value-added by all firms in e.g. Estonia and Italy, compared to 8% in the US and 15% in Germany (Figure 1.2, lower chart). Even within Europe, there are important differences: for example, the share of employment in the size class 0-9 employees is twice as large in Italy and Portugal than in Denmark or Germany (OECD, 2019[12]). Across sectors and within countries, SME employment is heavily concentrated in construction and specific service sectors, notably accommodation and food, real estate and advertising, and in a few manufacturing sectors like textiles and apparel, wood, paper and printing, and furniture manufacturing (Figure 1.3).

Figure 1.2. The relative weight of SMEs of different sizes varies across OECD countries

Share in total employment and value added by size class

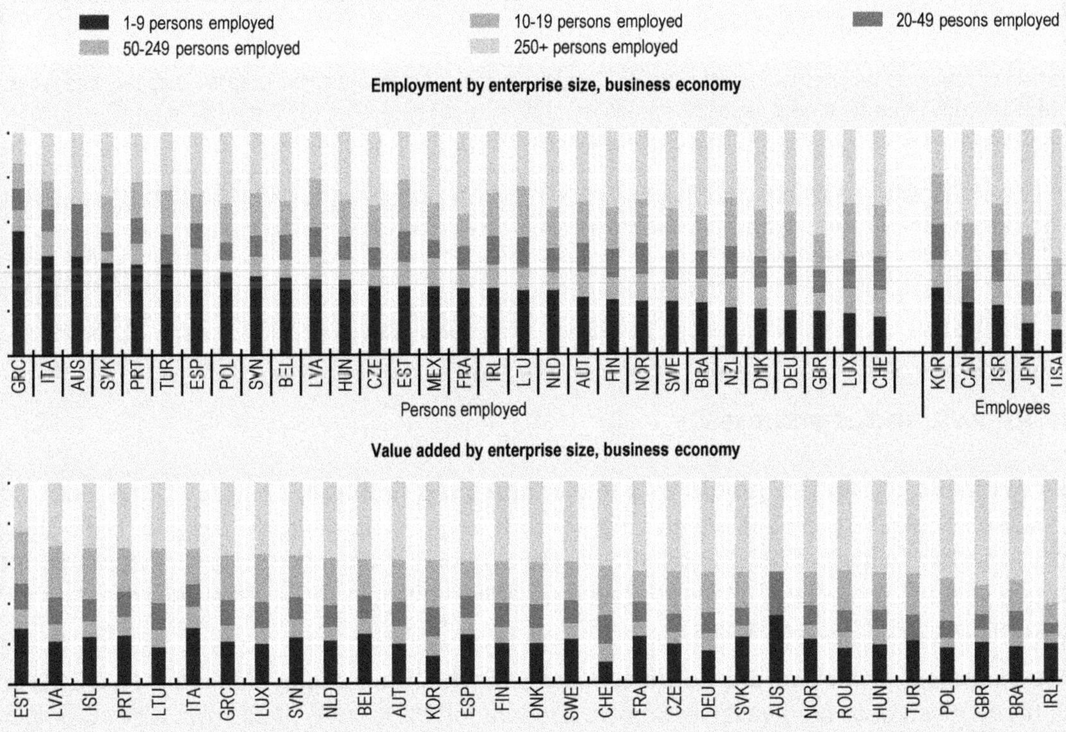

Note: Size classes are based on the number of persons employed. Data cover business economy excluding financial intermediation. Data refer to value-added at factor costs in European countries and value-added at basic prices for other countries, except the Russian Federation and the US, for which data refer to turnover.
Source: OECD (2018[13]), *Entrepreneurship at a Glance 2018 - Highlights*, https://www.oecd.org/sdd/business-stats/EAG-2018-Highlights.pdf.

Within countries and sectors, large productivity differences exist between SMEs of different sizes, with productivity typically growing with the size of the firm, especially in the manufacturing sector. Age is another important dimension of heterogeneity, with younger SMEs being more likely to grow but also to exit the market (Criscuolo, Gal and Menon, 2014[14]).

Figure 1.3. Share of SME employment differs across sectors

The average share of employment in SMEs by sector across 31 OECD countries, 2018

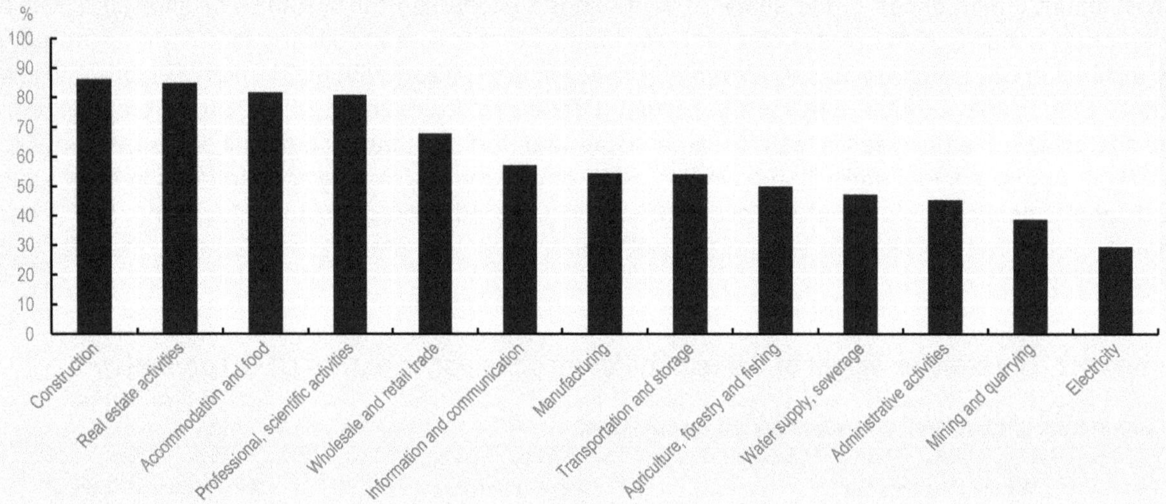

Note: The data by sector are weighted averages for 31 OECD countries. The unit of measurement used is enterprises and in case of lack thereof establishments. SMEs are defined as companies with less than 250 employees.
Source: OECD.stats (2021[15]), *Structural and Demographic Business Statistics (SDBS)*, OECD, Paris.

Source (box): OECD (2019[12]), *OECD SME and Entrepreneurship Outlook 2019*, https://dx.doi.org/10.1787/34907e9c-en; Criscuolo, C., P. Gal and C. Menon (2014[14]), "The Dynamics of Employment Growth: New Evidence from 18 Countries", https://dx.doi.org/10.1787/5jz417hj6hg6-en.

What is known about scalers?

Available evidence on scalers points to a few established findings. The OECD has been collecting country and sector statistics on scalers and high-growth firms for more than a decade. High-growth firms have also been the subject of several country-specific studies.[2] The comparison of available indicators across countries and the review of academic research allow defining a set of "established facts" that appear to hold consistently in different contexts.

The share of scalers differs across countries and over the business cycle. In the 15 OECD countries for which harmonised data are available, scalers account for 7% to 14% of all firms with 10 employees or more in 2017. Individual countries such as Denmark and the Netherlands show more within-country variation across sectors than Korea and Spain for example (in Figure 1.4, Panel A, the size of the box is proportional to the within-country variation). There is also large variation within countries with the business cycle. For example, between 2011 and 2018, the share of scalers ranges from 6% to 11% in Italy, from 9% to 16% in the Netherlands, and from 7% to 16% in Spain.[3] Cross-country empirical analyses also document a substantial variation across countries in firms' growth dispersion. Countries with faster productivity growth show a larger share of both fast-growing and fast-contracting firms. Countries with slower productivity growth have a higher share of zero-growth firms (Bravo-Biosca, 2010[16]). National policies and framework conditions, such as the functioning of the financial system and employment regulations, explain part of the differences in the distribution of employment growth across countries (Bravo-Biosca, Criscuolo and Menon, 2016[17]).

Box 1.2. Identifying scalers: The Eurostat-OECD definition of high-growth enterprises

The definition of scaling up adopted in this report is based on previous work on high-growth firms. The *Eurostat-OECD Manual on Business Demography Statistics* recommended the following definition of high-growth enterprises: "All enterprises with average annualised growth greater than 20% per annum, over a three-year period, and with ten or more employees at the beginning of the observation period. Growth is thus measured by the number of employees and by turnover" (2007, p. 61[18]). The definition has been widely adopted in the economic and business literature; one of its advantages, therefore, is its comparability.

The 20% threshold was set considering previous research from individual countries (Ahmad, 2008[19]). Further work by Eurostat focused on medium-growth firms, which include firms growing at an annualised growth rate of at least 10% for 3 consecutive years. The manual proposes a cut-off for firm size at the beginning of the high-growth period of 10 employees for both the turnover and employment measures of high-growth.[4] It does not define a minimum turnover cut-off to maintain consistency across countries.

High growth is calculated as follows:

$$\sqrt[3]{\frac{var_{t+3}}{var_t}} - 1 > 0.2$$

where var_t refers to employment or turnover at the beginning of the period and the subscript $t+3$ denotes values at the end of the three-year period. The 20% average yearly growth is equivalent to 72.8% growth if the growth is calculated between the starting period and end period. The 10% annual growth rate results in 33.1% growth over 3 years. In the report, "scalers" are firms that meet the 10% threshold, while firms that meet the 20% threshold are defined as "high-growth firms" or "high-growth scalers".

Source: OECD/Eurostat (2007[18]), *OECD-Eurostat Manual on Business Demography Statistics*, https://www.oecd.org/sdd/39974460.pdf (accessed on 5 August 2019); Ahmad, N. (2008[19]), "A proposed framework for business demography statistics", http://dx.doi.org/10.1007/978-0-387-72288-7_7.

The share of scalers is higher in the service sector than in manufacturing. Across OECD countries, the incidence of scalers is higher in knowledge-intensive services, notably in information and communications, and financial and insurance activities. Instead, high-growth firms are not more common in technology-intensive manufacturing sectors, which means that the typical scaler is not a high-tech firm (Coad et al., 2014[20]). Such sectoral pattern tends to replicate across all countries in the sample, as there are small differences across countries in the ranking of sectors by the share of scalers (Figure 1.4, Panel B).

For many firms, high-growth spurts are isolated episodes in their lifetime. Research for Portugal, Sweden and the UK shows that repeated high-growth phases are rare.[5] However, scalers may scale up again later during their lifetime. Evidence from a cohort of young scalers born in 1998 in the UK shows that, on average, they scale twice over a 15-year period (Anyadike-Danes and Hart, 2019[21]). This finding highlights the importance of mapping the transformation process that scalers undertake before, during and after the high-growth period, to isolate the activities and dynamic factors that are associated with high-growth (e.g. exporting or innovation). The analysis of the different transformation processes that prepare and accompany scaling is the subject of the analysis presented in Chapter 4 of the report. The fact that high growth comes from a wide group of firms during an exceptional phase of their lifetime rather than by a small group of exceptional firms that is constantly growing fast is overlooked in the policy debate, as available statistics and most studies do not track scalers over time.

Figure 1.4. The share of scalers differs considerably across both countries and sectors

Share of employment scalers in all non-micro SMEs in 2017

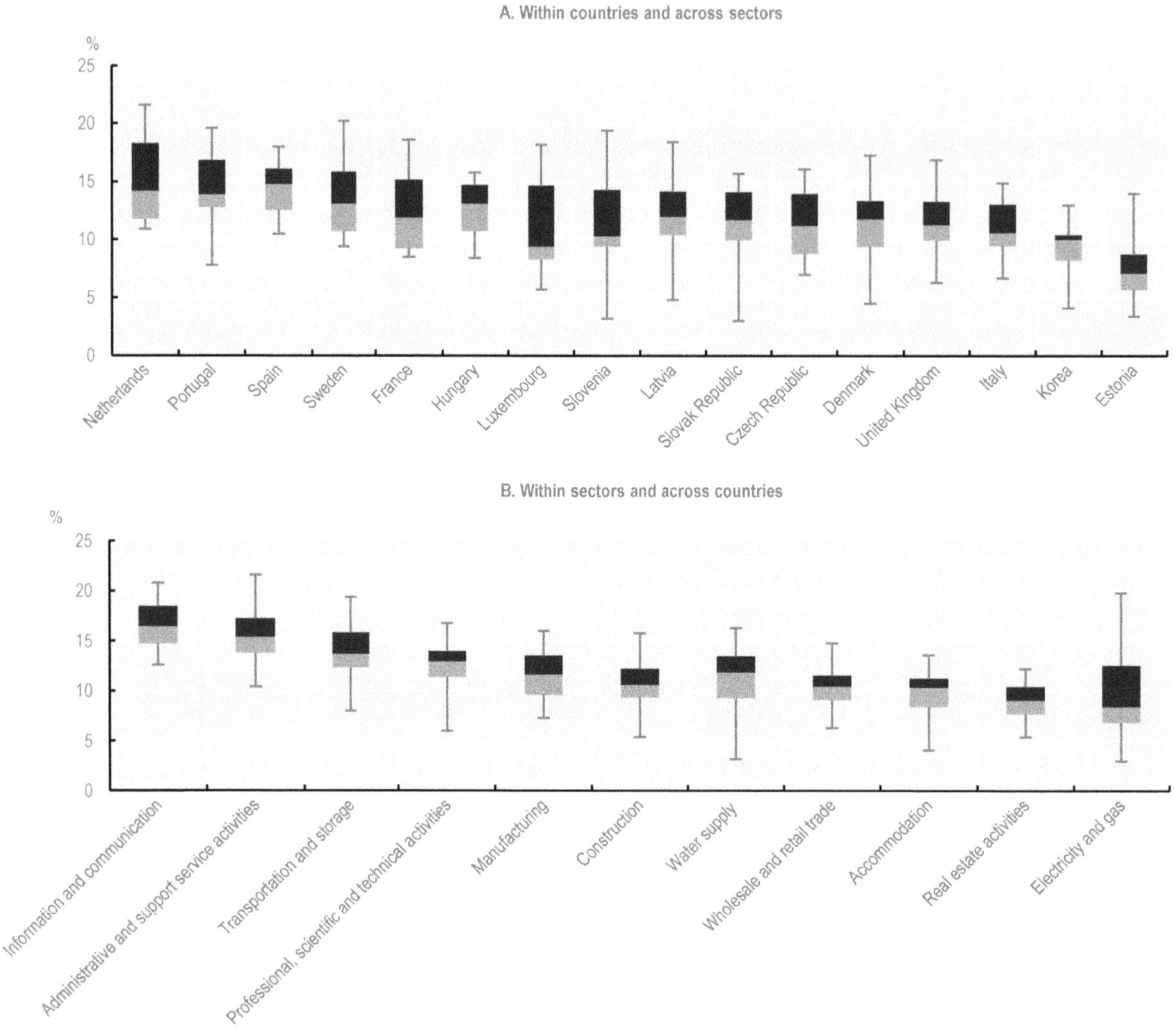

Note: Scalers are firms that grow in employment at an average rate of 10% or more a year over a 3-year period (see Box 1.2). Panel A displays the variation in shares of high-growth firms across sectors within each of the 16 countries. Panel B displays the variation in shares of high-growth firms across countries within each of the 11 sectors (NACE 2.1, 1-digit). The boxes represent the values of high-growth shares from first to third quantiles. The line inside the box represents the median value. The whiskers mark the minimum and maximum values.
Source: OECD.stats (2021[15]), *Structural and Demographic Business Statistics (SDBS)*, OECD, Paris.

Young firms are more likely to scale but most scalers are mature businesses. Most studies agree that young firms have more chance of growing faster than mature or old firms. The empirical evidence of the disproportionate contribution to employment growth of young, small firms is extensive and covers both OECD (Criscuolo, Gal and Menon, 2014[22]; Haltiwanger et al., 2017[23]) and emerging countries (Grover Goswami, Medvedev and Olafsen, 2019[7]). However, assuming that young age coincides with high growth is misleading. Start-ups are characterised by higher variability in growth performance and a lower survival rate ("up-or-out dynamics"), so the larger share of high-growth firms is counterbalanced by a larger number of shrinking or exiting businesses. Evidence from OECD countries shows that over the first five years of activity, most start-ups either stay small or exit the market (Calvino, Criscuolo and Menon, 2018[11]).

Innovative start-ups backed by venture capital (VC) investments and "unicorns" play an important role in aggregate growth but they account for a tiny share of all scalers. VC financing is key for economic growth in OECD countries. For example, recent evidence for the US shows that the absence of VC funding would lower aggregate growth by 28% (Akcigit et al., 2019[24]) and employment generated by VC-backed firms represents around 10% of employment in the late 1990s and early 2000s (Puri and Zarutskie, 2012[25]). However, only a tiny share of firms are VC-backed. For instance, in the US, where VC markets are relatively well developed, only 0.31% of new start-ups are backed by VC (Gornall and Strebulaev, 2021[26]). In most OECD countries VC is below 0.05% of gross domestic product (GDP) (OECD, 2018[13]). The so-called "unicorns", i.e. companies backed by VC that reach a capitalisation of more than USD 1 billion, are only a few hundred globally. This implies that the large majority of scalers – even the younger ones – are not relying on VC to support growth.

Box 1.3. Scalers in the Nordics

A 2019 study on high-growth scalers in the Nordic countries (Denmark, Finland, Iceland, Norway, Sweden) provides evidence to improve the ecosystem for scale-ups across the region. Nordic Innovation – an institution that promotes cross-border trade and innovation between Nordic countries – analysed the characteristics of scalers in those countries for the period 2013-16. The analysis defines high-growth scalers as firms that grow at 20% or more per annum over 3 consecutive years in both employment and turnover, and have an annual turnover of at least EUR 2 million and at least 10 full-time equivalent employees at the beginning of the 3-year growth period.

The findings point to the disproportionate role of scalers in job creation. The analysis focuses on scalers in knowledge-intensive sectors, where most scalers are active, manufacturing and firms in construction and other services. Key findings are that scalers account for a disproportionally large share of employment (5.2%) compared to their number (0.19% of all enterprises, including micro businesses) and created nearly 200 000 jobs between 2013 and 2016. The majority of scalers are turnover scalers (51%), followed by turnover and employment scalers (30%) and employment scalers (19%). Turnover scalers increase their value-added productivity, becoming the most productive among the three types of scalers at the end of the observation period.

Nordic Innovation also provides an evaluation of the Nordic Scalers support scheme. The scheme included 33 companies, selected on the basis of being a scaler (according to the definition above) and through interviews with individual companies, to determine the "disruptiveness" of the business idea as well as motivations, ambitions and fit for the programme. The purpose of the Nordic Scalers programme is to help the best Nordic companies in the scale-up phase to prepare and accelerate their next stages of growth through access to competence building. The main findings of the evaluation are the following:

- Programmes for scalers should be aligned with national and regional economic strategies.
- They should react to changes in firms' needs in a timely manner.

- They should provide a mix of financial and non-financial assistance.
- They should foster peer-to-peer support.
- They should have fixed and appropriate selection criteria for programme participation.
- They should customise support for individual firms.

Nordic Innovation proposes a list of policy areas in support of scaling up. At the national level, policies should focus on increasing the talent pool, improving access to growth capital and enhancing access to international business partners. At the regional level, policy makers can strengthen the scale-up environment by enhancing access to the network of scale-up expertise and private and public innovation partners. Additionally, regions should follow similar paths as the national policy by building strong channels for talent recruitment and acquiring venture capital. Finally, regional support should ensure affordable access to laboratories, test and production facilities.

Source: Nordic Innovation (2019[27]) *Mini Evaluation of the Nordic Scalers Programme*, https://www.diva-portal.org/smash/get/diva2:1372693/FULLTEXT01.pdf (accessed on 10 March 2021); Nordic Council (2019[28]), *Scale-ups in the Nordics*.

Scalers are not necessarily small. The higher propensity of small firms to grow fast found in older studies (Birch, 1987[29]) is explained by the fact that younger firms grow faster and are typically very small. A recent paper using firm-level data for the US on the universe of businesses shows that once firm age is also considered, there is no systematic relationship between firm size and relative growth (Haltiwanger, Jarmin and Miranda, 2011[30]). However, other studies on Italian and Portuguese firms instead show that small firms still tend to grow faster, even when age is taken into account (Lotti and Santarelli, 2001[31]; Neumark, Wall and Zhang, 2011[32]; Geurts and Van Biesebroeck, 2016[33]).

Scalers tend to be more productive than similar firms just before the high-growth period. Studies on French and Italian firms show that labour productivity, profitability and investment intensity is higher in firms that will scale up in the next period in either employment or turnover (Moschella, Tamagni and Yu, 2019[34]; Coad, 2010[35]). Another study on Italian firms also shows that businesses that start with higher productivity also tend to turn into high-growth firms in their lifetime (Arrighetti and Lasagni, 2013[36]). Similarly, evidence from the UK shows that firms with higher productivity growth are likely to become turnover high-growth firms (Du and Temouri, 2015[37]).

The review of available evidence on scalers highlights several open questions which are addressed in this report. The next chapters of the report complement the established facts discussed above with new evidence from five pilot countries (Finland, Italy, Portugal, the Slovak Republic, Spain), building upon the analysis of firm-level data sources. A non-exhaustive summary of some of the new findings, compared to what is known from previous research, is reported in Table 1.1. The new evidence fills in important knowledge gaps. For instance, the disproportionate contribution of scalers to job and value creation is confirmed across the five pilot countries, with new evidence on the leading role of mature scalers. The analysis of growth trajectories of scalers in the 3 years after scaling show that around 60% of them are able to maintain or consolidate the new scale. However, differences exist between scalers of different age and across sectors. The analysis of the transformation that scalers undertake shows that scaling is much more than growth. The transformation deeply affects the way scalers operate along several dimensions, including innovation and digitalisation, workforce composition, integration in global markets, access to finance and productivity. For many firms, scaling is a forward-looking strategy as in several dimensions the transformation begins before scaling.

Table 1.1. What we know and what we learn about scalers

What is known	What we learn
The share of scalers differs across countries and sectors.	Scalers contribute more than half of job and value creation across all pilot countries.
The typical scaler is not a high-tech firm.	Most jobs created by scalers come from mature scalers operating in less knowledge-intensive services.
For many scalers, high growth is an isolated episode in their lifetime.	Scaling is sustainable. Three years after scaling, the majority of scalers maintain the new size or continue to grow at a slower pace.
Scalers appear to be "one-hit wonders" as it is hard to predict which firms will grow fast.	Many scalers start transforming before growing, e.g. by investing more in innovation or by accessing global markets.

Box 1.4. Employment and turnover measures for high growth

In economic research and business demographics statistics, high growth and scaling up are defined using either employment or turnover to measure firm growth. Each approach has its own advantages and limitations. Both metrics are used in this report and differences in findings are discussed when informative.

Employment-based metrics are more common, as employee headcount is available in almost every administrative dataset on enterprises. Change in employment is the most straightforward way of signalling a firm's success and policy makers prioritise employment outcomes, with (good) jobs directly related to income and welfare. However, some methodological issues may still limit the extent to which data can be compared across countries, especially if employment is measured in headcount rather than in hours worked or full-time equivalent units. For example, differences in the share of part-time workers across countries may lead to a different number of employed workers for the same number of full-time equivalent units. The inclusion of temporary workers in the headcount may also differ across national sources.

Focusing solely on employment growth excludes a large share of firms that reach another scale of economic activity without exceptional employment growth. Turnover scale-up is often generated via improvements in firm productivity, which increase the efficiency of resources used. Such a "scale without mass" business model is generated via process innovation or specific technology adoption that permits firms to scale their business with only minimal or no employment growth.

Turnover is more in line with dimensions businesses use to measure their own success. Total turnover (i.e. sales) is one of the targets that firms set for themselves and leadership outcomes are often evaluated considering turnover performance. Profit-maximising firms actively seek to increase turnover (Mert, 2018[38]), along with other measures such as stock returns, yet rarely target to increase employment.

Some firms may grow in employment abroad and in turnover domestically. This is a second possible reason for a "scale without mass" growth model, especially in high-income countries in which some firms – including SMEs – outsource abroad the most labour-intensive phases of the production process. For example, a survey of Danish and Swedish SMEs in the early 2000s' show that around 25% of them are offshoring (Waehrens, Slepniov and Johansen, 2015[39]).

Turnover is more volatile and more sensitive to the economic cycle. Large fluctuations – both negative and positive – in turnover are more frequent than in employment. Labour adjustments are more costly compared to other inputs and the lower cyclicality of employment makes employment a less erratic measure of firm growth. As a result, there are more firms that scale in turnover than in employment. Employment expansions may also expect persistent and fast growth in turnover. The economic theory first suggested that firms prepare for future growth by hiring the right workforce (Penrose, 1959[40]) and empirical research has shown that employment growth leads to future increases in sales (Coad, 2010[35]).

Source: Krasniqi, B. and S. Desai (2016[41]), "Institutional drivers of high-growth firms: Country-level evidence from 26 transition economies", http://dx.doi.org/10.1007/s11187-016-9736-7; Mert, M. (2018[38]), "What does a firm maximize? A simple explanation with regard to economic growth", https://doi.org/10.1177/1847979018815296; Waehrens, B., D. Slepniov and J. Johansen (2015[39]), "Offshoring practices of Danish and Swedish SMEs: Effects on operations configuration", http://dx.doi.org/10.1080/09537287.2014.971519; Coad, A. (2010[35]), "Exploring the processes of firm growth: Evidence from a vector auto-regression", http://dx.doi.org/10.1093/icc/dtq018; Penrose, E. (1959[40]), *The Theory of the Growth of the Firm*, https://books.google.fr/books/about/The_Theory_of_the_Growth_of_the_Firm (accessed on 1 August 2019).

More evidence on scalers' characteristics and the transformation process they undertake is needed

Understanding how policies can effectively support scalers requires more dedicated work. Given their important role in creating jobs, how to support high-growth firms is a central theme in the entrepreneurship policy debate. The question is particularly important for the recovery from the COVID-19 crisis, given the large degree of structural change that it will entail and the role that scalers can play to transform new growth opportunities into jobs, economic value and resilience (OECD, 2021[2]). However, there is little available evidence to help policy makers allocate scarce resources toward their most effective use. Broadly, three types of analysis are required:

- **The first type is general studies that provide useful knowledge on the characteristics of scalers, their heterogeneity and the barriers that they face in scaling.** To be effective, SME policies need to take into account the diversity of the SME population, as discussed in Box 1.1. Scaling-up policies are no exception. Currently, there is a limited understanding of the specific characteristics of scalers, with the results that scale-up policies often lack their own identity and are blended with innovation, entrepreneurship and equity finance policies (Flachenecker et al., 2020[42]; Mason and Brown, 2011[43]). Policy makers may look for scalers in the wrong place and support them with the wrong tools, based on assumptions on their characteristics – e.g. that they are young, high-technology firms operating in the manufacturing sector and that they are often equity-backed – that do not correspond to reality (Mason and Brown, 2011[43]). Many scaling-up policies are also based on the assumption that the supported company will continue to grow. Policy studies need to help understand which firms should be supported and how. There are at least three different policy questions that should be addressed: i) how much do scalers contribute to aggregate growth across OECD countries and are there differences among types of scalers?; ii) how sustainable is the new scale in the long term?; iii) how do scalers differ from non-scalers?
- **The second type of analysis should assess how national and regional policies support or hamper the growth of scalers.** Scalers may react differently to specific policy regulations and business framework conditions than the general population of SMEs. A set of comparable metrics on scalers across countries, combined with a comprehensive database of harmonised policy indicators, would enable a stream of cross-country studies aimed at understanding how the policy and business environment can be reformed to enhance scalers' role in the economy. The policy indicators could cover policy initiatives and institutions in areas such as access to finance, innovation policies for SMEs, digitalisation and data governance by SMEs and size-contingent regulations (i.e. regulations that kick in when firms reach a given size threshold) (OECD, forthcoming[44]).

- **The third type is properly designed programme evaluations that compare the performance of supported firms against a suitable control group of comparable but unsupported firms.** These studies help select those programmes that are reaching the expected outcome. Unfortunately, these studies are very rare, if not absent, in the context of scaling-up policies (Bosma and Stam, 2012[45]). Compared to other areas of economic policy such as active labour market policies or development, in which rigorous programme evaluation is now an essential component of the policy design cycle, there is a dearth of studies on policies that support SMEs (Bravo-Biosca, 2016[46]). Even evaluations of small programmes can produce important policy findings, as the example of the evaluation of the Nordic Scalers programme shows, as described in Box 1.3.

The policy interest in scalers is motivated by their disproportionate role in net job creation but it is unclear whether all scalers are contributing equally. Country-specific studies provide some information on the matter but systematic evidence covering a large number of OECD countries is still missing. For instance, there are no internationally comparable statistics available on the contribution to net job creation by scalers of different sizes or sectors.

Very little is known on whether scalers are systematically different from non-scalers. While some information is available on the structural characteristics of scalers, such as size and age, the dynamic transformation process that scalers undertake may be more important for policy. Likely, an SME that increases its size by more than one-third in three years has to face several new challenges. For example, about 5% to 14% of high-growth firms engage in some innovative activity while they scale up (Vértesy, Sorbo and Damioli, 2017[47]). SMEs may also start exporting and change the composition of their workforce to support their high-growth phase and adapt to the new scale. Deep organisational changes and new human resources practices might be required. Except for country-level studies that consider selected factors – such as access to the global market or external finance – in isolation, there is no available empirical evidence on the transformation process of scalers as they experience a high-growth period.

The mapping of the different transformation patterns of scalers may point to several areas in which policy support may be highly effective. Chapter 4 of the report discusses how the transformation that scalers undertake may follow different models, depending on the factors that trigger scaling. For some firms, scaling is the result of a forward-looking growth strategy grounded on innovation and productivity improvements that involves a deep transformation of the inner structure of the firm. For other firms, the scaling transformation may be driven by an external increase in demand or it may entail the replication of existing business processes that leaves the core structure of the firm unaltered. The timing and nature of the transformation provide useful indications on which scaling models prevail. Chapter 4 thus presents new evidence on the transformation process that distinguishes SMEs that scale up from comparable firms that do not scale. The analysis focuses on dynamic factors that may change as firms age and grow, such as innovation, integration in global markets, digitalisation and workforce characteristics.

Do scalers differ in their growth trajectories after their initial growth phase? Evidence on whether scalers maintain or consolidate the new scale, or rather reverse to their initial size, is important to understand which types of scalers will lead toward a sustained and resilient recovery. For policy makers, additional evidence on the heterogeneous growth patterns of scalers could be valuable for at least two reasons. First, the evidence can be useful to tackle possible market or policy failures that make it difficult for specific types of scalers to maintain or consolidate the new scale. Second, support policies may become more effective if they target the subset of scalers that are intrinsically more likely to maintain and consolidate their scale.

Size-contingent regulations that increase the regulatory burden on firms when they reach a given size may also represent an obstacle to growth. Evidence from France shows that firms are much more likely to stay at the 49-employee level and not grow because of additional regulations that are enforced on firms with at least 50 employees (Garicano, Lelarge and Reenen, 2016[48]). Evidence from Italy on additional firing restrictions that used to apply to firms with over 15 employees shows that the probability of firm growth is reduced by around 2 percentage points near the threshold (Schivardi and Torrini, 2008[49]). Although this evidence does not directly relate to the incidence of scaling up, it provides a cautionary note on the unintended consequences that size-contingent regulations may have on potential scalers.

Box 1.5. Public policies should take stock of SME diversity

The fact that SMEs are a very diverse group of firms and belong to a diversity of business ecosystems calls for a fundamental rethinking of entrepreneurship and SME policy (OECD, 2019[12]). Policies that do not fully acknowledge SME heterogeneity, in particular regarding growth, are likely to miss their targets (Shane, 2009[50]; Schoar, 2010[51]). The economic and business literature has proposed many different classifications of SMEs, based, for example, on the personal traits and objectives of the entrepreneurs leading them or on their growth trajectories (Raes, forthcoming[52]). A seminal stylised framework identifies two different groups of entrepreneurs: those who become entrepreneurs to provide subsistence income (subsistence entrepreneurs) and those who aim to create large businesses which will provide jobs and income for others (transformative entrepreneurs). These individuals respond differently to policy changes and economic cycles. Evidence suggests that only a negligible fraction of entrepreneurs transition from one type to the other. Thus, policies supporting one type of entrepreneur (or their companies) may have a different impact on the other group of entrepreneurs (Schoar, 2010[51]).

Public policies should be endowed with the tools to identify and understand the needs of different types of SMEs and entrepreneurs. This does not mean that policies should only "pick winners" and focus only on "transformative" businesses. Non-transformative entrepreneurs and their companies are also important for the economy: the figures reported above imply that most of the stock of employment in our economies is accounted for by this broad category of SMEs. While these companies may not create new jobs or introduce new services or products, they contribute to a variety of different needs and provide the bulk of goods and services that consumers and other businesses buy or use daily. However, the type of policy support these companies may need, as well as the objectives of such policy interventions, may be diametrically different from those of policies targeting high-growth firms and scalers. Therefore, policy makers should take account of the diversity of SMEs (and entrepreneurs) in policy making, including through the development and use of policy-relevant SME and entrepreneurship typologies and the collection of granular data to inform decisions (OECD, 2021[53]).

Source: OECD (2019[12]), *OECD SME and Entrepreneurship Outlook 2019*, https://dx.doi.org/10.1787/34907e9c-en; Shane, S. (2009[50]), "Why encouraging more people to become entrepreneurs is bad public policy", http://dx.doi.org/10.1007/s11187-009-9215-5; Raes, S. (forthcoming[52]), *Understanding SME Heterogeneity: Towards policy relevant typologies for SMEs and entrepreneurship*, OECD Publishing, Paris; Schoar, A. (2010[51]), "The divide between subsistence and transformational entrepreneurship", http://dx.doi.org/10.1086/605853; OECD (2021[53]), "SME and entrepreneurship policy frameworks across OECD countries: An OECD Strategy for SMEs and Entrepreneurship", OECD SME and Entrepreneurship Papers, No. 29, OECD Publishing, Paris, https://doi.org/10.1787/9f6c41ce-en

Support for scalers is hindered by the difficulty to predict which SMEs will become high-growth firms. The diffusion of "big data" and the recent improvement of machine learning have spurred interest in analyses aimed at identifying firms that are likely to grow fast in the future (Coad and Srhoj, 2019[54]; McKenzie and Sansone, 2019[55]). Providing targeted support to scalers based on this information may appear like a promising policy option. However, until now, there has been limited success in identifying firm or entrepreneur characteristics that predict subsequent growth, as the components that appear to matter are very hard to measure. The measurable components of growth and performance are overshadowed by the random or unmeasurable component (McKelvie and Wiklund, 2010[56]). A recent study on SMEs in the UK shows that firm observable characteristics such as productivity, size, age or investment levels showed no correlation with future productivity growth, defined as growth in turnover or value-added per employee (Jibril, Stanfield and Roper, 2020[57]). Instead, qualitative indicators on good leadership are a much stronger predictor of productivity gains over time. However, this information is harder to collect, as it requires detailed interviews.

Scaling out of the crisis

Scalers can play an important role in the COVID-19 recovery period

The COVID-19 crisis speeds up the transformation of the business sector but may also leave some permanent scars. The pandemic has induced permanent changes in OECD economies and accelerated existing trends such as digitalisation (OECD, 2021[1]). While some businesses and sectors will face structurally weaker demand and more adverse market conditions, many new opportunities and markets will arise. The enhanced uptake of digital tools by firms and households opens new markets and creates room for new products and services, as well as cost-saving measures. The diffusion of e-commerce has improved access to viable markets without the need for large investments in marketing and distribution. Demand for online services and goods during the crisis opened up opportunities for existing firms and new entrepreneurs. Cheaper access to shared IT resources in the "cloud" and the potential of continued homeworking promise productivity gains or cost savings (e.g. as less office space is required). As a result, the business sector that will emerge from the recovery will be fundamentally different from the one that entered the crisis (G30, 2020[58]).

Crises trigger a process of "creative destruction" but can also permanently "scar" the economy. The worst-performing firms, typically those with the lowest productivity, are more likely to struggle during a downturn and go bankrupt. Labour and capital employed by these firms could then become available for firms that have the potential to scale and for new entrants. However, crises can also "scar" the economy and slow down productivity growth, e.g. by limiting the availability of external finance and forcing high-potential businesses to close down (Hallward-Driemeier and Rijkers, 2013[59]). The 2008 global financial crisis did induce a sharp increase in the bankruptcy rate, both in Europe and the US. However, in contrast to previous recessions, there is no clear evidence that this translated into the entry of new firms or the expansion of the most productive ones, i.e. there is no evidence that destruction was followed by "creativity".[6]

With the right policy mix in place, scalers can play a key role in transforming new opportunities into jobs, economic value and resilience, contributing to a fast and sustainable recovery. Scalers contribute with the majority of new jobs and economic value, and the recovery crisis will not be an exception. Rather, innovative and risk-taking scalers may face more growth opportunities than in normal times, if properly supported. Therefore, jointly with a broad spectrum of support measures for viable businesses that risk failing because of the crisis, the right recovery policy mix should include support for firms with high growth potential (Lambert and Van Reenen, 2021[60]). Beyond the creation of jobs and economic value, the scaling of highly productive businesses is also key to increasing productivity. Indeed, more than half of productivity growth in industrialised countries is due to the expansion of the most productive firms, as they absorb capital and labour from less productive firms (allocative efficiency), rather than to the growth in productivity of the average firm (Disney, Haskel and Heden, 2003[61]; Baldwin and Gu, 2006[62]). As the COVID-19 crisis highlighted, a sole view on economic performance might fall short in ensuring sustainable growth. Resilience and the ability of firms to adapt to important transitions, such as the transition towards net-zero greenhouse gas emissions should be considerations as well.

Governments need to ensure that business transformations and the reallocation of financial resources can happen smoothly. Reforming and streamlining insolvency procedures can accelerate the flow of financial resources from closing businesses to new ventures or by helping SMEs keep their assets by better identifying viable from non-viable businesses (OECD, 2021[2]). Governments should also support retraining and assist the transition of workers who need to change jobs. In the EU, scalers are also expected to play an important role in the "twin transitions", i.e. the synergic process of greening and digitalisation of the economy (Box 1.6).

Entry and exit dynamics differ from those of previous recessions

The recession following the 2007-08 crisis had a strong negative impact on scalers. Aggregate data for the last recession show that the number of high-growth scalers in the 7 OECD countries for which data are available dropped by up to 65% in 2011 compared to 2008 (Figure 1.5). In four out of seven countries, the recovery in the crisis' aftermath was only partial, as the number of high-growth scalers in the year 2013 was still lower than in 2008.[7] Empirical evidence for the US also shows that the number of high-growth scalers contracted significantly in the aftermath of the 2008 financial crisis (Decker et al., 2016[63]). Similarly, an analysis of firm-level data from the Community Innovation Survey (CIS) for European countries in the period 2006-14 shows that the recession reduced the share of turnover scalers sharply. Furthermore, the crisis reduced the likelihood to scale more for large firms than small firms, as measured by turnover volume. Therefore, the share of turnover growth by scalers contracted even more than the share of scalers in all firms (Benedetti Fasil et al., 2021[64]). There are at least two reasons why the 2007-08 crisis had such a large impact on scalers. First, the crisis resulted in a severe tightening of credit conditions for SMEs, with high-potential but high-risk businesses being the most vulnerable. Second, in several markets, unsustainable growth predated (and caused) the crisis itself, e.g. because of expansionary policies in some countries that injected a large amount of "easy" money in the private sector or loose regulation in the financial sector. Such unstainable growth explains the high number of existing scalers when the crisis suddenly kicked in, with the collapse of the financial services firm Lehman Brothers. Therefore, the number of scalers not only reduced sharply in the aftermath of the crisis but also started from an inflated benchmark level.

Figure 1.5. The number of high-growth scalers decreased in the aftermath of the 2007-08 global financial crisis

Number of high-growth scalers by country in 2011 and 2013, relative to the number of high-growth scalers in 2008

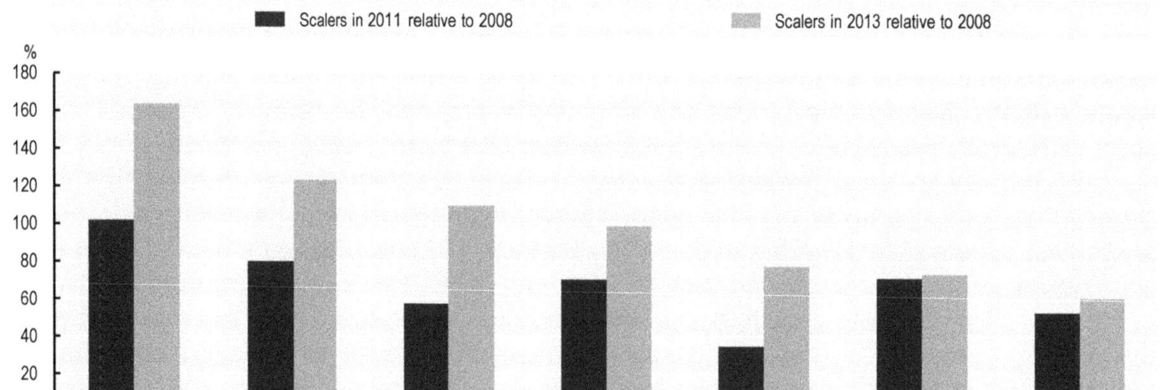

Note: High-growth scalers are defined as those firms that completed 3 years of employment growth at an average yearly rate of 20% or more; see Box 1.2 for further details on the definition of scalers.
Source: OECD.stats (2021[15]), *Structural and Demographic Business Statistics (SDBS)*, OECD, Paris.

Preliminary evidence for OECD countries shows that entry rates differ widely across countries during the COVID-19 crisis. Some of the new entrants today are tomorrow's scalers. The rate of new business formation is an important indicator to understand what will happen to scalers in the aftermath of the COVID-19 crisis. Some dynamism in creating new businesses would be an indicator that a process of creative destruction could be in motion. In some countries, like Australia, Canada, Norway, the UK and the US, the entry rate in 2020 was higher than in 2019, despite an initial decrease in the second quarter of the year (coincidental with the first lockdowns in OECD countries). In the US in particular, the number of new business formations was the highest since records exist.[8] Conversely, in Italy, Portugal and Spain, the entry rate was substantially lower in 2020 than in previous years. Other large countries in continental Europe show an intermediate pattern, with entry rates in 2020 that are similar to those of previous years or even higher by the end of 2020, as it is the case, for example, in Finland or Germany (OECD (2021[65]), Figure 1.6). This is substantially different from what happened in previous recessions, during which the entry rates dropped substantially.[9]

Figure 1.6. Firm entries increased in the second half of 2020, following a dip in the second quarter

Number of entries of new enterprise in Finland, Germany, Italy, Japan, the Netherlands and the US, quarterly series, 2007-20, 2007=100

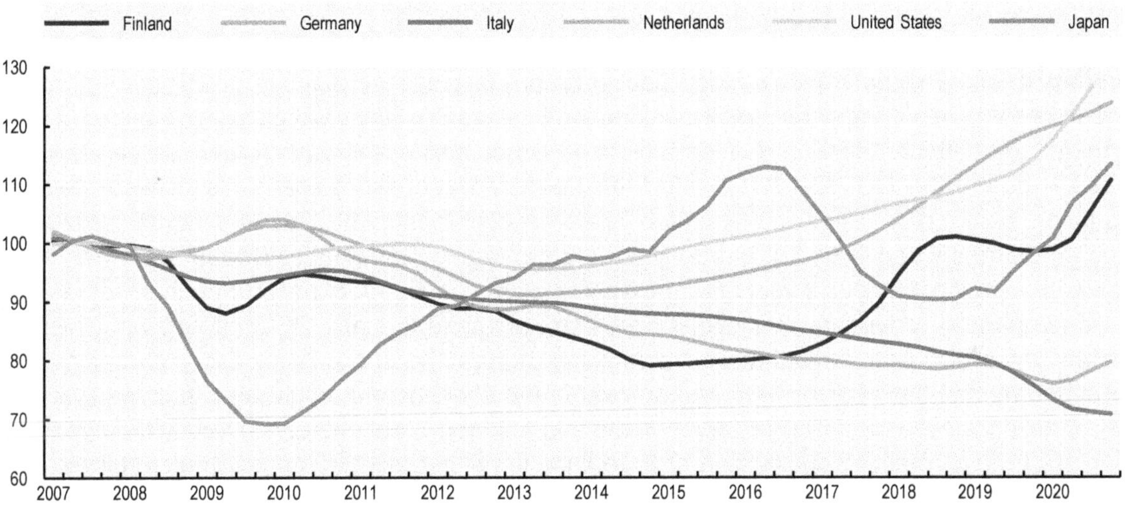

Note: For the purpose of presentation of quarterly series, seasonal adjustment is applied using TramoSeats algorithm with five regressors: log/level, trading days, Easter, outlier detection and automatic model identification. Series are log-transformed and decomposed into a trend component. The index is calculated based on 2007 (2007 = average of 2007 quarters) in order to present movements between the base year and a given quarter.
Source: OECD.stats (2021[66]), *Timely Indicators of Entrepreneurship*, OECD, Paris.

Some sectors thrived despite the crisis but "brick and mortar" activities suffered throughout 2020. In the US, out of the 19 major industry sectors, new business applications grew by more than 10% in 13 of them in the first 10 months of 2020. Wholesale trade and other services (a general category that includes personal care services and laundry services) were among the sectors that grew. Conversely, other traditional "brick and mortar" activities show a drop. For example, business applications in the real estate sector and the oil and gas extraction industry fell by 11% and 24% respectively (O'Donnell, Newman and Fikri, 2021[67]). Data from four other OECD countries for which entry statistics for 2020 are available (Belgium, Finland, Netherlands, Portugal) show that, in the first part of the year, the worst-hit sectors were transportation and storage, hotel and restaurants, and arts and entertainment, with a rather similar pattern across countries. Conversely, industries that rely less on face-to-face contacts and make more use of digital skills, such as information and communication and professional services, have been partially sheltered from the crisis. However, countries differ in the speed of recovery in the worst-hit sectors. For example, transportation and storage show a robust rebound in entry rates in France in the second part of 2020, while in Portugal further reduced (OECD, 2021[65]).

The surge in entrepreneurship observed in some countries may point to self-employment being a "survival" option for many workers. For instance, evidence from the UK suggests that some "solo" self-employed – i.e. sole traders or company owner-managers without employees – opt for this alternative form of work because they cannot find suitable opportunities in traditional employment. They are more likely than employees to want to work more hours than they currently are working and to have recently been unemployed or inactive (Giupponi and Xu, 2020[68]). In the US, the number of new business applications was higher in 2020 than the year before for both likely non-employer businesses and likely employer businesses but the increase was stronger for the former. Furthermore, the number of new likely employer businesses is a forward-looking indicator, as it takes time for an application to turn into a new business and the pace at which high-propensity applications are translating into true active firms is slower in 2020 than after the 2008 financial crisis (O'Donnell, Newman and Fikri, 2021[67]). A recent report by the Kaufmann Foundation shows that, in the US, the "opportunity" share of new entrepreneurs – i.e. the percentage of the total number of new entrepreneurs who were not unemployed and not looking for a job as they started a new business – was the lowest in 2020 since at least records exist (1995) (Fairlie and Desai, 2021[69]).

Support measures kept viable businesses afloat, preserving assets for some potential scalers, but may have also delayed the exit of unproductive firms, which limits the resources available to new or growing firms. The emergency policy packages put in place by national governments have been effective in keeping afloat viable but credit-constrained businesses, which would have defaulted in absence of the measures (OECD, 2020[70]). Across advanced economies, bankruptcies have fallen – rather than increased – during the COVID-19 recession, unlike during past recessions; this decline also reflects moratoria on bankruptcy filings implemented in some countries (IMF, 2021[71]; OECD, 2020[70]). For instance, in Germany and Italy, the quarterly average enterprise bankruptcy rate in 2020 was 18% and 35% lower than in the previous 2 years respectively (Figure 1.7). Extraordinary furlough schemes to cover wages of temporarily redundant employees were also launched in many OECD countries, which limited the outflow of workers from firms that were struggling through the crisis. While this is overall good news for the economy and the affected workers, at least in the short term, it might also indicate that the high number of new business formation observed in the same period is not entirely driven by the opportunity to hire workers from contracting businesses or to replace firms that exit the market. It also raises concerns that chronically unproductive businesses may delay their exit from the market longer than it would be socially desirable, as their workforce and capital could be put to better use in more productive firms. However, preliminary evidence from Australia, New Zealand and the UK suggests this may not be the case, as the flow of workers from low to high productivity firms continued during the crisis (Andrews, Charlton and More, 2021[72]; Andrews, Hambur and Bahar, 2021[73]).

The risk of a lost generation of scalers

A lost generation of new scalers would have long-term implications for the economy. Some of the new firms that are founded today are tomorrow's scalers. Crises may negatively affect the entry of future scalers along three different margins. The first margin is the number of start-ups if the crisis leads to a lower number of entries of high-potential new businesses. The second margin is the growth potential of these new companies, as firms born during past recessions not only start smaller but also tend to stay smaller in future years, even when the aggregate economy recovers. The reason for the smaller firm size might be the fact that it is more difficult to start a scalable business during a crisis because, for example, supply chains are distorted, credit conditions are poor and customer demand is more difficult to acquire. The third margin is the survival rate: start-ups and young firms have a lower survival rate generally and it tends to decrease during recessions (Sedláček and Sterk, 2017[74]).

The sectors that have been more negatively affected by the crisis have a higher incidence of scalers. A recent report by the European Commission (EC) Joint Research Centre (JRC), focusing on European scalers in the COVID-19 crisis context, shows that, in the EU, the share of high-growth scalers in the sectors that contracted the most during 2020 is higher than the average share of high-growth scalers in the business economy as a whole (Box 1.6). This highlights the risk that the pandemic is creating a business environment that is less conducive to scaling, with long-lasting negative repercussions on the recovery. Therefore, the policy response should not only focus on the immediate survival of viable firms but also on deploying longer-term measures geared to reduce barriers for potential scalers.

Prompt action by governments was and is important to avoid a lost generation of scalers. The rapid introduction of public financial support during the COVID-19 pandemic played a key role to ensure viable businesses remained in the market, implementing lessons learned from the last global financial crisis. Beyond the immediate response, many countries already use investment packages supporting recovery to help firms with growth potential. Several OECD countries, including France, Germany and the UK, have already taken action in this direction, e.g. through the creation of dedicated funds to support equity investments in innovative entrepreneurship (OECD, 2020[75]). Credit constraints can be another major barrier for firms with high-growth potential, which are perceived as riskier by investors. Generally, OECD countries have many different policy instruments in place to help overcome this barrier, such as credit guarantee schemes (Cusmano, 2018[76]; OECD, 2020[77]). Recovery might require governments to absorb more risk but also to improve the targeting of support to make the best use of limited resources. Measures to alleviate credit constraints are particularly important for young firms that struggle to provide adequate collateral and do not have a lending track record. They would be crucial to avoid bankruptcies of promising young firms born just before the crisis, once the current waivers are lifted.

Figure 1.7. Firms went bankrupt at a lower rate in 2020 than during the previous crisis

The number of bankruptcies in Finland, Germany, Italy, Japan, Netherlands, Spain and the US, quarterly series, 2007-20, 2007=100

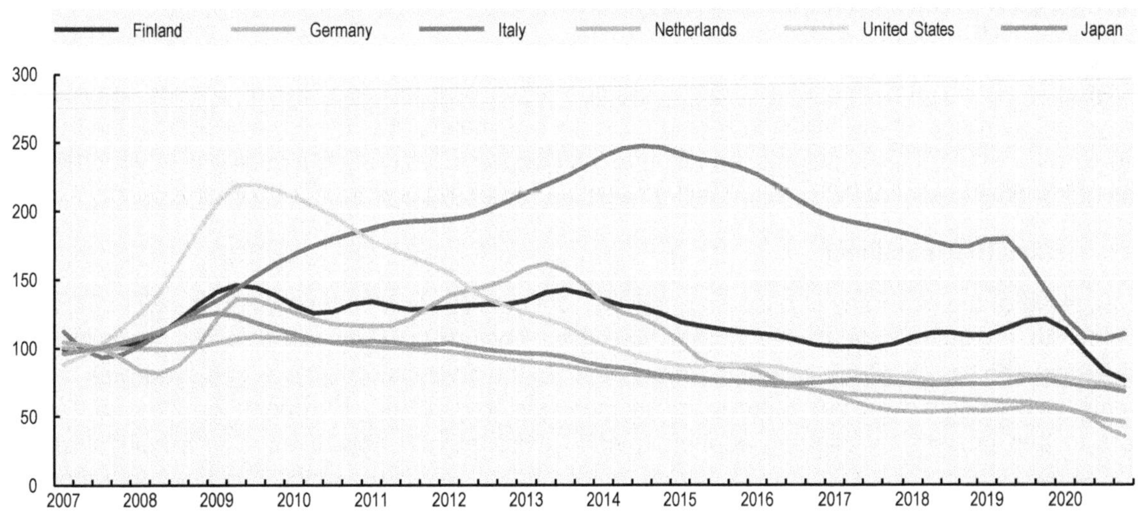

Note: Data for bankruptcies in Japan and the US consider only incorporated businesses (natural persons and sole proprietorships are excluded). The bankruptcy in the remaining countries is reported for all enterprises. For the purpose of presentation of quarterly series, seasonal adjustment is applied using the TramoSeats algorithm with five regressors: log/level, trading days, Easter, outlier detection and automatic model identification. Series are log-transformed and decomposed into a trend component. The index is calculated based on 2007 (2007 = average of 2007 quarters) in order to present movements between the base year and a given quarter.
Source: OECD.stats (2021[66]), *Timely Indicators of Entrepreneurship*, OECD, Paris.

A new wave of digitally enabled entrepreneurship may be on the rise

The crisis makes it urgent to address the divide between SMEs that can benefit from digitalisation and those that lag behind. The health crisis exposed a divide across SMEs in their ability to use digital technologies such as remote working, online sales and remote communications with suppliers and customers. Such a divide exists also for other digital technologies – such as the Internet of Things, cloud computing and data analytics – that are revolutionising firms' potential capacity for simulation, prototyping, decision making and automation. These digital technologies are creating unprecedented opportunities for SMEs (OECD, 2021[1]). However, a significant share of SMEs lag in the adoption of digital tools and employing IT specialists that could help implement the digital transition. Cross-firm divides were already growing before the crisis (OECD, 2021[2]). For example, 28% of firms in France with 20-49 employees used cloud storage services in 2018, compared to 70% of firms with 250 to 499 employees (Nevoux et al., 2019[3]). It is still unclear whether the divide has widened or narrowed during the crisis but the new digital impetus has certainly further weakened the position of SMEs lagging behind.

New digitally-enabled entrepreneurship can be the silver lining of the crisis. The steep acceleration in the digital transition induced by the COVID-19 crisis may have reduced barriers to starting a business or opting for self-employment. Similarly, it may be easier for new and small businesses to access a viable market without large investments in marketing and distribution, thanks to the diffusion of e-commerce. This may have induced many "latent" entrepreneurs to eventually start their businesses during the crisis. It would also explain part of the surge in new business formations observed in some countries.

Box 1.6. European scalers in the COVID-19 crisis context

A recent report by the EC's JRC analyses the possible impact of the COVID-19 crisis on European scalers, highlighting the role of scalers in delivering on the "twin transitions", i.e. the greening and the digitalisation of the European economy.

COVID-19's uneven effect across sectors and types of firms

The COVID-19 crisis has uneven effects across the business economy. The most affected sectors – such as advertising and market research, transportation and storage, travel agency services and employment activities – have traditionally higher shares of scalers than the EU average for the business economy as a whole. This highlights the risk that the pandemic is creating a business environment that is less conducive to scaling, with long-lasting negative repercussions on the recovery.

Scalers and the twin transitions

The greening of the economy is a leading policy priority for the recovery phase in the EU and scalers can play an important role to reach this objective. The productivity advantages associated with digitalisation can be a strategic complementary asset to the greening objective. The synergies between greening and digitalisation are referred to as the "twin transitions". European policies can support scalers in this process by aligning economic with environmental objectives. The empirical analysis indeed shows that publicly supported environmental innovations increase the likelihood for enterprises to become employment scalers. The report also finds that scalers and firms that plan to grow show a considerably larger adoption rate of digital technologies than other enterprises. However, there are large differences across EU countries and the shares of growth-oriented firms adopting advanced digital technologies are lower in the EU than in the UK and the US.

Policy measures

Across the EU, swift policy action has provided liquidity and employment support that is crucial to withstand the negative economic effects of the COVID-19 pandemic crisis. A concern is that policies focus on the immediate survival of viable firms miss opportunities for deploying longer-term measures geared to improve the business environment for scalers. Examples for such policies range from providing the right framework conditions that will help SMEs to grow to addressing country-specific bottlenecks, such as improving access to finance or increasing the skill levels of the workforce. In this regard, and as an example on the European level, the Recovery and Resiliency Facility (RRF) provides an important reform and investment impetus to foster the digital and ecological transition in Europe.

Source: Benedetti Fasil, C. et al. (2021[64]), *High Growth Enterprises in the COVID-19 Crisis Context*, https://publications.jrc.ec.europa.eu/repository/handle/JRC124469 (accessed on 17 June 2021).

References

Ahmad, N. (2008), "A proposed framework for business demography statistics", *Measuring Entrepreneurship*, pp. 113-174, http://dx.doi.org/10.1007/978-0-387-72288-7_7. [19]

Akcigit, U. et al. (2019), "Synergizing ventures", http://dx.doi.org/10.3386/W26196. [24]

Andrews, D., A. Charlton and A. More (2021), "COVID-19, productivity and reallocation: Timely evidence from three OECD countries", *OECD Economics Department Working Papers*, No. 1676, OECD Publishing, Paris, https://doi.org/10.1787/d2c4b89c-en (accessed on 30 September 2021). [72]

Andrews, D., J. Hambur and E. Bahar (2021), "The COVID-19 shock and productivity-enhancing reallocation in Australia: Real-time evidence from Single Touch Payroll", *OECD Economics Department Working Papers*, No. 1677, OECD Publishing, Paris, https://dx.doi.org/10.1787/2f6e7cb1-en. [73]

Anyadike-Danes, M. and M. Hart (2019), "Fecundity, fertility, survival and growth: High-growth firms in the UK and their contribution to job creation, a demographic perspective", No. 74, ERC Research Paper, https://www.enterpriseresearch.ac.uk/publications/fecundity-fertility-survival-growth-research-paper-no-74/ (accessed on 26 July 2021). [21]

Arrighetti, A. and A. Lasagni (2013), "Assessing the determinants of high-growth manufacturing firms in Italy", *International Journal of the Economics of Business*, Vol. 20/2, pp. 245-267, http://dx.doi.org/10.1080/13571516.2013.783456. [36]

Baldwin, J. and W. Gu (2006), "Plant turnover and productivity growth in Canadian manufacturing", *Industrial and Corporate Change*, Vol. 15/3, pp. 417-465, http://dx.doi.org/10.1093/icc/dtj017. [62]

Benedetti Fasil, C. et al. (2021), *High Growth Enterprises in the COVID-19 Crisis Context*, Publications Office of the European Union, https://publications.jrc.ec.europa.eu/repository/handle/JRC124469 (accessed on 17 June 2021). [64]

Birch, D. (1987), "Job creation in America: How our smallest companies put the most people to work", University of Illinois at Urbana-Champaign's Academy for Entrepreneurial Leadership Historical Research Reference in Entrepreneurship, https://papers.ssrn.com/abstract=1496185 (accessed on 9 March 2021). [29]

Bosma, N. and E. Stam (2012), "Local Policies for High-Employment Growth Enterprises", *Report prepared for the OECD/DBA International Workshop on "High-growth firms: local policies and local determinants"*. [45]

Bravo-Biosca, A. (2016), "Experimental innovation and growth policy: why do we need it?", NESTA, London, https://www.nesta.org.uk/report/experimental-innovation-and-growth-policy-why-do-we-need-it/ (accessed on 19 July 2021). [46]

Bravo-Biosca, A. (2010), *Growth Dynamics: Exploring Business Growth and Contraction in Europe and the US*, UK Research Report, NESTA. [16]

Bravo-Biosca, A., C. Criscuolo and C. Menon (2016), "What drives the dynamics of business growth?", *Economic Policy*, Vol. 31/88, pp. 703–742, http://dx.doi.org/10.1093/epolic/eiw013. [17]

Cabral, L. and J. Mata (2003), "On the evolution of the firm size distribution: Facts and theory", *American Economic Review*, Vol. 93/4, pp. 1075-1090, https://pubs.aeaweb.org/doi/pdfplus/10.1257/000282803769206205 (accessed on 18 July 2019). [79]

Calvino, F., C. Criscuolo and C. Menon (2018), "Cross-country evidence on start-up dynamics", *Industrial and Corporate Change*, Vol. 27/4, pp. 677-698, http://dx.doi.org/10.1093/icc/dty006. [11]

Carreira, C. and P. Teixeira (2016), "Entry and exit in severe recessions: Lessons from the 2008-2013 Portuguese economic crisis", *Small Business Economics*, Vol. 46/4, pp. 591-617, http://dx.doi.org/10.1007/S11187-016-9703-3. [80]

Coad, A. (2010), "Exploring the processes of firm growth: Evidence from a vector auto-regression", *Industrial and Corporate Change*, Vol. 19/6, pp. 1677-1703, http://dx.doi.org/10.1093/icc/dtq018. [35]

Coad, A. et al. (2014), "High-growth firms: Introduction to the special section", *Industrial and Corporate Change*, Vol. 23/1, pp. 91–112, http://dx.doi.org/10.1093/icc/dtt052. [20]

Coad, A. and S. Srhoj (2019), "Catching gazelles with a lasso: Big data techniques for the prediction of high-growth firms", *Small Business Economics*, Vol. 55/3, pp. 541-565, http://dx.doi.org/10.1007/s11187-019-00203-3. [54]

Criscuolo, C., P. Gal and C. Menon (2014), *The Dynamics of Employment Growth: New Evidence from 18 Countries*, OECD Publishing, Paris, https://doi.org/10.1787/5jz417hj6hg6-en. [22]

Criscuolo, C., P. Gal and C. Menon (2014), "The Dynamics of Employment Growth: New Evidence from 18 Countries", *OECD Science, Technology and Industry Policy Papers*, No. 14, OECD Publishing, Paris, https://dx.doi.org/10.1787/5jz417hj6hg6-en. [14]

Cusmano, L. (2018), "SME and Entrepreneurship Financing: The Role of Credit Guarantee Schemes and Mutual Guarantee Societies in supporting finance for small and medium-sized enterprises", *OECD SME and Entrepreneurship Papers*, No. 1, OECD Publishing, Paris, https://doi.org/10.1787/35b8fece-en (accessed on 24 September 2021). [76]

Daunfeldt, S., N. Elert and D. Johansson (2014), "The economic contribution of high-growth firms: Do policy implications depend on the choice of growth indicator?", *Journal of Industry, Competition and Trade*, Vol. 14/3, pp. 337-365, http://dx.doi.org/10.1007/s10842-013-0168-7. [81]

Davis, S., J. Haltiwanger and S. Schuh (1996), *Job Creation and Destruction*, MIT Press, Cambridge, MA. [82]

Decker, R. et al. (2016), "Where has all the skewness gone? The decline in high-growth (young) firms in the U.S.", *European Economic Review*, Vol. 86, pp. 4-23, http://dx.doi.org/10.1016/J.EUROECOREV.2015.12.013. [63]

Deschryvere, M. (2008), "High growth firms and job creation in Finland", *Keskusteluaiheita – Discussion papers*, No. 1144, Research Institute of the Finnish Economy, https://www.etla.fi/wp-content/uploads/2012/09/dp1144.pdf (accessed on 2 October 2019). [5]

Disney, R., J. Haskel and Y. Heden (2003), "Restructuring and productivity growth in UK manufacturing", *The Economic Journal*, Vol. 113/489, pp. 666-694, http://dx.doi.org/10.1111/1468-0297.t01-1-00145. [61]

Du, J. and Y. Temouri (2015), "High-growth firms and productivity: Evidence from the United Kingdom", *Small Business Economics*, Vol. 44/1, pp. 123-143, http://dx.doi.org/10.1007/s11187-014-9584-2. [37]

EC/Kantar (2020), *SMEs, Start-ups, Scale-ups, and Entrepreneurship*, Flash Eurobarometer Survey, European Commission. [9]

Fairlie, R. and S. Desai (2021), *National Report on Early-stage Entrepreneurship in the United States: 2020*, Kauffman Foundation, http://www.kauffman.org/indicators (accessed on 15 March 2021). [69]

Flachenecker, F. et al. (2020), "High growth enterprises: Demographics, finance & policy measures", No. JRC119788, Publications Office of the European Union, Luxembourg, http://dx.doi.org/10.2760/34219 (accessed on 19 July 2021). [42]

Foster, L., C. Grim and J. Haltiwanger (2015), "Reallocation in the great recession: Cleansing or not?", *Journal of Labor Economics*, Vol. 34/S1, pp. 293-331, http://dx.doi.org/10.1086/682397. [83]

France Stratégie (2021), *The Effects of the Covid-19 Crisis on Productivity and Competitiveness - Second Report*, https://www.strategie.gouv.fr/english-articles/effects-covid-19-crisis-productivity-and-competitiveness-second-report (accessed on 10 March 2021). [78]

G30 (2020), *Reviving and Restructuring the Corporate Sector Post-Covid: Designing Public Policy Interventions*, G30 Working Group on Corporate Sector Revitalization, https://group30.org/publications/detail/4820 (accessed on 4 March 2021). [58]

Garicano, L., C. Lelarge and J. Reenen (2016), "Firm size distortions and the productivity distribution: Evidence from France", *American Economic Review*, Vol. 106/11, pp. 3439-3479, http://dx.doi.org/10.1257/aer.20130232. [48]

Geurts, K. and J. Van Biesebroeck (2016), "Firm creation and post-entry dynamics of de novo entrants", *International Journal of Industrial Organization*, Vol. 49, pp. 59-104, http://dx.doi.org/10.1016/j.ijindorg.2016.08.002. [33]

Giupponi, G. and X. Xu (2020), "What does the rise of self-employment tell us about the UK labour market?", Inequality: the IFS Deaton Review, https://www.ifs.org.uk/inequality/what-does-the-rise-of-self-employment-tell-us-about-the-uk-labour-market/ (accessed on 8 March 2021). [68]

Gornall, W. and I. Strebulaev (2021), "The economic impact of venture capital: Evidence from public companies", *SSRN Electronic Journal*, http://dx.doi.org/10.2139/SSRN.2681841. [26]

Grover Goswami, A., D. Medvedev and E. Olafsen (2019), *High-growth Firms: Facts, Fiction, and Policy Options for Emerging Economies*, World Bank, Washington, DC. [7]

Hallak, I. and P. Harasztosi (2019), *Job Creation in Europe: A Firm-level Analysis*, Publications Office of the European Union, Luxembourg. [84]

Hallward-Driemeier, M. and B. Rijkers (2013), "Do crises catalyze creative destruction? Firm-level evidence from Indonesia", *The Review of Economics and Statistics*, Vol. 95/1, pp. 1788-1810, http://dx.doi.org/10.1162/REST_A_00407. [59]

Haltiwanger, J. et al. (2017), *High growth young firms: Contribution to job, output and productivity growth*, Center for Administrative Records Research and Applications, U.S. Census Bureau, Washington, DC, https://www.census.gov/content/dam/Census/library/working-papers/2017/adrm/carra-wp-2017-03.pdf (accessed on 18 July 2019). [23]

Haltiwanger, J., R. Jarmin and J. Miranda (2011), "Who creates jobs? Small vs. large vs. young", *NBER Working Paper*, No. 16300, http://econweb.umd.edu/~haltiwan/size_age_paper_R&R_Aug_16_2011.pdf (accessed on 11 October 2019). [30]

Hurst, E. and B. Pugsley (2012), "What do small businesses do?", *Brookings Papers on Economic Activity*, Vol. 43/2, pp. 73-142. [8]

IMF (2021), *World Economic Outlook Update, January 2021: Policy Support and Vaccines Expected to Lift Activity*, International Monetary Fund, https://www.imf.org/en/Publications/WEO/Issues/2021/01/26/2021-world-economic-outlook-update (accessed on 8 March 2021). [71]

Jibril, H., C. Stanfield and S. Roper (2020), "What drives productivity growth behind the frontier? A mixed-methods investigation into UK SMEs", *ERC Research Paper*, No. 89. [57]

Jovanovic, B. (1982), "Selection and the evolution of industry", *Econometrica*, Vol. 50/3, http://dx.doi.org/10.2307/1912606. [10]

Krasniqi, B. and S. Desai (2016), "Institutional drivers of high-growth firms: Country-level evidence from 26 transition economies", *Small Business Economics*, Vol. 47/4, pp. 1075-1094, http://dx.doi.org/10.1007/s11187-016-9736-7. [41]

Lambert, P. and J. Van Reenen (2021), "A major wave of UK business closures by April 2021? The scale of the problem and what can be done", Centre for Economic Performance. [60]

Lotti, F. and E. Santarelli (2001), "Is firm growth proportional? An appraisal of firm size distribution", *Economics Bulletin*, Vol. 12/6, pp. 1-7. [31]

Mason, C. and R. Brown (2011), "Creating good public policy to support high-growth firms", *Small Business Economics*, Vol. 40/2, pp. 211-225, http://dx.doi.org/10.1007/S11187-011-9369-9. [43]

McKelvie, A. and J. Wiklund (2010), "Advancing firm growth research: A focus on growth mode instead of growth rate", *Entrepreneurship Theory and Practice*, Vol. 34/2, pp. 261-288. [56]

McKenzie, D. and D. Sansone (2019), "Predicting entrepreneurial success is hard: Evidence from a business plan competition in Nigeria", *Journal of Development Economics*, Vol. 141, p. 102369, http://dx.doi.org/10.1016/j.jdeveco.2019.07.002. [55]

Mert, M. (2018), "What does a firm maximize? A simple explanation with regard to economic growth", *International Journal of Engineering Business Management*, Vol. 10, https://doi.org/10.1177/1847979018815296. [38]

Moschella, D., F. Tamagni and X. Yu (2019), "Persistent high-growth firms in China's manufacturing", *Small Business Economics*, Vol. 52/3, pp. 573-594, http://dx.doi.org/10.1007/s11187-017-9973-4. [34]

NESTA (2009), *The Vital 6 Per Cent*, National Endowment for Science, Technology and the Arts, https://media.nesta.org.uk/documents/vital-six-per-cent.pdf (accessed on 2 October 2019). [4]

Neumark, D., B. Wall and J. Zhang (2011), "Do Small Businesses Create More Jobs? New Evidence for the United States from the National Establishment Time Series", *The Review of Economics and Statistics*, Vol. 93/1, pp. 16-29, http://dx.doi.org/10.1162/REST_A_00060. [32]

Nevoux, S. et al. (2019), "La durée d'utilisation des équipements continue de progresser en 2018. Résultats de l'enquête menée par la Banque de France (Productive capital operating times continued to increase in 2018 - Findings of the annual Banque de France survey)", *Bulletin de la Banque de France* 222, https://ideas.repec.org/a/bfr/bullbf/201922202.html (accessed on 11 March 2021). [3]

Nordic Council (2019), *Scale-ups in the Nordics*. [28]

Nordic Innovation (2019), *Mini Evaluation of the Nordic Scalers Programme*, https://www.diva-portal.org/smash/get/diva2:1372693/FULLTEXT01.pdf (accessed on 10 March 2021). [27]

O'Donnell, J., D. Newman and K. Fikri (2021), "The startup surge? Unpacking 2020 trends in business formation", Economic Innovation Group, https://eig.org/news/the-startup-surge-business-formation-trends-in-2020 (accessed on 8 March 2021). [67]

OECD (2021), "Business dynamism during the COVID-19 pandemic", *OECD Policy Responses to Coronavirus (COVID-19)*, OECD Publishing, Paris, https://doi.org/10.1787/f08af011-en (accessed on 5 March 2021). [65]

OECD (2021), *OECD SME and Entrepreneurship Outlook 2021*, OECD Publishing, Paris, https://dx.doi.org/10.1787/97a5bbfe-en. [2]

OECD (2021), *SME and entrepreneurship policy frameworks across OECD countries: An OECD Strategy for SMEs and Entrepreneurship*, OECD Publishing. [53]

OECD (2021), *The Digital Transformation of SMEs*, OECD Studies on SMEs and Entrepreneurship, OECD Publishing, Paris, https://dx.doi.org/10.1787/bdb9256a-en. [1]

OECD (2020), "Coronavirus (COVID-19): SME policy responses", *OECD Policy Responses to Coronavirus (COVID-19)*. [70]

OECD (2020), *Financing SMEs and Entrepreneurs 2020: An OECD Scoreboard*, OECD Publishing, Paris, https://dx.doi.org/10.1787/061fe03d-en. [77]

OECD (2020), "Start-ups in the time of COVID-19: Facing the challenges, seizing the opportunities", *OECD Policy Responses to Coronavirus (COVID-19)*, OECD, Paris, http://www.oecd.org/coronavirus/policy-responses/start-ups-in-the-time-of-covid-19-facing-the-challenges-seizing-the-opportunities-87219267/ (accessed on 10 March 2021). [75]

OECD (2019), *OECD SME and Entrepreneurship Outlook 2019*, OECD Publishing, Paris, https://dx.doi.org/10.1787/34907e9c-en. [12]

OECD (2018), *Entrepreneurship at a Glance 2018 - Highlights*, OECD, Paris, https://www.oecd.org/sdd/business-stats/EAG-2018-Highlights.pdf. [13]

OECD (forthcoming), "Pilot on unleashing SME potential to scale up: New evidence on scale up policies and institutions", OECD, Paris. [44]

OECD.stats (2021), *Structural and Demographic Business Statistics (SDBS)*, OECD, Paris. [15]

OECD.stats (2021), *Timely Indicators of Entrepreneurship*, OECD, Paris. [66]

OECD/Eurostat (2007), *OECD-Eurostat Manual on Business Demography Statistics*, OECD and European Commission, https://www.oecd.org/sdd/39974460.pdf (accessed on 5 August 2019). [18]

Parker, S., D. Storey and A. van Witteloostuijn (2010), "What happens to gazelles? The importance of dynamic management strategy", *Small Business Economics*, Vol. 35/2, pp. 203-226, http://dx.doi.org/10.1007/s11187-009-9250-2. [85]

Penrose, E. (1959), *The Theory of the Growth of the Firm*, OUP Oxford, https://books.google.fr/books/about/The_Theory_of_the_Growth_of_the_Firm.html?id=85FLx2NQlaoC&redir_esc=y (accessed on 1 August 2019). [40]

Puri, M. and R. Zarutskie (2012), "On the life cycle dynamics of venture-capital- and non-venture-capital-financed firms", *Journal of Finance*, Vol. 67/6, pp. 2247-2293, http://dx.doi.org/10.1111/J.1540-6261.2012.01786.X. [25]

Raes, S. (forthcoming), *Understanding SME Heterogeneity: Towards policy relevant typologies for SMEs and entrepreneurship*, OECD Publishing, Paris. [52]

Rivard, P. (2020), *High-growth Firm Characteristics in Canada*, Innovation, Science and Economic Development Canada, https://www.ic.gc.ca/eic/site/061.nsf/vwapj/High-Growth-Firms-Characteristics-Canada.pdf/$file/High-Growth-Firms-Characteristics-Canada.pdf (accessed on 29 March 2021). [6]

Rodrigues, F., N. Tavares and G. de Barros (2021), “Drivers of exceptional job creation – A dynamic probit approach using portuguese firm-level data”, *Portuguese Economic Journal*, Vol. 20/1, pp. 45-69, https://web.b.ebscohost.com/abstract?direct=true&profile=ehost&scope=site&authtype=crawler&jrnl=1617982X&AN=147968465&h=0fJP72zcd%2fsF1YFMbgt14F3EHT0HbmPVEadbwGsuwf4lXTgTl0wenrVUdVyPmfrtMD3Ax%2bJ6hO5yVpCQkc6DOA%3d%3d&crl=c&resultNs=AdminWebAuth&resultLocal=ErrCrlNoProfile&crlhashurl=login.aspx%3fdirect%3dtrue%26profile%3dehost%26scope%3dsite%26authtype%3dcrawler%26jrnl%3d1617982X%26AN%3d147968465 (accessed on 19 July 2021). [86]

Schivardi, F. and R. Torrini (2008), “Identifying the effects of firing restrictions through size-contingent differences in regulation”, *Labour Economics*, Vol. 15/3, pp. 482-511, http://dx.doi.org/10.1016/J.LABECO.2007.03.003. [49]

Schoar, A. (2010), “The divide between subsistence and transformational entrepreneurship”, *Innovation Policy and the Economy*, Vol. 10, pp. 57-81, http://dx.doi.org/10.1086/605853. [51]

Schreyer, P. (2000), “High-Growth Firms and Employment”, *OECD Science, Technology and Industry Working Papers*, No. 2000/03, OECD Publishing, Paris, https://doi.org/10.1787/861275538813 (accessed on 18 May 2021). [87]

Sedláček, P. and V. Sterk (2017), “The growth potential of startups over the business cycle”, *American Economic Review*, Vol. 107/10, pp. 3182-3210, http://dx.doi.org/10.1257/aer.20141280. [74]

Shane, S. (2009), “Why encouraging more people to become entrepreneurs is bad public policy”, *Small Business Economics*, Vol. 33/2, pp. 141-149, http://dx.doi.org/10.1007/s11187-009-9215-5. [50]

Vértesy, D., D. Sorbo and M. Damioli (2017), “High-growth, innovative enterprises in Europe - Counting them across countries and sectors”, http://dx.doi.org/10.2760/328958. [47]

Waehrens, B., D. Slepniov and J. Johansen (2015), “Offshoring practices of Danish and Swedish SMEs: Effects on operations configuration”, *The Management of Operations*, Vol. 26/9, pp. 693-705, http://dx.doi.org/10.1080/09537287.2014.971519. [39]

Notes

[1] See, for example, Criscuolo, Gal and Menon (2014[22]), Haltiwanger et al. (2017[23]), NESTA (2009[4]) and Schreyer (2000[87]). While these statistics typically include firms of all sizes, the evidence shows that large firms are as likely to grow fast as SMEs, which implies that almost the entire population of scalers are SMEs. E.g., between 2013 and 2016, 92% of high-growth firms in Nordic countries were SMEs with 10 to 99 employees (Nordic Council, 2019[28]).

[2] See Coad et al. (2014[20]) for a critical review of available evidence.

[3] See OECD.stats (2021[15]).

[4] The 10-employee threshold may introduce a "mean-reversion" bias. As employment levels tend to converge toward the average value in the long period, random positive and negative fluctuations tend to alternate over time – i.e. a firm is statistically more likely to contract after growing. Thus, by imposing a size constraint at the beginning of the period, there is the possibility that the sample is slightly biased toward contracting firms. A possible solution to both limitations could be to use a size threshold that is calculated on average over the three years, rather than at the beginning of the period (Davis, Haltiwanger and Schuh, 1996[82]; Hallak and Harasztosi, 2019[84]).

[5] See, for example, Parker, Storey and van Witteloostuijn (2010[85]), Daunfeldt, Elert and Johansson (2014[81]) and Rodrigues, Tavares and de Barros (Rodrigues, Tavares and de Barros, 2021[86]).

[6] See, for example, Foster, Grim and Haltiwanger (2015[83]); Carreira and Teixeira (2016[80]); France Stratégie (2021[78]).

[7] The number of scalers is an indicator that is quite inertial over time, as scalers are defined based on a three-year growth period (e.g. scalers in 2013 are companies that experienced a high-growth period in the 2010-13 triennium; see Box 1.2 for further details on the definition of scaling-up firms). Therefore, the number of scalers in 2013 is directly affected by market conditions in year 2010.

[8] Statistics on new business formation are available from at www.census.gov/econ/bfs. The Business Formation Statistics (BFS) are an experimental data product of the U.S. Census Bureau developed in research collaboration with economists affiliated with Board of Governors of the Federal Reserve System, Federal Reserve Bank of Atlanta, University of Maryland, and University of Notre Dame.

[9] In the United States, for instance, the number of start-ups in 2009 was 30 percent below its pre-crisis level in 2006 (Sedláček and Sterk, 2017[74]). Among European countries, the overall enterprise entry rate in 2009 varied from 45% below the 2007 levels in Spain, 7% lower in Italy, about unchanged in Germany (Figure 1.6).

2 How do scalers contribute to economic growth?

This chapter provides new evidence on scalers' growth dynamics for five OECD countries – Finland, Italy, Portugal, the Slovak Republic and Spain. The evidence is based on a pilot exercise using firm-level microdata and focuses on the scaling of small- and medium-sized enterprises (SMEs). The contribution of scalers to economic growth depends on the employment and value they create during their high-growth phase and on their ability to sustain their new scale beyond that phase. The analysis confirms that the contribution of scalers is crucial for economic and employment growth, and provides new evidence on their ability to maintain the new scale and the role played by different types of scalers.

In Brief

Scalers create the majority of new jobs in the five OECD pilot countries; most scalers remain at their new scale or continue to grow in the three years after scaling up

New evidence shows that employment scalers make up only around 15% of SMEs with at least 10 employees (non-micro SMEs) but account for 50% or more of jobs created. Scalers are firms growing in employment or turnover at an average annual rate of at least 10% per year over a 3-year period. Over the 2015-17 period, scalers in employment accounted for 13% to 15% of all non-micro SMEs and contributed 47% (Italy) to 69% (Finland) of all jobs created by growing non-micro SMEs. Even among scalers, the fastest-growing firms make the largest contribution to job creation. About one-third of scalers are "high-growth scalers", i.e. they grow faster than 20% per year on average. High-growth scalers contribute 53% to 72% of all jobs created by scalers. New firms entering the market account for most of the other new jobs, while surviving businesses that do not scale up contribute only marginally. In Portugal, for example, around 5 000 SMEs scaled up in employment during the 2014-16 triennium, creating more than 120 000 jobs. Among those, around 1 500 high-growth scalers created about 70 000 jobs.

The majority of scalers are "mature" SMEs that are at least six years old at the beginning of their growth spell. On average across the 5 pilot countries, mature scalers represent over 80% of all employment scalers and they account for more than 70% of new jobs created by scalers over the 2015-17 period (2014-16 for Portugal). "Young" SMEs (five years old or younger) are twice as likely to scale up than mature SMEs but they account for only about 20% of all (non-micro) SMEs, which explains their smaller share among scalers and the lower contribution to job creation.

Scalers in turnover contribute disproportionately to value creation. Scalers in turnover contribute between 51% (in Spain) and 71% (in Finland and Portugal) to growth in total sales by non-micro SMEs. Turnover scalers also create jobs as they account for 40-65% of gross job creation. Such a large contribution to employment growth is due to two main reasons. First, about one-third of turnover scalers are also employment scalers at the same time. Second, turnover scalers are 50% to 80% more numerous than employment scalers.

The majority of scalers are able to consolidate their new scale or even continue to grow. About 60% of employment scalers continue to add jobs or at least maintain their new scale in the 3 years after their initial high-growth phase. Scalers in turnover are equally likely to scale up again but they are also slightly more likely to reverse their growth trajectory.

The share of scalers that continue to grow differs between economic sectors. At the upper end, between 66% and 75% of employment scalers in high-tech manufacturing maintain their new scale or continue to grow. The typical lower end of rates for successful scalers are in construction but even in this sector around 50% of employment scalers continue to operate at least at their new scale. Importantly, the aggregate contribution to job growth for scalers continues to be positive in the years following scaling up. Support for scalers, therefore, continues to "pay off" beyond the scale-up phase despite some scalers falling "victim to their own success", i.e. they shrink or even exit the market in the three years post scaling.

Young employment scalers are more likely to scale up twice over a six-year period than mature firms. Between 11% (Spain) and 29% (Portugal) of young scalers follow their first high growth phase with a second one. For mature firms, the share of continuing scalers ranges from 10% (Spain) to 20% (Portugal), with an average gap of around five percentage points compared to young scalers across all countries. At the same time, the growth paths of young firms tend to diverge more than for mature firms. Young scalers are more likely to continue to expand but they are also more likely to fail. Around 45% of young firms shrink to go back to a smaller size or exit the market in the three years following their initial high growth. For mature firms, the average is about 7 percentage points lower.

Employment scalers often become turnover scalers and vice versa. Between 14% of scalers in employment in Spain and up to one-third in Portugal continued scaling in turnover in the next three-year period. The opposite growth dynamics, from employment to turnover scaling, are also evident: about 10% to 20% of turnover scalers turn into employment scalers. This suggests that for some firms the scaling-up process is an enduring one that involves a transformation of the way the firm operates.

Introduction

The contribution of scalers to job creation and economic growth depends on the employment and value they create during their high-growth phase and on whether they can subsequently maintain their new scale. Scalers are firms growing in employment or turnover at an average annual rate of at least 10% per year over a 3-year period (Box 2.1). While the contemporaneous contribution to job and value creation by scalers has been widely discussed by economic and policy research, there is less evidence available on the role of scalers in supporting growth beyond their high-growth phase. In light of that, the analysis of this chapter combines two sets of indicators to consider both aspects. The first part of the chapter looks at the contribution to net job creation and net turnover creation by different types of scalers; the second part looks at the growth patterns of different types of scalers in the three years that follow their high-growth phase.

This chapter leverages firm-level data from five pilot countries. The findings build upon harmonised analysis of confidential firm-level data sources from Finland, Italy, Portugal, Spain and the Slovak Republic. The exploitation of firm-level data is a "gold mine" for policy analysis but access is still a bottleneck. Box 2.2 discusses the main advantages that firm-level data bring to the analysis, which include the possibility to flexibly aggregate firms along many different dimensions, to track firms over time and to analyse the evolution of their growth pattern, and to customise indicators and variables to specific policy questions. The analysis confirms that the contribution of scalers is crucial for economic and employment growth and that the contribution is persistent over time. The chapter provides further evidence on the contribution to job and value creation by different groups of scalers, such as firms in different sectors or of different ages, and goes beyond the high-growth phase by considering subsequent growth patterns. After scaling up, most scalers are able to maintain the new scale and their aggregate contribution to job and value creation continues to be positive.

Box 2.1. Definitions of scalers

The definition of "scalers" adopted in this report mirrors the Eurostat-OECD definition of "high-growth firms" illustrated in the *Eurostat-OECD Manual on Business Demography Statistics* (2007[1]). An exhaustive definition is reported in Chapter 1.

- Scalers are non-micro firms that grow in employment and turnover at a minimum yearly rate of 10% over a period of 3 consecutive years.
- "Employment scalers" refers to firms that scale up in employment.
- "Turnover scalers" are firms that scale up in turnover, i.e. the total sales of the products and services by the firm within a given year.
- "High-growth" (employment or turnover) scalers are firms that grow in employment or turnover at a yearly rate of more than 20% over 3 consecutive years.

For all definitions, there is the additional condition that the firm must have at least 10 employees in the year in which the fast growth begins.

Source: OECD/Eurostat (2007[1]), *OECD-Eurostat Manual on Business Demography Statistics*, https://www.oecd.org/sdd/39974460.pdf (accessed on 5 August 2019).

The contribution to job and value creation by scalers

Employment growth is concentrated in a few firms that play a crucial role in aggregate growth. Scalers are firms with 10 employees or more that grow in employment or turnover at an average annual rate of at least 10% per year over a 3-year period (Box 2.1). Over the 2015-17 period (2014-16 in Portugal), employment scalers account for 13% to 15% of non-micro SMEs (SMEs with at least 10 employees) but contribute 47% to 69% of gross job creation, i.e. the sum of jobs created by growing firms in the non-financial business economy[1] (the definitions of the metrics of job creation are described in Box 2.3). New SMEs that enter the market (entrants) also contribute significantly to new jobs; however, some of these entries are likely to be the result of changes in the legal form of the company, such as mergers or acquisitions (*de alio* entrants), which are known to represent a non-trivial share of all entries among non-micro SMEs (Geurts and Van Biesebroeck, 2016[2]). SMEs that close operations account for the largest share of gross job destruction in Italy, Portugal and Spain, while surviving SMEs that contract play a larger role in Finland and the Slovak Republic (Figure 2.1). For instance, scaling SMEs added over 132 000 jobs to the Portuguese economy between 2015 and 2017. Other SMEs growing at a slower pace added around 60 000 jobs, while other surviving SMEs that contracted over the same period accounted for a reduction of about 72 000 jobs, adding to 107 000 jobs lost by exiting firms. New SMEs entering during the triennium contributed with 35 000 jobs.

Most new jobs added by employment scalers are due to firms that are more than five years old. On average, mature scalers, i.e. those who start scaling more than 5 years after entering the market, represent over 70% of all employment scalers and they account for more than 40% of gross job creation across 5 countries.[2] Mature scalers are especially important for job creation in Finland and Portugal, where they are responsible for 50% and 43% respectively of gross job creation among all non-micro SMEs. Young firms are more likely to scale than mature businesses but they account for a smaller share of all firms. Therefore, only around one out of four scalers is a young firm. Young scalers are responsible for 14% to 20% of gross job creation of all SMEs in Finland, Italy, Portugal and the Slovak Republic and for about 7% in Spain (Figure 2.1).

Figure 2.1. Mature employment scalers account for the largest share of gross job creation

Gross job creation and destruction by young and mature scalers and other non-micro SMEs, 2015-17

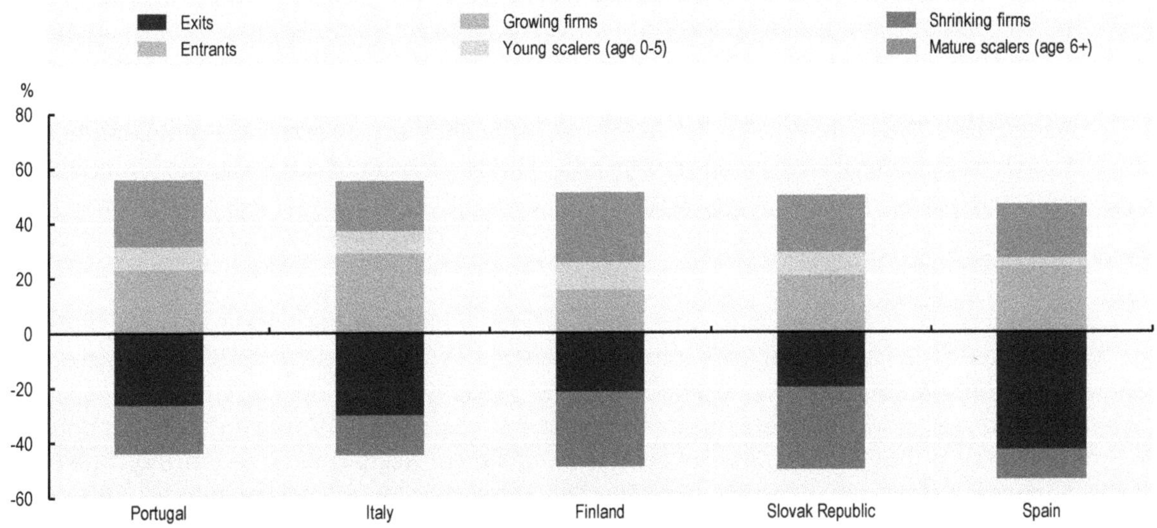

Note: The contribution by each group of firms is reported as a percentage of the sum of gross job creation and gross job destruction in absolute value, which implies that, for each country, the positive and negative segments of the bars sum to 100 in absolute values. Employment scalers grow in employment by at least 10% per year over 3 consecutive years on average, as defined in Box 1.2. The sample includes firms with at least 10 and at most 249 employees. The same chart that also includes micro firms with less than 10 employees is reported in Annex A. The sample is limited to the non-financial business economy. Owing to methodological differences, figures may differ from official statistics.
Source: Calculations based on microdata sources from five countries. See Annex B for details.

Box 2.2. Advantages of analyses based on firm-level data

Statistical agencies have made substantial progress over the last decades in developing business demographic indicators that also cover "high-growth firms" and scalers. Nevertheless, available data still do not allow to systematically compare countries and assess the role played by different groups of scalers. However, this information is important to design effective scaling-up policies. The analysis of microdata from national sources on firms and their employees allows to significantly expand the evidence base on scalers as it brings a number of advantages.

- Firm-level data allow to flexibly aggregate firms along many different dimensions, which is essential to understand heterogeneity. Firms differ substantially even within sector and size classes, thus traditional disaggregation that is commonly available, while useful, rarely proves to be resolutive. With firm-level data, it is possible to analyse different phenomena along with a wider array of dimensions, including age, location, detailed size class, etc. On a more technical note, the analysis of a granular and large dataset (for a large OECD country a longitudinal firm-level dataset contains several millions of observations) also allows disentangling the effect of variables that are strongly correlated among each other (e.g. size and age), which would be impossible to do with aggregated data (Haltiwanger, Jarmin and Miranda, 2011[3]).
- With longitudinal firm-level data, it is possible to track firms over time and analyse the evolution of their growth pattern. This is important to assess the sustainability of the scaling-up process, i.e. to understand the extent to which scaling up is a temporary or stable phenomenon. It also allows studying the transformative process that scalers undertake before, during and after the high-growth phase.

- It is possible to customise indicators and variables to specific policy questions. These include access to global markets, workforce characteristics and location for example. While the economic and business literature has so far focused on a restricted number of sources – typically business registers and balance-sheet repositories – maintained by national statistical offices (NSOs), there is a large wealth of additional data sources that are potentially accessible. In particular, datasets that link annual fiscal statistics of firms with the annual declaration of social security data, as well as other sources such as customs declarations, research and development (R&D) investment surveys or surveys on financial links between enterprises, are of main interest for investigating firm growth. The availability of a wide spectrum of variables and indicators for many firms also provides an ideal setting to apply innovative machine learning techniques. This enables to uncover new findings compared to traditional statistical and econometric techniques.

The exploitation of firm-level data is a "gold mine" for policy analysis but access is still a bottleneck. One of the reasons is that databases are collected and maintained by different administrations (e.g. custom agencies, social security agencies, etc), whose primary mandate is not producing statistics or economic analysis. However, there has been significant progress in this area and commendable best practices exist across OECD countries. For instance, France has established a secure data hub (*Centre d'accès sécurisé distant aux données,* CASD). The CASD facilitates access to over 350 different datasets maintained by different public sector agencies, including the Ministries of Health, the Environment, Education, Finance, Labour, the National Statistical Office and the central agency for social security. Firm-level data are linkable across original sources via a unique identifier, which significantly expands the detail and scope of the analysis. As a result, a wealth of evidence based on firm-level data is now available to policy makers and researchers.

Source: Haltiwanger, J., R. Jarmin and J. Miranda (2011[3]), "Who creates jobs? Small vs. large vs. young", http://econweb.umd.edu/~haltiwan/size_age_paper_R&R_Aug_16_2011.pdf (accessed on 11 October 2019).

Among scalers, those that grow very fast account for most new jobs. About one-third of employment scalers grow faster than 20% annually and are defined as high-growth scalers. More than half of gross job creation by scalers is generated by high-growth scalers across the five pilot countries (Figure 2.2). The same pattern applies to turnover scalers. These figures further illustrate that employment and turnover growth is concentrated in a small number of firms, at a specific point in time.

Scalers play an even more important role in aggregate turnover growth than job creation. Turnover scalers generate 51% to 71% of gross turnover growth (see definition in Box 2.3) across the examined countries (Figure 2.3). As with jobs, surviving non-scalers (in turnover) are contributing only marginally to aggregate turnover growth. For example, in Finland, scalers generated EUR 28 billion of turnover growth between 2015 and 2017, which represents 71% of the total gross turnover growth generated by SMEs. Mature scalers dominate aggregate turnover creation and account for about 80% of gross turnover growth by all turnover scalers, on average across the countries in the sample (Figure 2.3). This makes mature scalers even larger contributors for turnover growth than is the case for job creation.

Figure 2.2. High-growth scalers create the majority of jobs among scalers

Share of gross job creation by high-growth scalers in employment (left) and turnover (right) in all gross job creation by scalers, 2015-17

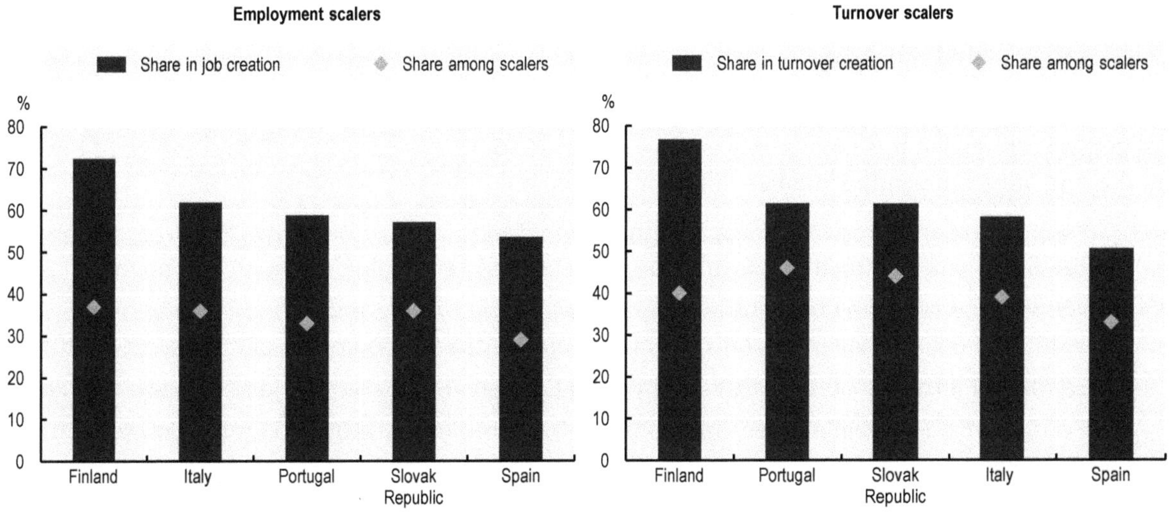

Note: Scalers grow in employment or turnover by 10-20% (medium-growth enterprises) per year and over 20% (high-growth enterprises) per year over 3 consecutive years on average, as defined in Box 1.2. High-growth firms in employment represent 29% of scalers in Spain, 33% in Portugal, 36% in Italy and the Slovak Republic, and 37% in Finland. High-growth firms in turnover represent 33% of scalers in Spain, 46% in Portugal, 39% in Italy and 40% in Finland. The sample is limited to the non-financial business economy. Owing to methodological differences, figures may differ from official statistics.
Source: Calculations based on microdata sources from five countries. See Annex B for more information.

Box 2.3. Measuring the contribution of different groups of firms to employment and turnover growth

Common metrics to quantify the contribution of a group of firms to employment growth are gross job creation, gross job destruction and net job creation. They all build upon the concept of net employment change at the firm level, i.e. the change in employment level for a given firm over a period. The three metrics are defined as follows:

- *Gross job creation:* Sum of all positive net employment changes across a group of firms, i.e. the sum of employment gains of all firms with positive employment growth.
- *Gross job destruction*: Sum of all negative net employment changes across a group of firms, i.e. the sum (in absolute values) of all employment losses of all firms with negative employment growth.
- *Net job creation*: The difference between gross job creation and gross job destruction.

An example of a group of three firms can clarify how these metrics work in practice. The first firm grows from 10 to 15 employees, the second shrinks from 12 to 10 and the third is stable. It results that the gross job creation is equal to five, the gross job destruction is equal to two and the net job creation is equal to three.

An important limitation of these metrics is that they do not take into account the amount of job "churning" inside the firm. Only the net balance between total hires and separations for each firm at the end of the period matters, irrespective of the volume of hires and separations. For example, the three metrics are identical if the first firm is hiring five workers and dismissing none or if it is hiring ten workers and dismissing five.

The same definitions are also applied to turnover growth. For example, gross turnover growth refers to the sum of all positive net turnover changes across a group of firms, i.e. the sum of turnover increases of all firms with positive turnover growth.

Definitions adopted in this report

In this report, the metrics are calculated over three years, to match the high-growth period of scalers. The graphs reported in this section are relative to the 2015-17 period (2014-16 for Portugal). For each country, the firms are divided into five different groups:

- *Young scalers*: Firms that finish a high-growth period at the end of the three-year interval, in 2017, and entered the market less than six years before the start of the growth period (in 2014).
- *Mature scalers*: Firms that finish a high-growth period at the end of the three-year interval, in 2017, and entered the market six years or more before the beginning of the period (in 2014).
- *Entrants:* Firms born in the three-year period (2015-17) for which the job flows are calculated.
- *Exiting firms*: Firms that close operations in the three years (2015-17) for which the job flows are calculated.
- *Other firms:* All other surviving non-scalers.

Figure 2.3. Scalers account for the majority of gross turnover growth

Gross turnover creation and destruction by young and mature turnover scalers and other non-micro SMEs, 2015-17

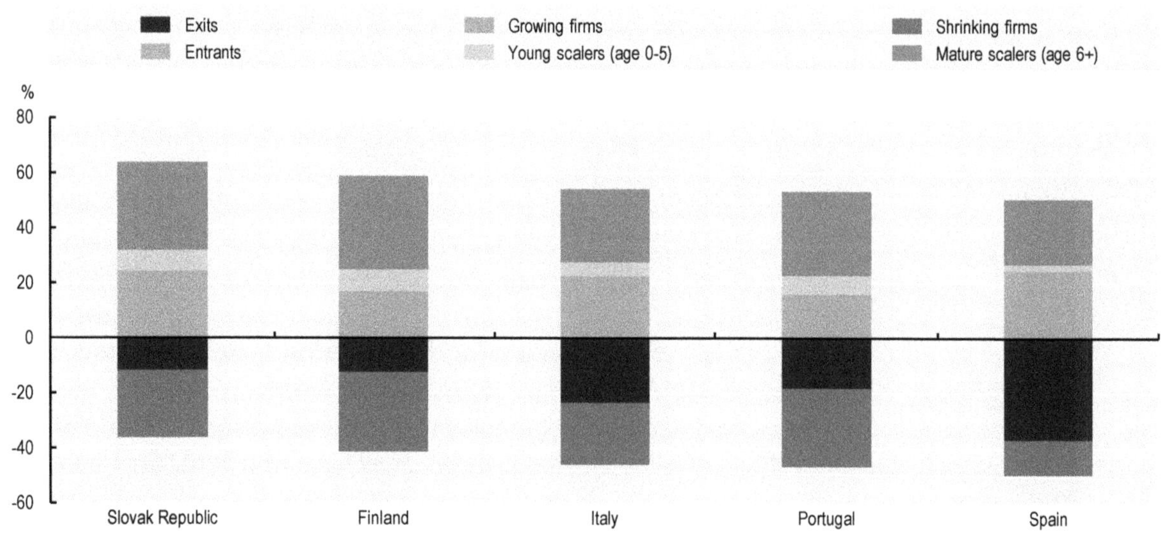

Note: Gross turnover creation is calculated as the total turnover added by all non-micro SMEs growing in turnover over the triennium. The contribution by each group of firms is reported as a percentage of the sum of gross job creation and gross job destruction in absolute value, which implies that for each country the positive and negative segments of the bars sum to 100 in absolute values. Scalers grow in employment or turnover by at least 10% per year over 3 consecutive years on average, as defined in Box 1.2. The sample includes firms with at least 10 and at most 249 employees. The sample is limited to the non-financial business economy. Owing to methodological differences, figures may differ from official statistics. The turnover creation by employment scalers is portrayed in Annex A.

Source: Calculations based on microdata sources from five countries. See Annex B for more information.

Turnover scalers contribute significantly to job creation. Turnover scalers contribute to 38% to 65% of gross job creation by non-micro SMEs across the 5 countries in the sample (Figure 2.4). There are two main reasons that explain the large contribution to employment growth by turnover scalers. First, they are more numerous than employment scalers. For each employment scaler, there are 1.5 to 1.8 turnover scalers across the 5 pilot countries. Second, one-third of turnover scalers also scale up in employment.

Figure 2.4. Scalers in turnover also contribute substantially to job creation

Gross job creation and destruction by young and mature turnover scalers and other firms, 2015-17

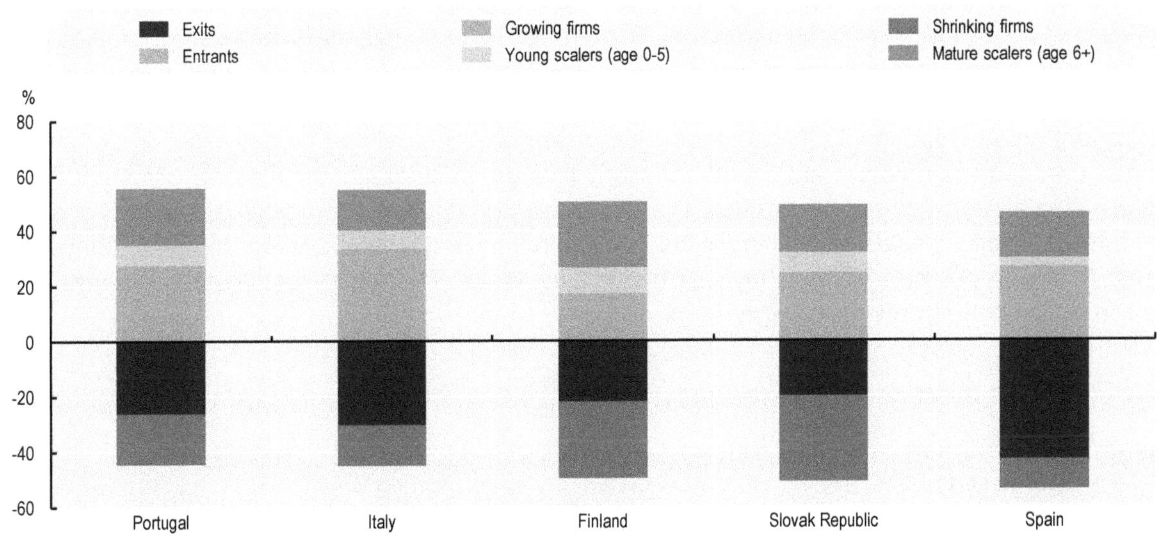

Note: The contribution by each group of firms is reported as a percentage of the sum of gross job creation and gross job destruction in absolute value, which implies that for each country the positive and negative segments of the bars sum to 100 in absolute values. Turnover scalers grow in turnover by at least 10% per year over 3 consecutive years on average, as defined in Box 1.2. The sample includes firms with at least 10 and at most 249 employees. Job creation among SMEs including micro firms with less than 10 employees is reported in Annex A. The sample is limited to the non-financial business economy. Owing to methodological differences, figures may differ from official statistics.
Source: Calculations based on microdata sources from five countries. See Annex B.

Beyond scalers: Micro firms' contribution to job creation

Micro firms are excluded from the definition of scalers as it is difficult to compare their relative growth with that of larger firms. As the definition of scalers is based on a relative growth threshold, even a small absolute increase in a firm's workforce, i.e. hiring one or two additional employees, would cause a micro-sized firm with between one and nine employees to become a high-growth firm. Their inclusion would therefore make it harder to distinguish and compare firms that undertake a transformative process and those that are following a slow and gradual path. The drawback of excluding micro firms is, however, that despite their individually small size they make up a large part of the firm population and total employment. The focus on firms with ten or more employees, therefore, excludes a considerable contribution to job creation by micro firms.[3] Beyond the challenge related to the relative growth definition of scalers, measuring the contribution of micro firms is hampered by incomplete coverage in administrative data sources in some countries. Micro firms may not be incorporated or may be registered as simplified legal entities (e.g. sole proprietorship), benefitting from reduced accounting requirements. Therefore, administrative data sources may not cover all micro firms in a country or provide data that is limited in both the time coverage and the type of information available. For instance, the data for Italy and Spain used in this report are sourced from balance-sheet repositories that cover only shareholder companies, thus providing only partial coverage of micro firms, and in particular of self-employed.

Including job creation from micro firms, SMEs with at least ten employees that scale up account for one-third of gross job creation by incumbent firms. On average across the 5 pilot countries in the period 2015-17 (2014-16 for Portugal), scalers account for 29% of gross job creation when micro firms are included. Growing micro firms account for 31% and growing non-micro SMEs for 11%. The remaining share of gross job creation is due to newly entering micro firms over the triennium (18%) and new entering non-micro SMEs (11%). Even though micro firms are not included in the definition of scalers, some of them do grow rapidly to reach a new scale. Therefore, the contribution by scalers measured including micro firms is a lower bound of the actual contribution of all fast-growing businesses in the economy.

The majority of surviving micro firms are stable in employment over time. The contribution of micro firms to gross job creation among all SMEs with 1 to 249 employees is highest in the Slovak Republic (61%) and lowest in Italy (42%) (Figure 2.5). Every year, around 10% of firms exit the market and are replaced by a similar percentage of new firms, most of which are micro firms. New micro entrants by definition can only create jobs in the year they enter and their contribution accounts for a large share of employment growth across OECD countries.[4] Incumbent micro firms that do not enter or exit in a given year also contribute to employment growth. Similarly to larger businesses, the majority of incumbent micro firms are stable in employment over time. The aggregate contribution to employment growth of surviving micro firms is positive because declining micro firms do not have any "employment buffer" to contract, thus they often have to exit the market if they experience a downturn. Therefore, conditional on surviving, micro firms are more likely to grow than larger firms.

Figure 2.5. When micro firms are included, scalers account for one-third of gross job creation

Gross job creation and destruction by young and mature employment scalers and other SMEs with 1 to 249 employees, 2015-17

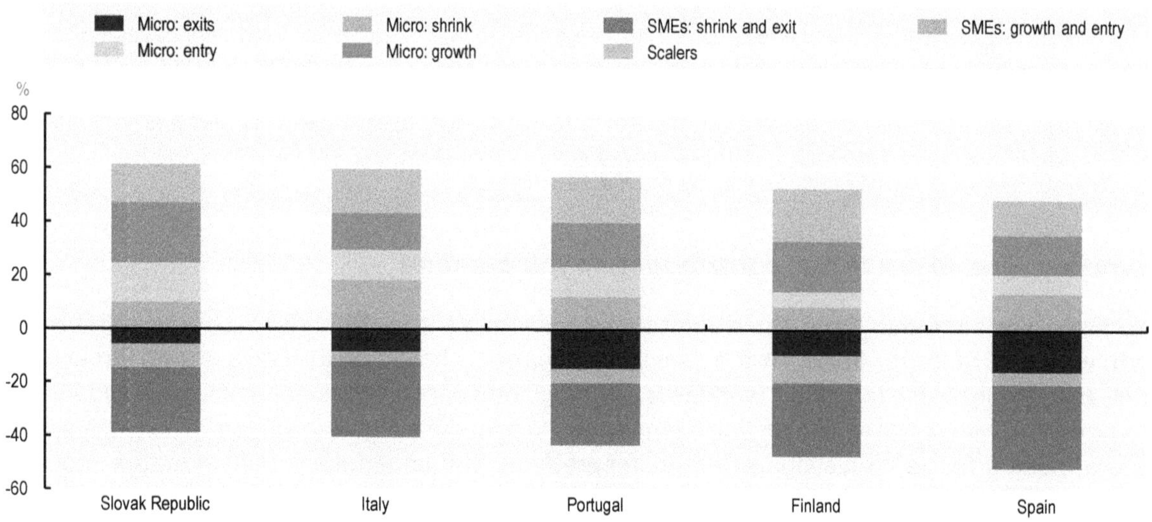

Note: The contribution by each group of firms is reported as a percentage of the sum of gross job creation and gross job destruction in absolute value, which implies that, for each country, the positive and negative segments of the bars sum to 100 in absolute values. Employment scalers grow in employment by at least 10% per year over 3 consecutive years on average, as defined in Box 1.2. The sample includes firms with at least 1 and at most 249 employees. The sample is limited to the non-financial business economy. Owing to methodological differences, figures may differ from official statistics.
Source: Calculations based on microdata sources from five countries. See Annex B for more information.

Extending the definition of scalers to micro firms shows that their propensity to scale is similar to those of non-micro SMEs. Statistical agencies, and notably Eurostat, are making progress in measuring the contribution of "micro scalers". In a recent pilot exercise involving 12 European countries, Eurostat applies a new methodology that requires that the minimum growth in absolute numbers for a micro high-growth enterprise (HGE) is 3.31 employees in 3 years. With this threshold, micro HGEs experience the same absolute growth as an HGE starting the high-growth period with 10 employees and growing on average at 10% per year. The resulting statistics show that around 15% of enterprises with 5 to 9 employees and around 5% of enterprises with 1 to 4 employees are classified as micro HGEs. In addition, micro HGEs are younger than non-micro HGEs: approximately 25-30% of micro HGEs are at most 5 years old, compared to 15-20% of non-micro HGEs.[5]

Scaling up through mergers and acquisitions (M&A)

Firms can grow in employment or turnover either through expansion of their existing business (organic growth) or through acquiring other companies, i.e. through M&A (see Box 2.4). M&A events can have both positive and negative effects on employment growth in the medium to long term. The positive effects may arise from productivity gains after the merger, which translates into employment growth. These productivity gains may materialise because of synergies between activities in the two former entities, technology and knowledge transfer and/or adoption of new management practices (Guadalupe, Kuzmina and Thomas, 2012[4]) The negative effects on employment arise as M&A events create room for rationalisations in the use of labour and opportunity to reduce redundancies.

The definition of scaling up considers both organic and non-organic growth when calculating high growth in terms of employment and turnover. Organic and non-organic growth are two different margins along which SMEs can expand and both should be taken into account in the analysis of scaling patterns. There is however additional value in distinguishing M&A from organic growth because barriers and required support for M&A activity differs substantially from supporting hiring and expansion of existing businesses.

M&A could account for a non-trivial share of scaling-up episodes, at least in larger firms. For instance, evidence from Finland shows that M&A account for about 60% of high-growth episodes in firms with 250 and more employees, compared to about 10% for firms between 10 and 19 employees. Overall, around 15% of high-growth scalers (growing at 20% per annum or more over a period of 3 years) appear to be involved in M&A events in correspondence with the high-growth period (Deschryvere, 2008[5]). M&A also affect the measurement of firm age, as the latter is typically calculated using the entry year, which may not correspond to the actual age of the business for entities originating from an M&A.[6]

Box 2.4. Detecting mergers and acquisitions (M&A) using linked employer-employee data

Traditional firm-level data sources normally do not allow to identify mergers of two distinct companies or the acquisition of a company by another one. A merger is often recorded as the entry of a new business, even if the businesses are not new to the market ("de alio" entry). An acquisition instead results in an existing firm sharply increasing its employment and turnover because of the transfer of a branch of business, an establishment or a whole firm from another entity. The growth by acquisition contrasts with the process of growing by gradually hiring additional employees and expanding the turnover by gaining market share – which is defined as "organic growth".

M&A events can be identified in the data using detailed employer-employee data, which allow tracking large groups of workers that move simultaneously from a company to another. The methodology adopted in this report follows the approach developed by researchers working on Belgian firm-level data (Geurts and Van Biesebroeck, 2016[2]). An M&A is identified if there is a collective transfer of workers from two entities that involves more than half of the workers of at least one of the two entities and more than five individual workers. The approach entails a degree of error and does not allow to precisely track all events. The methodology may also produce some "false positives", i.e. it may classify as M&A events some peculiar cases of organic growth. However, in absence of official administrative data on ownership transfers, the analysis proves to be useful to understand the extent to which scaling up depends on non-organic growth.

Source: Geurts, K. and J. Van Biesebroeck (2016[2]), "Firm creation and post-entry dynamics of de novo entrants", http://dx.doi.org/10.1016/j.ijindorg.2016.08.002.

Nine out of ten scaling-up episodes are not linked to an M&A event and are thus driven by organic growth.[7] The analysis of Portuguese data show that M&As are a relatively rare phenomenon. The procedure used to identify M&As, described in Box 2.4, identifies around 600-700 events per year in Portugal over the period 2011-17, which compares to a sample of more than 30 000 non-micro firms, of which around 4 000 scale in employment. Therefore, 89% of scaling episodes happen because of organic growth. However, M&A events have a stronger association with the scaling-up of bigger firms (which account for a small share in all firms). For around 30% of scaling up in firms with 100 to 249 employees and for half of scaling up of firms with more than 250 employees, it is possible to track an M&A event happening during the 3 years of the high-growth period.

Four out of 10 M&A events involve a firm that scale. Among all M&A events identified in the data, in 40% of cases, the acquiring firm is classified as an employment scaler and in 37% of cases as a turnover scaler in the year in which the event took place or in the following 2 years. The shares are slightly lower (20% and 21% for employment and turnover scalers respectively) for high-growth scalers growing at 20% yearly. Therefore, scaling in most cases is due to organic growth, not to M&A. However, if there is an M&A, it is likely that the acquiring firm is identified as a scaler within the following three years.

What happens after scaling?

Scaling up is a persistent transformation for many scalers. Between 40% and 70% of employment or turnover scalers remain at their newly achieved scale or continue to grow further in the three years after the scaling.[8] Scaling is therefore a sustainable process for many SMEs. A considerable share of scalers even repeats their exceptional high growth. Between 20% and 25% of scalers scale again in Finland, Italy and Portugal (Figure 2.6). The share is lower, at about 11%, in Spain; however, this is because of the high frequency of missing employment information in Spanish firm-level data, which does not allow to track the post-growth trajectory of around 30% of scalers. For firms scaling up over the 2012-14 period, the share of repeated high growth in Spain remains comparable to other countries when the analysis is restricted to firms for which data are available over the full period. Conversely, across the 4 countries, between 20% and 30% of scalers reverse the dynamics of their growth and contract after scaling.

SMEs that scale twice are particularly important for employment growth. These companies increase their employment level by more than 80% over a 6-year period. For example, around 800 SMEs that scaled twice in employment over the 2011-16 period in Portugal created more than 52 000 jobs, with a median growth rate of 170% over the same period. The probability to scale again falls rapidly for scalers that grow at a higher rate. For the high-growth scalers that grow at least 20% on average for 3 years, only about 8% grow at the same rate again for another 3 years.[9]

For around 10% of scalers, no information is available 3 years after scaling; in most cases, it is likely that the company ceased operations. The lack of information is due to the firm not being present in the firm-level repositories used for the analysis or being present with missing information on employment (or turnover, in the case of turnover scalers). The lack of information is open to different interpretations. First, the firm may be closed or about to close, which is typically associated with the business not being successful. Second, the company may have been acquired by another entity, which typically indicates success rather than failure. Third, the lack of information may simply be a "nuisance" in the data, e.g. due to reporting errors. In this case, it is reasonable to assume that the issue affects successful and unsuccessful businesses to a similar extent. It is not possible to know the exact incidence of each of the three alternatives. However, it is known that acquisitions are rare even for growth-oriented businesses (Breschi, Lassebie and Menon, 2018[6]). Conversely, around 8-10% of businesses close down each year and the percentage is not much lower for former scalers, at least based on evidence from the United Kingdom (Anyadike-Danes and Hart, 2019[7]; Coad, 2007[8]). Therefore, it is likely that the majority of former scalers with missing information have ceased operations. Spain can be an exception in this analysis, as information on the post-scaling status is missing for 30% of scalers. This is due to the source data being carefully scrutinised by experts at the Bank of Spain, resulting in blanking of implausible values. In this case, data issues are likely to explain the majority of missing information occurrences.

Figure 2.6. The majority of employment scalers maintain the new scale

Growth dynamics of employment scalers in the three years after scaling

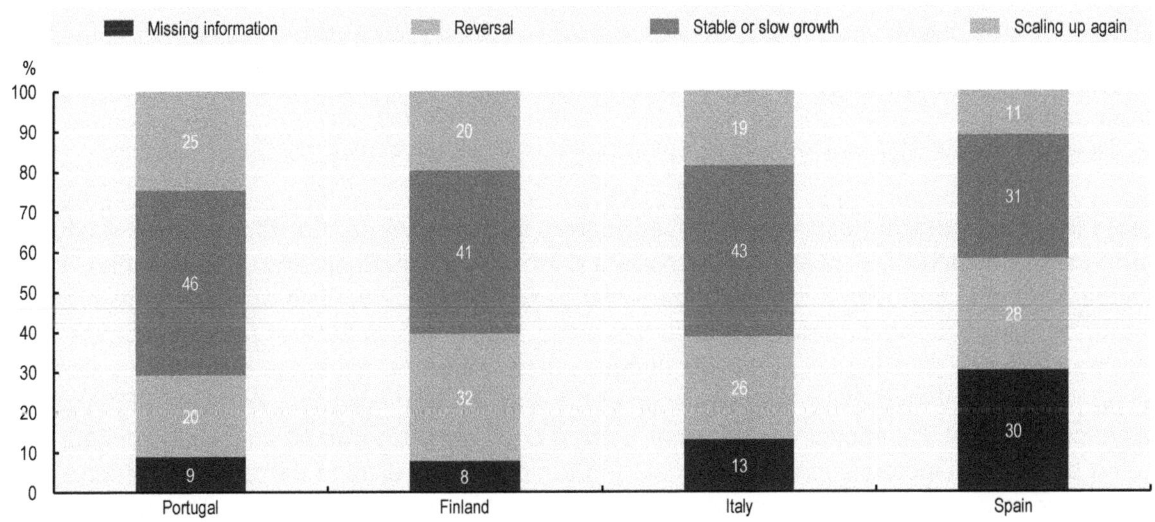

Note: Employment scalers grow in employment by at least 10% per year over 3 consecutive years on average, as defined in Box 1.2. The sample includes scalers that end their first 3-year scaling period between 2011 and 2015 in Finland, 2004 to 2015 in Italy, 2013 to 2014 in Portugal and 2006 to 2015 in Spain. The sample is limited to the non-financial business economy. Owing to methodological differences, figures may differ from official statistics.
Source: Calculations based on microdata sources from five countries. See Annex B for more information.

Scalers in turnover are slightly less likely to consolidate their scale than scalers in employment. About 20% of scalers continue scaling in turnover, compared to 18% of employment scalers. Yet, 37% of turnover scalers remain at the new scale or continue to grow (compared to 40% of employment scalers) and 29% (compared to 26% of employment scalers) reverse the growth dynamics (Figure 2.7). Easier downscaling in turnover stands in contrast to employment downscaling, which can be much costlier for firms. While turnover adapts instantly to the new market conditions, dismissing workers can be costly because of severance pay and related regulations. It can also entail the loss of know-how and of skills that would be difficult and costly to reacquire, should the market conditions improve. Therefore, employment adjustments are smoother and more inertial than turnover fluctuations in SMEs.

Figure 2.7. Turnover scalers are slightly more likely to scale up again

Growth dynamics of turnover scalers in the three years after scaling

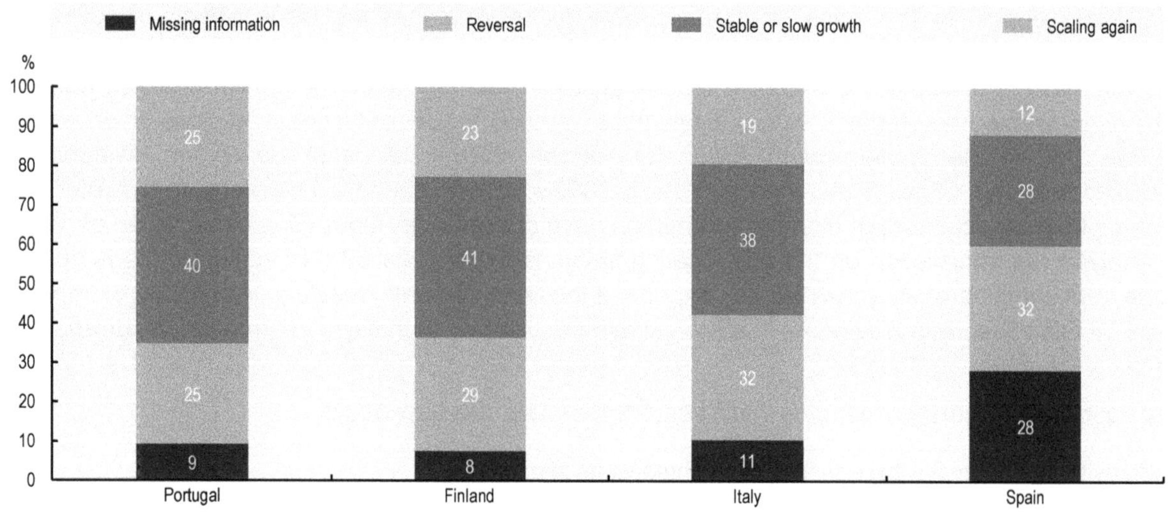

Note: Turnover scalers grow in turnover by at least 10% per year over 3 consecutive years on average, as defined in Box 1.2. The sample includes scalers that end their first 3-year scaling period between 2011 and 2015 in Finland, 2004 to 2015 in Italy, 2013 to 2014 in Portugal and 2006 to 2015 in Spain. The sample is limited to the non-financial business economy. Owing to methodological differences, figures may differ from official statistics.
Source: Calculations based on microdata sources from five countries. See Annex B for more information.

Employment scalers often become turnover scalers and vice versa. For those firms, scaling is an enduring transformation. Between 14% of scalers in employment in Spain and up to one-third in Portugal continued scaling in turnover in the next three-year period (Figure 2.8). The opposite growth dynamics, from employment to turnover scaling, are also evident: about 10% to 20% of turnover scalers turn into employment scalers (see Figure A.1). This suggests that, for some firms, the scaling-up process is an enduring process that involves a transformation of the way the firm operates. For firms that first scale in employment and then in turnover or vice versa, scaling does not appear to be an isolated phase, possibly triggered by external factors such as a sudden and temporary increase in demand but rather a strategy that builds upon an internal transformation in the way in which the firm operates. This points to scaling being predominantly a firm's strategic choice, rather than a random event that makes scalers "one-hit wonders", as part of previous research maintained. Such transformation may not be confined to the years in which scaling in employment or turnover takes place but may rather be part of a firm's long-term strategy, which involves a phase of preparation that may last for several years. A detailed analysis of the transformation process that scalers undertake before, during or after scaling leveraging firm-level sources is the subject of Chapter 4 of this report.

Figure 2.8. Up to one-third of employment scalers become turnover scalers

Turnover growth dynamics of employment scalers in the three years after scaling

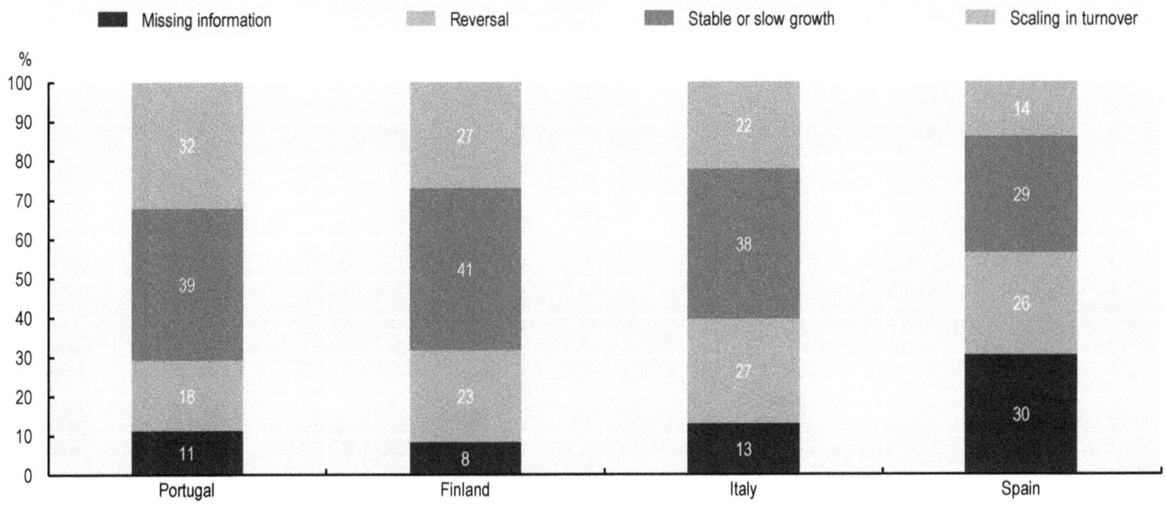

Note: Employment scalers grow in employment by at least 10% per year over 3 consecutive years on average, as defined in Box 1.2. The figure displays employment scalers and their performance in turnover after the initial growth. The sample includes scalers that end their first 3-year scaling period between 2011 and 2015 in Finland, 2004 to 2015 in Italy, 2013 to 2014 in Portugal and 2006 to 2015 in Spain. The equivalent figure for turnover scalers can be found in Annex A. The sample is limited to the non-financial business economy. Owing to methodological differences, figures may differ from official statistics.
Source: Calculations based on microdata sources from five countries. See Annex B for more information.

The sustainability of scaling depends on the sector and the age of scalers

Scalers in the information and communication technology (ICT) sector often repeat scaling. Scalers in construction are the least likely to continue growing. Between 18% (Spain) and 39% (Portugal) of employment scalers in the ICT sector continue exceptional growth in the 3 years following the first expansion across the 4 countries analysed. ICT sector scalers are also less likely to "downscale", underlining the overall lower volatility of employment growth of the sector: 20% to 24% of scalers reverse the growth pattern after scaling (Figure 2.9, right panel). In the construction sector, 7% to 24% of scalers continue scaling, while 35% to 50% of them reverse to a smaller size (Figure 2.9, left panel). The pattern observed suggests that for many SMEs in the construction sector, scaling may be linked to specific characteristics of the market, such as the procurement of public works organised around large contracts or "boom-and-bust" cycles in real estate investments. Scalers in construction may therefore often follow a scaling-up model that is driven by an erratic external demand, rather than by internal improvements in productivity and competitiveness. Chapter 4 of the report discusses in depth the different transformation models that scalers can follow, depending on the different factors that can trigger fast growth, such as disruptive technological innovations or internal improvements in productivity.

Younger scalers in employment are more likely to both scale up again and reverse than mature scalers. Between 11% to 29% of young scalers scale up again, compared to 11% to 23% of mature scalers, the share of scalers that scale again is larger among young scalers than among mature scalers in all countries analysed. Young scalers are also more likely to revert the scaling or exit the market than mature firms, and are less likely to be stable after scaling than mature scalers (Figure 2.9, left panel). The evidence recalls the "up or out" growth pattern that the economic literature attributes to new and young businesses. Young businesses enter small as they need to experiment with their model in real market conditions. Those that are viable need to grow quickly to reach a minimum scale and compete with older firms; those that are not successful instead tend to shrink and exit quickly (Jovanovic, 1982[9]).

Figure 2.9. Scalers in the construction sector are more likely to reverse to a smaller size

Employment growth dynamics of employment scalers in construction and ICT in the three years after scaling

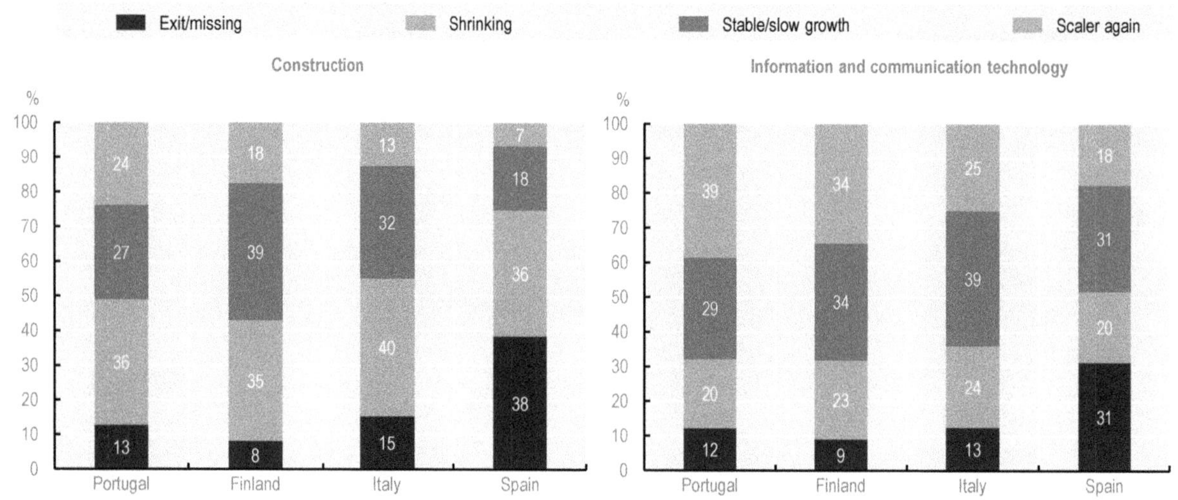

Note: Employment scalers grow in employment by at least 10% per year over 3 consecutive years on average, as defined in Box 1.2. The sample includes scalers that end their first 3-year scaling period between 2011 and 2015 in Finland, 2004 to 2015 in Italy, 2013 to 2014 in Portugal and 2006 to 2015 in Spain. The sample is limited to the non-financial business economy. Owing to methodological differences, figures may differ from official statistics.
Source: Calculations based on microdata sources from five countries. See Annex B for more information.

Figure 2.10. Young employment scalers are more likely to scale up again but also to exit or reverse

Growth dynamics of scalers in the three years after scaling

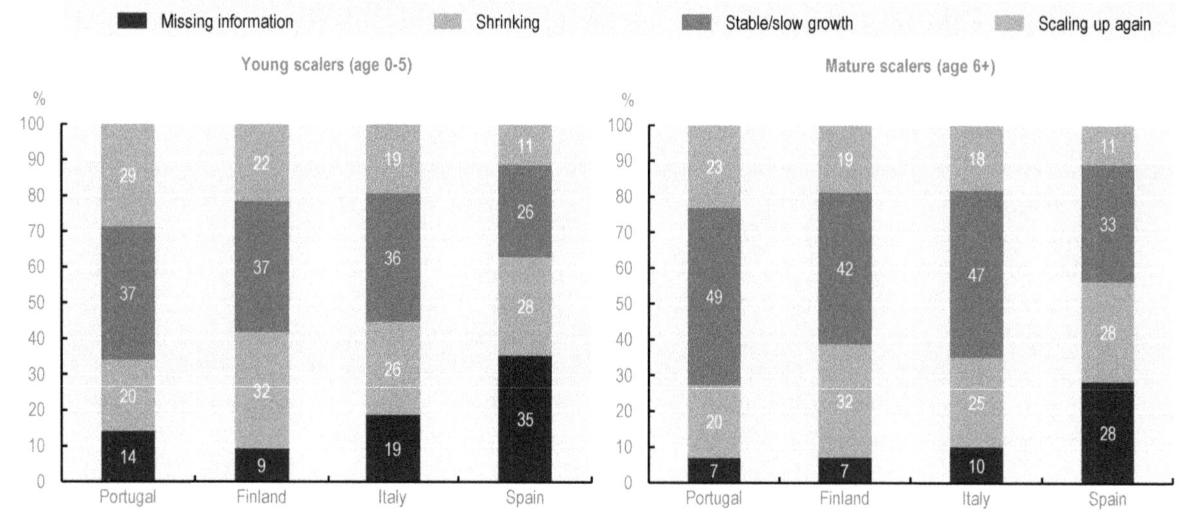

Note: Employment scalers grow in employment by at least 10% per year over three consecutive years on average, as defined in Box 1.2. The sample includes scalers that end their first 3-year scaling period between 2011 and 2015 in Finland, 2004 to 2015 in Italy, 2013 to 2014 in Portugal and 2006 to 2015 in Spain. The sample is limited to the non-financial business economy. Owing to methodological differences, figures may differ from official statistics.
Source: Calculations based on microdata sources from five countries. See Annex B for more information.

Conversely, younger scalers in turnover are less likely to scale up again and to reverse than mature scalers. The "up or out dynamics" that appear to characterise scaling in employment for young firms is less evident for scaling in turnover. Rather, continued scaling seems to be more achievable for firms that have a longer presence in the market. For example, in Portugal, 28% of mature scalers in turnover scale again, compared to about 24% of young scalers. Mature turnover scalers are, however, also likely to exit the market, possibly also because of acquisition by other firms. Between 9% to 34% of mature scalers cannot be followed in the period of 3 years after their exceptional growth period (Figure 2.11).

Figure 2.11. Mature turnover scalers are more likely to scale again than younger ones

Growth dynamics of turnover scalers in the three years after scaling

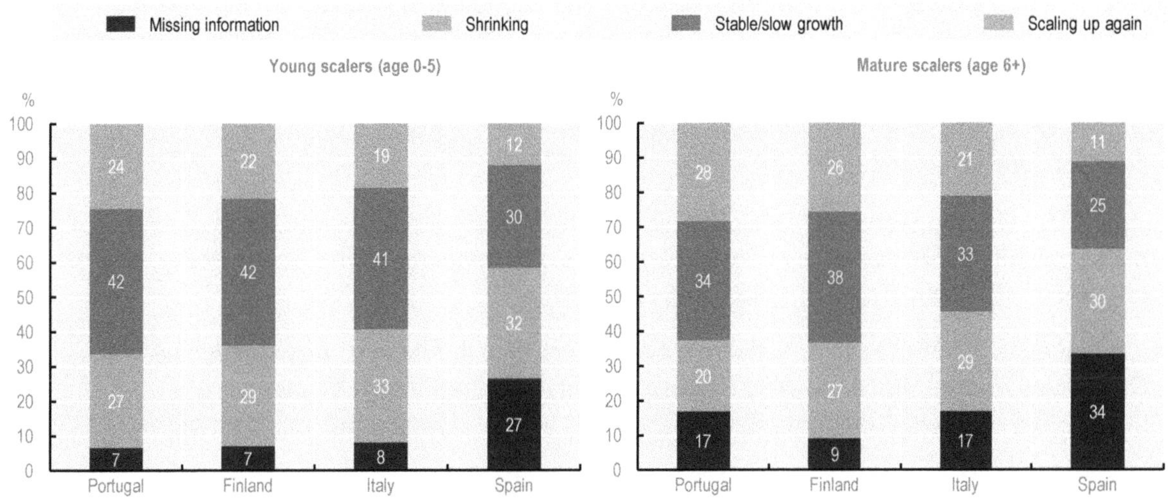

Note: Turnover scalers grow in employment by at least 10% per year over 3 consecutive years on average, as defined in Box 1.2. The sample includes scalers that end their first 3-year scaling period between 2011 and 2015 in Finland, 2004 to 2015 in Italy, 2013 to 2014 in Portugal, and 2006 to 2015 in Spain. The sample is limited to the non-financial business economy. Owing to methodological differences, figures may differ from official statistics.
Source: Calculations based on microdata sources from five countries. See Annex B for more information.

References

Anadyke-Danes, M. and M. Hart (2018), "All grown up? The fate after 15 years of a quarter of a million UK firms born in 1998", *Journal of Evolutionary Economics*, Vol. 28/1, pp. 45-76, http://dx.doi.org/10.1007/s00191-017-0549-x. [11]

Anyadike-Danes, M. and M. Hart (2019), "Fecundity, fertility, survival and growth: High-growth firms in the UK and their contribution to job creation, a demographic perspective.", *ERC Research Paper*, No. 74, https://www.enterpriseresearch.ac.uk/publications/fecundity-fertility-survival-growth-research-paper-no-74/ (accessed on 26 July 2021). [7]

Breschi, S., J. Lassebie and C. Menon (2018), "A portrait of innovative start-ups across countries", *OECD Science, Technology and Industry Working Papers*, No. 2018/02, OECD Publishing, Paris, https://doi.org/10.1787/f9ff02f4-en. [6]

Calvino, F., C. Criscuolo and C. Menon (2018), "Cross-country evidence on start-up dynamics", *Industrial and Corporate Change*, Vol. 27/4, pp. 677–698, http://dx.doi.org/10.1093/icc/dty006. [12]

Coad, A. (2007), "Testing the principle of 'growth of the fitter': The relationship between profits and firm growth", *Structural Change and Economic Dynamics*, Vol. 18/3, pp. 370-386, http://dx.doi.org/10.1016/j.strueco.2007.05.001. [8]

Coad, A., J. Frankish and A. Link (2020), "The economic contribution of a cohort of new firms over time", *Review of Industrial Organization*, Vol. 57/3, pp. 519-536, http://dx.doi.org/10.1007/S11151-020-09777-9. [13]

Daunfeldt, S., N. Elert and D. Johansson (2014), "The economic contribution of high-growth firms: Do policy implications depend on the choice of growth indicator?", *Journal of Industry, Competition and Trade*, Vol. 14/3, pp. 337-365, http://dx.doi.org/10.1007/s10842-013-0168-7. [14]

Daunfeldt, S., N. Elert and D. Johansson (2013), "The economic contribution of high-growth firms: Do definitions matter?". [16]

Daunfeldt, S., D. Johansson and D. Halvarsson (2015), "Using the Eurostat-OECD definition of high-growth firms: A cautionary note", *Journal of Entrepreneurship and Public Policy*, Vol. 4/1, pp. 50-56, http://dx.doi.org/10.1108/JEPP-05-2013-0020. [15]

Deschryvere, M. (2008), "High growth firms and job creation in Finland", *Keskusteluaiheita – Discussion Papers*, No. 1144, The Research Institute of the Finnish Economy, https://www.etla.fi/wp-content/uploads/2012/09/dp1144.pdf (accessed on 2 October 2019). [5]

Geurts, K. and J. Van Biesebroeck (2016), "Firm creation and post-entry dynamics of de novo entrants", *International Journal of Industrial Organization*, Vol. 49, pp. 59-104, http://dx.doi.org/10.1016/j.ijindorg.2016.08.002. [2]

Guadalupe, M., O. Kuzmina and C. Thomas (2012), "Innovation and foreign ownership", *American Economic Review*, Vol. 102/7, pp. 3594-3627, http://dx.doi.org/10.1257/aer.102.7.3594. [4]

Haltiwanger, J., R. Jarmin and J. Miranda (2011), "Who creates jobs? Small vs. large vs. young", *NBER Working Paper*, No. 16300, http://econweb.umd.edu/~haltiwan/size_age_paper_R&R_Aug_16_2011.pdf (accessed on 11 October 2019). [3]

Jarmin, R. and J. Miranda (2012), "The longitudinal business database", *SSRN Electronic Journal*, http://dx.doi.org/10.2139/ssrn.2128793. [17]

Jovanovic, B. (1982), "Selection and the evolution of industry", *Econometrica*, Vol. 50/3, http://dx.doi.org/10.2307/1912606. [9]

Nordic Council (2019), *Scale-ups in the Nordics*. [10]

OECD/Eurostat (2007), *OECD-Eurostat Manual on Business Demography Statistics*, https://www.oecd.org/sdd/39974460.pdf (accessed on 5 August 2019). [1]

Notes

[1] The non-financial business economy includes the sectors of industry, construction, distributive trades and services.

[2] Between 2011 and 2014 in Finland, 71% of scalers were mature firms, 66% in Italy, 78% in Spain and 73% in Portugal.

[3] See, for example, Daunfeldt, Elert and Johansson (2013[16]) and Daunfeldt, Johansson and Halvarsson (2015[15]).

[4] However, previous research shows that, over a time window of several years, the contribution of a given cohort of micro entrants becomes negative or very small, as most of them either fail in the first three to five years of the activity or do not grow. See, for example, Calvino, Criscuolo and Menon (2018[12]) for evidence on 18 OECD countries and Anadyke-Danes and Hart (2018[11]) and Coad, Frankish and Link (2020[13]) for evidence on the United Kingdom.

[5] See https://ec.europa.eu/eurostat/statistics-explained/index.php?title=Characteristics_of_micro_high-growth_enterprises (accessed on 26 July 2021).

[6] An analysis of Belgian data shows that most entrants with more than ten employees are pre-existing companies that reregister as a new firm and "de alio" entrants (Geurts and Van Biesebroeck, 2016[2]). High incidence of spurious entry also implies that firm age is underestimated. However, some of these spurious entries are often detected by national agencies maintaining business registers or similar database (Jarmin and Miranda, 2012[17]).

[7] The figure is consistent with findings from the Scandinavian countries for the period 2014-17, reporting that 85% of scalers grow due to organic growth and 15% due to mergers and acquisitions (Nordic Council, 2019[10]).

[8] As outlined in Chapter 1, the economic literature maintains that scaling is an isolated episode in the firms' lifecycles. High growth in employment over three years is found to not repeat itself for most scalers (Daunfeldt, Elert and Johansson, 2014[14]). However, this is partly due to research focusing on the narrower concept of high-growth scalers, e.g. firms growing at a yearly rate of 20% per annum.

[9] Data for the Slovak Republic is only available for years 2014-19, which is less than the required eight years to evaluate subsequent growth periods.

3 Which SMEs do scale up?

The chapter presents evidence on the incidence of scaling among small- and medium-sized enterprises (SMEs) of different sizes, ages, sectors of activity and locations. The analysis leverages firm-level data from five OECD countries (Finland, Italy, Portugal, the Slovak Republic and Spain).

In Brief

The typical scaler is a mature firm operating in low-technology services

One in 4 SMEs with 10 to 249 employees is an employment or a turnover scaler. Scalers are firms with at least 10 employees (non-micro SMEs) that grow at an average yearly rate of 10% or more in either employment or turnover for 3 consecutive years. Across the 5 countries analysed over the period 2015-17, 13% to 15% of non-micro SMEs scale in employment and 20% to 26% scale in turnover. Scaling in turnover happens more often than scaling in employment because turnover is an output of the production process, while employment is one of several possible inputs: not every firm that grows does so along the employment margin. Furthermore, employment may take some time to adjust to positive or negative trends in sales as firms face fixed costs in both hiring and dismissing workers.

The majority of employment scalers also scale in turnover at the same time. The share of these “double scalers” ranges between 9% (in Italy and Spain) to 12% (in Finland), which means that around two-thirds of employment scalers are also scaling in turnover over the same period (2015-17). The fact that scaling in employment and turnover tend to happen at the same time suggests that, for the majority of employment scalers, the increase in workforce does not lead to lower labour productivity.

Young firms are more likely to scale up than older firms. Young firms, defined as businesses founded no more than 5 years before they start scaling, are 2.5 to 3.5 times more likely to scale in employment and 1.8 to 2.3 times more likely to scale in turnover than old firms (defined as having been active for more than 20 years) in the 5 countries considered. Young firms are also 1.3 to 2.1 times more likely to scale in employment compared to firms of intermediate age (6 to 20 years old) as well as 1.2 to 1.7 in terms of turnover.

Most scalers are mature firms as young firms have a higher probability of scaling but are fewer in number: only one in five SMEs is a young firm. Therefore, even with their significantly higher propensity to scale, young firms still represent a minority of all scalers. About three-quarters of employment scalers have been established at least six years before the beginning of the high-growth phase. Young firms account for the remaining one-quarter of scalers.

Firms of all sizes are equally likely to scale in Italy, Portugal and Spain. The probability of scaling is lower for larger firms in Finland and the Slovak Republic. In Italy, Portugal and Spain, SMEs have a similar propensity to scale across size classes, while in Finland and the Slovak Republic the probability decreases with firm size. Firms with 10 to 19 employees have a 16% probability of scaling in employment in Finland and 11% in the Slovak Republic, compared to 8% for large firms with more than 250 employees in both countries. The propensity to scale in turnover follows a similar pattern.

The typical employment scaler is not a high-technology (high-tech) firm. The propensity to scale in employment across sector groups is highest in knowledge-intensive services, which account for around 12% to 23% of SMEs across the 5 countries in the sample. Larger sector groups such as less knowledge-intensive services represent 40% to 48% of all non-micro SMEs and, therefore, account for a higher number of scalers, even if they are characterised by a lower propensity to scale.

Construction and manufacturing firms have the highest probability of scaling in turnover. One in four firms scale up in turnover in construction and manufacturing, on average across the five countries analysed. The share in other sectors is slightly lower. About one in five SMEs in less knowledge-intensive services and education, social care and health services become a turnover scaler. There are, however, differences across countries. For example, SMEs in the education, social and healthcare sectors have a higher probability of scaling up in Finland and Italy than in the other countries.

All types of regions produce scalers. Across regions, the share of scalers in employment in all non-micro SMEs ranges from 10% to 17% in Italy, 8% to 13% in Spain, 8% to 14% in Portugal and 14% to 17% in the Slovak Republic. In Italy and Spain, several regions in the south of the country with a gross domestic product (GDP) per capita lower than the national average, such as Basilicata, Campania and Puglia in Italy and Andalusia and Murcia in Spain, are characterised by a higher incidence of scaling than wealthier regions in the same country.

Introduction

Available evidence on the distinctive characteristics of SMEs that are scaling up – or "scalers" – is limited. Most of it relates to a few national studies with limited comparability of results due to differences in methodologies and data sources. This chapter provides new harmonised evidence on the characteristics of scalers in Finland, Italy, Portugal, the Slovak Republic and Spain. The analysis can be expanded to several other OECD countries for which similar firm-level data sources are available.

Both pre-existing "structural" characteristics of a firm – such as age, size, sector and location – and dynamic factors that change as a firm transforms – such as integration in global markets or workforce composition – may explain why some SMEs scale up and others do not. Previous research has proposed different views on the role of structural (or *ex ante*) factors and dynamic (or time-variant) factors in explaining the propensity to scale up. Some studies maintain that most of the difference between high-growth and other firms is determined at the moment the company is created and is due to characteristics that do not change over time, e.g. the founders' skills and their motivation to become entrepreneurs.[1] Other studies argue that this view contrasts with evidence that firm growth is very volatile over time and point to the importance of dynamic factors that change over time to explore the nature of fast growth episodes.[2] By covering both structural and dynamic factors, the analysis in this report reconciles these different views and show that both sets of factors matter. This chapter focuses on structural differences, while the dynamic factors are considered in Chapter 4.

One out of four non-micro SMEs is an employment or turnover scaler

Most employment scalers also scale in turnover at the same time. Across the 5 pilot countries in the 2015-17 period, 13% to 15% of non-micro SMEs are employment scalers and 20% to 26% are turnover scalers. Around 10% to 14% of all non-micro SMEs are "double scalers", i.e. scale in both employment and turnover at the same time. Overall, 24% to 31% of non-micro SMEs are scaling along at least 1 of the 2 margins, i.e. at least 1 in 4 non-micro SMEs is an employment or turnover scaler in the 2015-17 period. Scalers in employment are more likely to be double scalers than scalers in turnover. Between 65% and 77% of employment scalers also scale in turnover, compared to 39% to 51% of turnover scalers that also scale in employment (Figure 3.1). The fact that scaling in employment and turnover tend to happen at the same time suggests that for the majority of employment scalers the increase in workforce does not come at the cost of productivity. Chapter 4 looks at productivity trends in scalers more closely, to find that employment scalers often experience an increase in labour productivity (revenue over employment) in the two years before the scaling phase. Higher productivity in turn can translate into higher wages for workers and support the "sustainability" of the larger scale over time.

There are at least three reasons why scaling in turnover is more frequent than scaling in employment. First, turnover is an output of the production process, while employment is one of several possible inputs. Not every firm that grows does so along the employment margin, as production can grow by adding other inputs – e.g., a firm may increase its sales by investing more in capital goods such as machinery or equipment, rather than in employment. Second, turnover is typically measured in nominal value and in domestic currency, thus the inflation rate translates into spurious growth. In the countries and periods under analysis, the yearly inflation rate was around 1-2%. Third, employment may take some time to adjust to positive or negative trends in sales, as firms face fixed costs in both hiring and dismissing workers. E.g., firms may struggle to find the staff with the right skills and, symmetrically, if they need to resize they may incur additional costs, due to e.g. severance pay. Firms may also decide to expand their workforce by subcontracting or outsourcing employment services in the short term. The comparison of scaling in employment with scaling in turnover points to the different ways in which firms can scale up, depending on the factors that trigger the fast growth. For instance, a sudden surge in demand due to external factors has very different implications for the company than a disruptive innovation developed inside the firm, even if both events may result in a similar fast growth in market share in the short term. The different scaling models that SMEs can follow are discussed in depth in Chapter 4 of this report.

Whether firms scale partly depends on the general performance of the economy. For example, following the 2007-08 global financial crisis, only around 5% of Spanish firms and about 10% of Italian SMEs scaled up over the 2009-11 period. By 2017, 13% of SMEs were at the end of the scaling phase in Spain and 14% in Italy. Similar to employment scaling, the share of turnover scalers in all non-micro SMEs has increased in the past decade, growing by around 50% from 2011 to 2017 in Finland and Italy, almost tripling in Spain.

Figure 3.1. Scaling in turnover is more frequent than scaling in employment

Share of scalers by type (employment, turnover or both) among all scalers

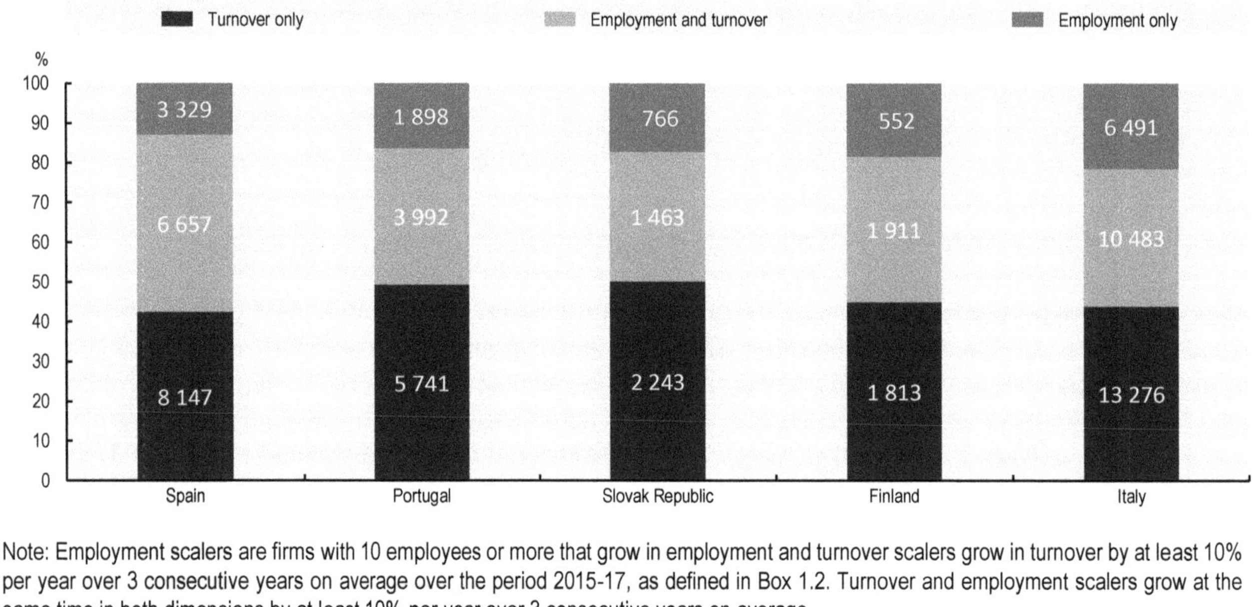

Note: Employment scalers are firms with 10 employees or more that grow in employment and turnover scalers grow in turnover by at least 10% per year over 3 consecutive years on average over the period 2015-17, as defined in Box 1.2. Turnover and employment scalers grow at the same time in both dimensions by at least 10% per year over 3 consecutive years on average.
Source: Calculations based on microdata sources from five countries. See Annex B for more information.

Younger firms are more likely to scale but most scalers are mature firms

Across all five countries analysed, young firms are two to three times more likely to scale up in employment than old firms. More than 20% of young firms with less than 6 years of activity scale in employment, compared to 7% of firms with more than 20 years of activity (Figure 3.2). The share of scalers for intermediate age classes – 6-10 and 11-20 years of activity – situates in the middle. "Up or out" dynamics characterise the growth and survival pattern of young firms and explain their disproportionate contribution to job creation. Young firms enter small because entrepreneurs are uncertain about the potential of their business in the market. Those who happen to be viable grow quickly to reach the same scale as their competitors, while those who do not succeed exit (Box 3.1).

Box 3.1. Young firms and "up or out" dynamics

The empirical evidence of the disproportionate contribution to employment growth of young small firms is extensive and covers the United States (US) (Haltiwanger, Jarmin and Miranda, 2011[1]), several OECD countries (Criscuolo, Gal and Menon, 2014[2]) as well as emerging economies (Grover Goswami, Medvedev and Olafsen, 2019[3]). Young firms can contribute to aggregate employment growth in their entry year by generating a new business entity and, in their post-entry year, by expanding the initial employment level. When disentangling the role of entry from the role of expansion, the evidence from the studies listed above shows that entry explains most of the contribution to job creation. Young firms also have very high job destruction rates from exit. However, young firms that survive grow more rapidly than mature firms.

Why do young firms grow faster but also show a higher mortality rate? Young firms are characterised by "up or out "dynamics (Haltiwanger, Jarmin and Miranda, 2011[1]; Jovanovic, 1982[4]). New entrants learn about their market potential as they operate in the industry. The successful ones survive and grow to reach the same scale as competitors; the unsuccessful decline and fail. The "up or out" dynamics are broadly confirmed by empirical evidence. This implies that the contribution to the economy of the group of young firms as a whole is not necessarily larger than the contribution of older firms.

Source: Haltiwanger, J., R. Jarmin and J. Miranda (2011[1]), "Who creates jobs? Small vs. large vs. young", http://econweb.umd.edu/~haltiwan/size_age_paper_R&R_Aug_16_2011.pdf (accessed on 11 October 2019); Criscuolo, C., P. Gal and C. Menon (2014[2]), "The Dynamics of Employment Growth: New Evidence from 18 Countries", https://doi.org/10.1787/5jz417hj6hg6-en; Grover Goswami, A., D. Medvedev and E. Olafsen (2019[3]), "High-growth firms: Facts, fiction, and policy options for emerging economies", World Bank, Washington, DC; Jovanovic, B. (1982[4]), "Selection and the evolution of Industry", http://dx.doi.org/10.2307/1912606.

Young firms scale more frequently but account for a small share of firms. Only one in five non-micro SMEs is a young firm. Therefore, even if they have a higher propensity to scale, young firms still represent a minority of all scalers: only about one-quarter of employment scalers are young, at the beginning of the high-growth phase. Mature scalers that have existed for at least six years make up the remaining three-quarters of employment scalers (Figure 3.2). Among them, the oldest firms, aged at least 21 years when they start scaling up, represent about one-fifth of scalers.

Firms are more likely to scale in turnover than in employment and more so as they age. About one-third of young firms are turnover scalers on average across countries. The probability of scaling falls to 16% for firms that are more than 20 years old (Figure 3.2). Thus, the decline in the probability of scaling with firm age mirrors the trend observed for scaling in employment. However, the younger the firm, the smaller the difference in the probability of scaling in turnover as compared to scaling in employment. Old firms are more than twice as likely to scale in turnover as in employment,[3] while young (0-5 years of activity) and medium-aged firms (6-10) are around 1.5 times more likely. One possible explanation of this finding is that, for some young firms, scaling in employment is a prerequisite to survive, as they need to quickly hire the necessary workforce that allows operating at a viable scale (Box 3.1). Later in their lifecycle, once firms have consolidated their workforce and reached a viable scale, firms may be able to accommodate an increase in demand without large adjustments to their employment level.

Figure 3.2. Younger firms are more likely than older firms to scale in employment

Share of non-micro firms that scale in employment, by age category

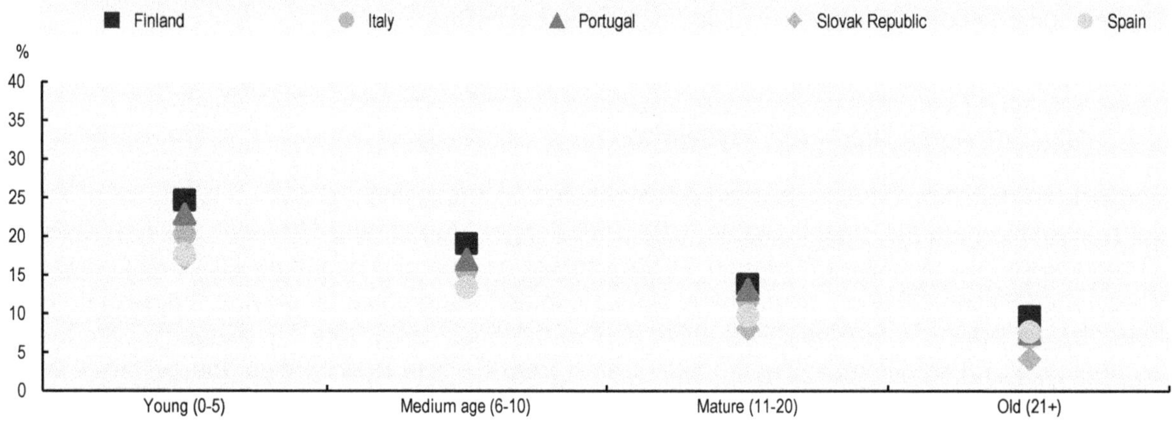

Note: Employment scalers are firms with 10 employees or more that grow in employment by at least 10% per year over 3 consecutive years on average, as defined in Box 1.2. The chart reports the share of scalers in the total number of firms with more than 10 employees in the same age category at the beginning of the period. The shares are calculated yearly and reported on average across the full period, weighted by the number of firms active in each year. The averages are computed on scalers that end their scaling-up period from 2011 to 2018 in Finland, 2004 to 2018 in Italy, 2013 to 2016 in Portugal, 2017 to 2018 in the Slovak Republic and 2006 to 2018 in Spain.
Source: Calculations based on microdata sources from five countries. See Annex B for more information.

Figure 3.3. The probability of scaling in turnover still falls with age but the difference between groups diminishes

Share of non-micro firms that scale in turnover by age category

Note: Turnover scalers are firms with 10 employees or more that grow in turnover by at least 10% per year over 3 consecutive years on average, as defined in Box 1.2. The chart reports the share of scalers in the total number of firms with more than 10 employees in the same age category at the beginning of the period. The shares are calculated yearly and reported on average across the full period, weighted by the number of firms active in each year. The averages are computed on scalers that end their scaling-up period from 2011 to 2018 in Finland, 2004 to 2018 in Italy, 2013 to 2016 in Portugal, 2017 to 2018 in the Slovak Republic and 2006 to 2018 in Spain.
Source: Calculations based on microdata sources from five countries. See Annex B for more information.

Figure 3.4. The majority of scalers are older firms that have operated for more than 11 years

Share of employment scalers in all scalers by age category

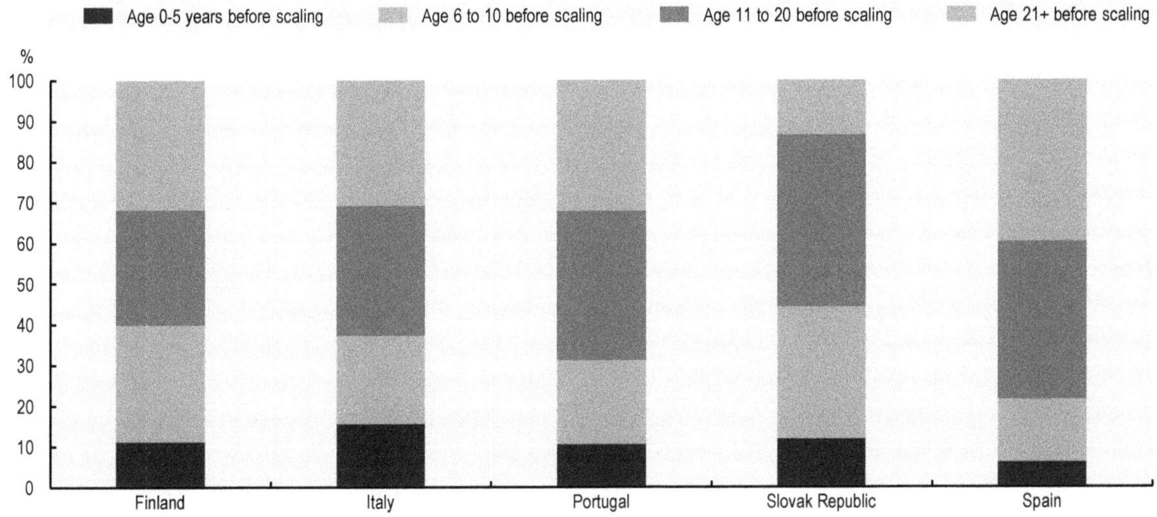

Note: Employment scalers are firms with 10 employees or more that grow in employment by at least 10% per year as defined in Box 1.2. The sample includes scalers that end their first 3-year scaling period between 2011 and 2015 in Finland, 2004 to 2015 in Italy, 2013 to 2014 in Portugal and 2006 to 2015 in Spain.

Source: Calculations based on microdata sources from five countries. See Annex B for more information.

Firms of different sizes are similarly likely to scale

Firms of different sizes tend to have similar propensities to scale in employment in Italy, Portugal and Spain. Across the 3 countries, the probability of firms to scale up is very similar across size classes, with differences amounting for about 1-2 percentage points, compared to a baseline probability of scaling up of around 11-12% (Figure 3.5).

In Finland and the Slovak Republic, larger firms are instead less likely to scale up. In the Slovak Republic, SMEs with 10 to 19 employees are around 2-3 percentage points more likely to scale than larger SMEs with 20 employees or more. In Finland, the differences across size classes are even more pronounced, with up to 16% of SMEs scaling up in the 10-19 employees size class, compared to 12% for SMEs in the 100-249 size class. As larger firms are also older and older firms scale less often as mentioned above, the declining pattern in the share of scalers for larger firms could actually be driven by age differences. However, the differences across size classes hold also in a more advanced analysis that takes into account firm age as well as the different sectoral composition across size classes.

Turnover scalers also show a similar pattern in the propensity to scale across size classes. In Italy and Spain, SMEs of different sizes have a similar probability of scaling up (around 20% in Italy, 18% in Spain). Large firms have the same (in Spain) or about two percentage points lower (in Italy) probability of scaling up than small firms within these countries. In Portugal, medium-sized firms with at least 100 and at most 249 employees have a 2-4 percentage-point lower probability of scaling up compared to the 20-22% share among small firms. In Finland and the Slovak Republic, the probability of scaling up in turnover decreases more rapidly with firm size. About 23% of firms between 10 and 49 employees in Finland scale up, compared to 15% of large firms. In the Slovak Republic, 29% of firms with 10-19 employees and around 26% of firms with 20-249 employees scale up, in contrast with 18% of large firms (Figure 3.6).

Figure 3.5. Firms of different sizes have a similar probability of scaling in employment in Italy, Portugal and Spain

Share of firms scaling in employment in the total number of non-micro firms, by size category

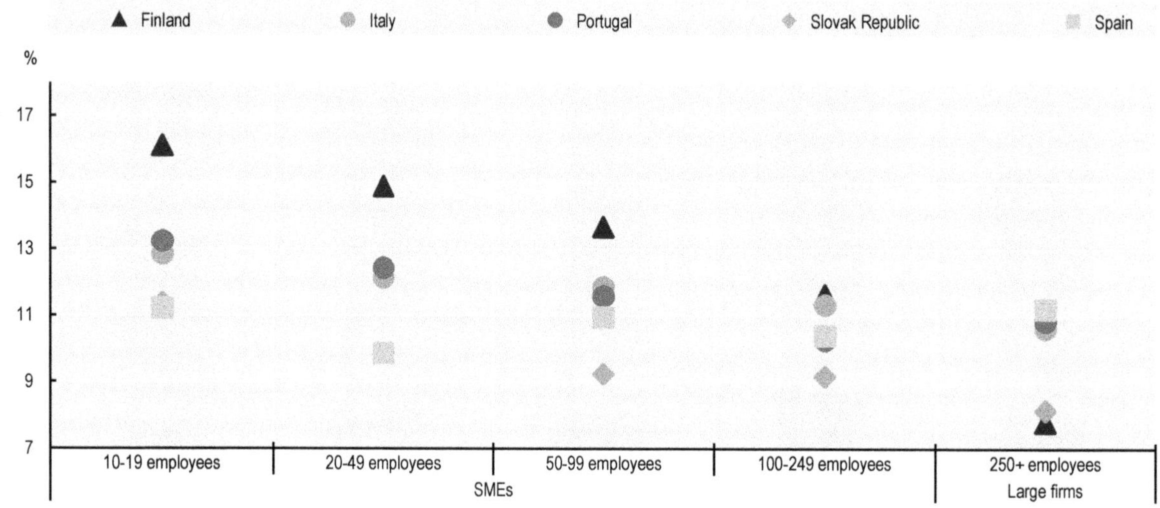

Note Employment scalers are firms with 10 employees or more that grow in employment by at least 10% per year on average, as defined in Box 1.2. The chart reports the share of scalers in the total number of firms with more than 10 employees in the same age category at the beginning of the period. The shares are calculated yearly and reported on average across the full period, weighted by the number of firms active in each year. The averages are computed on scalers that end their scaling-up period in 2011 to 2018 in Finland, 2004 to 2018 in Italy, 2013 to 2017 in Portugal, 2017 to 2018 in the Slovak Republic and 2006 to 2018 in Spain.
Source: Calculations based on microdata sources from five countries. See Annex B for more information.

Figure 3.6. Probability of scaling in turnover falls for the largest firms across all countries

Share of non-micro firms that scale in turnover by size category

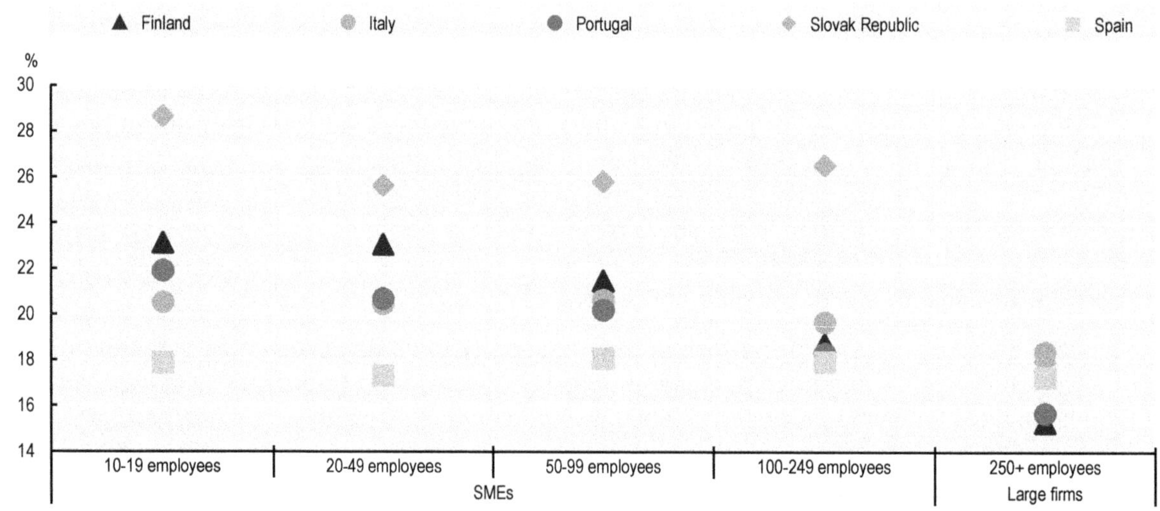

Note: Turnover scalers are firms with 10 employees or more that grow in turnover by at least 10% per year on average, as defined in Box 1.2. The chart reports the share of scalers in the total number of firms with more than 10 employees in the same age category at the beginning of the period. The shares are calculated yearly and reported on average across the full period, weighted by the number of firms active in each year. The averages are computed on scalers that end their scaling-up period in 2011 to 2018 in Finland, 2004 to 2018 in Italy, 2013 to 2017 in Portugal, 2017 to 2018 in the Slovak Republic and 2006 to 2018 in Spain.
Source: Calculations based on microdata sources from five countries. See Annex B for more information.

Small SMEs exploit lower co-ordination costs in the early stages of their growth, while large firms may be better at integrating in global markets and at innovating. The evidence presented above shows that there is not a conclusive answer on whether small firms grow faster and scale up more often, as the pattern differs across countries. Such debate has a long history in economic research (Gibrat, 1931[5]).[4] Small firms may, at least initially, grow faster as they face fewer internal co-ordination costs between managers and workers, which may hamper the growth of large(r) firms. However, in a knowledge-based economy, large firms may be advantaged in introducing innovations that have an increasing codified component that requires larger research teams (Jones, 2009[6]). Larger firms may also be better positioned to reach foreign markets with fixed entry costs, due to different regulations or the need to partner with a local distributor for example (Melitz, 2003[7]; OECD, 2019[8]).

Most scalers are in less knowledge-intensive services

The typical scaler is neither a knowledge-intensive nor a high-tech firm. The propensity to scale up across sectors is highest in knowledge-intensive services but firms in this sector account for only a small share of all firms with at least 10 employees, i.e. 9% of firms in Italy and Portugal, up to 20% in Finland. Larger sectors such as less knowledge-intensive services represent 38% to 46% of all non-micro SMEs and, therefore, account for a higher number of scalers even if they are characterised by a lower propensity to scale. For instance, more than one-third of employment scalers in Portugal and 46% of employment scalers in Spain operate in less knowledge-intensive services (Figure 3.7).[5]

SMEs in knowledge-intensive services have a high propensity to scale up in employment. In Finland, Portugal and Spain, 15% to 23% of firms in knowledge-intensive services are employment scalers – more than in any of the other five sectoral groups (high- and medium-high tech manufacturing; low- and medium-low tech manufacturing; less knowledge-intensive services; education, social, and health; and construction) (Figure 3.8). In Italy and the Slovak Republic, the share of employment scalers in knowledge-intensive services is the second-highest, with 18% and 12% respectively. Knowledge-intensive services include activities with high digital content, such as telecommunications and computer programming, consultancy and related activities, that have been able to grab the productivity benefits of information technologies over the last decade (OECD, 2021[9]). Knowledge-intensive services also include business service activities, such as management consultancy, advertising and employment activities, which employ many highly educated workers. Previous research shows that education and investments in human capital, such as training, play an important role in explaining firm growth and the probability of scaling (Daunfeldt, Elert and Johansson, 2016[10]).

The shares of scalers in other sector groups differ across countries and no common pattern emerges. For instance, the education, social and health service sectors are the group with the highest incidence of employment scalers in Italy and the lowest share in Portugal and the Slovak Republic. Given that these sectors are mainly producing non-tradable services (OECD, 2018[11]), these differences may reflect the orientation toward the local internal market of Italian scalers and a stronger specialisation in tradable goods and services for Portuguese and Slovak scalers.

Construction and manufacturing firms have the highest probability of scaling in turnover. One in four non-micro SMEs operating in construction or in high- and medium-high tech manufacturing scale up, on average across the five countries analysed. The share of turnover scalers in other sectors is slightly lower: about one in five SMEs in less-knowledge intensive services or education, social care and health services become a turnover scaler. There are, however, differences across countries. For example, SMEs in less-knowledge intensive services have a higher probability of scaling up in Portugal and the Slovak Republic than in the other countries (Figure 3.9).

Figure 3.7. Most scalers are in less knowledge-intensive services

Share of employment scalers by their main sector of activity

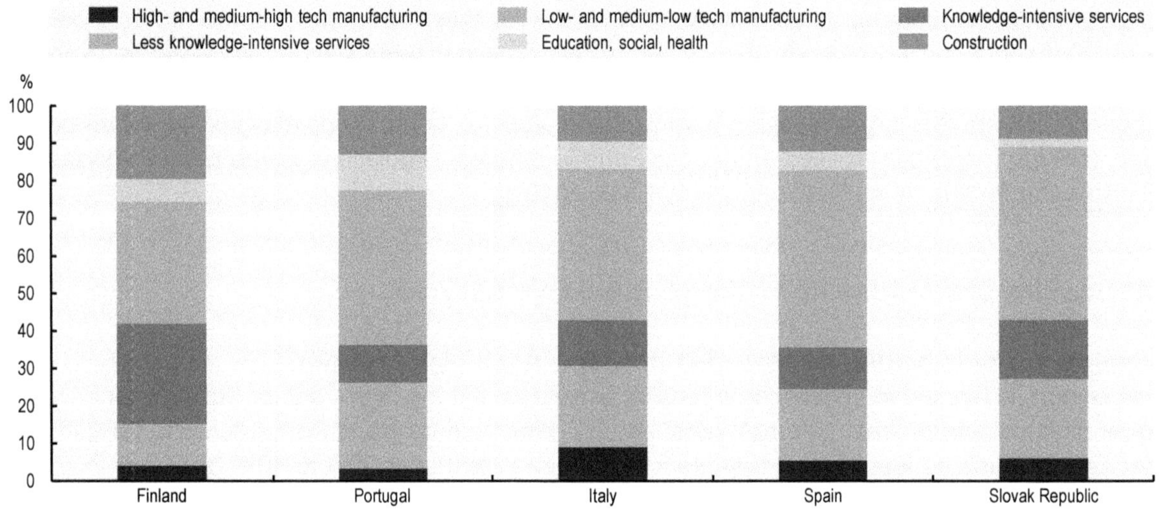

Note: For each country, the chart reports the average share of scalers of a given sector group among all scalers. Employment and turnover scalers are firms with 10 employees or more that grow in employment on in turnover respectively, by at least 10% per year over 3 consecutive years on average over the period 2015-17, as defined in Box 1.2. See Annex C for a detailed list of the two-digit sectors included in each sector group.
Source: Calculations based on microdata sources from five countries. See Annex B for more information.

Figure 3.8. SMEs in knowledge-intensive services have a high probability of scaling up in employment

Share of firms scaling in employment in all non-micro firms in the same sector

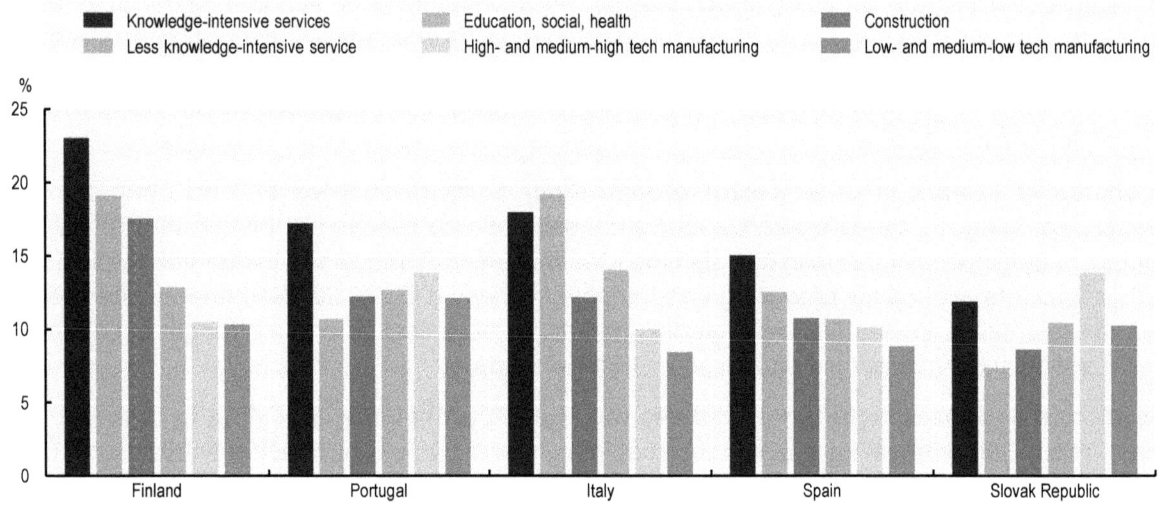

Note: The chart reports the share of scalers in the total number of firms in the same size category with more than 10 employees at the beginning of the period. Employment scalers are firms with 10 employees or more that grow in employment by at least 10% per year, as defined in Box 1.2. The shares are calculated yearly and reported on average across the full period, weighted by the number of firms active in each year. The averages are computed on scalers that end their scaling-up period in 2011 to 2018 in Finland, 2004 to 2018 in Italy, 2013 to 2017 in Portugal, 2017 to 2018 in the Slovak Republic and 2006 to 2018 in Spain. The sector groups are defined in Annex C.
Source: Calculations based on microdata sources from five countries. See Annex B for more information.

Technological factors and a high incidence of subcontracting may explain the higher probability of scaling in turnover than in employment in high-tech manufacturing and construction. The disconnect between scaling in turnover and scaling in employment in medium-high tech manufacturing is likely to be driven by the higher capital intensity of the production process and a lower reliance on labour. High-medium tech manufacturing firms can expand production and gain market shares by investing in machinery and equipment to increase labour productivity for example, without necessarily expanding the workforce. This explanation, however, is less likely to hold in the construction sector, which is typically more labour-intensive. Rather, the higher share of scalers in turnover than in employment may be explained by the high incidence of subcontracting and outsourcing of employment services in this sector (Fellini, Ferro and Fullin, 2016[12]).[6] Turnover scalers in construction may still result in new jobs, which may not fully appear in the statistics, as they are not employed directly by the scaling company.

Figure 3.9. Construction and manufacturing firms are more likely to scale in turnover than employment

Share of firms scaling in employment in all non-micro firms in the same sector

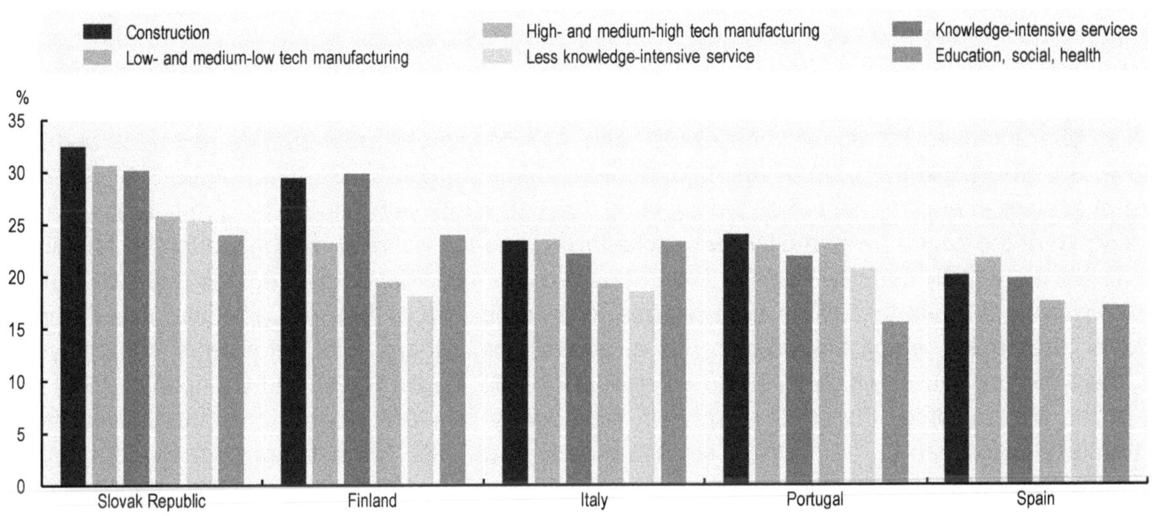

Note: Turnover scalers are firms with 10 employees or more that grow in turnover by at least 10% per year on average, as defined in Box 1.2. The shares are calculated yearly and reported on average across the full period, weighted by the number of firms active in each year. The averages are computed on scalers that end their scaling-up period in 2011 to 2018 in Finland, 2004 to 2018 in Italy, 2013 to 2017 in Portugal, 2017 to 2018 in the Slovak Republic and 2006 to 2018 in Spain. The sector groups are defined in Annex C.
Source: Calculations based on microdata sources from five countries. See Annex B for more information.

All types of regions can produce scalers

All regions have a sizeable share of scalers, with some variation in the propensity to scale across regions. The share of scalers in employment in all non-micro SMEs in the region ranges from 10% to 17% in Italy, 8% to 13% in Spain, 8% to 14% in Portugal and 14% to 17% in the Slovak Republic (where differences are not statistically significant when the sectoral and size compositions are also taken into account). The differences in propensity to scale in turnover across regions are similar in magnitude. The regional shares range from 19% to 25% in Italy, 15% to 19% in Spain, 18% to 25% in Portugal and 24% to 28% in the Slovak Republic.[7]

The share of scalers may vary across regions because of differences in local demand, factors affecting local productivity or the cost of inputs. The opportunities for scaling may differ regionally, due to the local pool of talents and skills, the possibility of interacting closely with other firms or the access to local public goods – such as transport infrastructure and universities – that affect local productivity. Institutional conditions like entrepreneurship culture, networks and regulations also affect the health of a local entrepreneurship ecosystem (OECD, 2021[13]). Firms choose their location depending on their specific needs. Some firms may prefer to be located in diverse and dynamic urban agglomerations where they can access a large variety of different skills in the labour force and where interactions with other businesses are easier and more frequent. Other firms may instead find it more suitable to be located in cities or regions that are specialised in a specific activity (OECD, 2017[14]). Firms may also relocate just before or during a high-growth phase to reduce the costs of their core inputs (Duranton and Puga, 2001[15]). For instance, a firm that plans to expand production may need to open a new establishment in a locality with lower real estate prices or lower wages. Although places are different, market prices can compensate for attractiveness, which means that, often, there is a little observable linkage between attractiveness factors such as local tax rate or local civil justice efficiency for example and firm location choices (Duranton, Gobillon and Overman, 2011[16]; Giacomelli and Menon, 2017[17]). Despite a large body of research on the location determinants of firms, there is a dearth of evidence looking at the case of scalers.[8]

Both wealthy and less-developed regions can have a high share of scalers. The firm-level data sources allow calculating the share of scalers in each TL2 region[9] across the four countries (the regional breakdown is not available for Finland; see Box 3.2 for a discussion of a possible "headquarter bias" that may affect the interpretation of the results). The region with the highest share of both employment (14%) and turnover (25%) scalers in Portugal is the Algarve, a wealthy region[10] in the south of Portugal with dynamic real estate and tourism sectors. The capital city region Lisbon and the northern region of Norte are also characterised by higher values (12% and 13% for employment scalers and 19% and 22% for turnover scalers respectively) than Alentejo, Azores, Centro and Madeira (see Figure 3.10 reporting the share of scalers in employment in all firms with at least 10 employees). In Spain, firms located in regions in the south of the country with a GDP per capita lower than the national average, such as Andalusia and Murcia, are more likely to scale than firms headquartered in more developed regions (the share of scalers in employment is equal to 12% in both regions, compared to e.g. 10% in Catalonia; see Figure 3.11). However, the capital region Madrid also has a relatively high share (12%) of scalers in employment. In Italy, the 3 regions with the highest share – Basilicata (17%), Puglia (15%) and Campania (15%) – are all part of the Mezzogiorno, the southern part of the country in which income and productivity levels are substantially lower than in the northern regions (see Figure 3.12).[11] Low factor prices in lagging regions may therefore play a relatively more important role for scaling than the competitive advantages of wealthier regions access, such as a larger local market, a pool of skilled workers, etc.

Differences in the propensity of local firms to scale may be more evident at a different geography. Differences in the share of scalers may depend on factors that vary within large (TL2) regions rather than across them. For instance, wages and housing costs differ widely between prime urban locations and rural areas. Local labour markets, as defined by areas within which workers can commute on a daily basis, are often smaller than TL2 regions, which means that differences in access to skills and educated workforce tend to vary significantly also within regions. The analysis of local differences in scaling at different spatial scales and using different definitions of spatial units is an interesting avenue for future research.

Box 3.2. The "headquarter bias" in regional business demography

The share of scalers by TL2 region is calculated based on the location of the firm (or the enterprise). Large, multi-plant firms (which tend to have headquarters in cities) may operate a substantial number of plants (and employ workers) outside of the region where the headquarters are located. If all workers employed in multi-plant firms are attributed to the headquarters' regions (as is the case with firm-level indicators), the regional scale-up indicators suffer from a "headquarter bias". In fact, employment indicators based on the enterprise approach do not reflect regional employment but rather the employment controlled by firms with headquarters in a given region. The headquarter bias could be eliminated by using plant or establishment-level information. Establishment-level data were not available for the current analysis but are collected in some OECD countries and are a promising avenue of future research.

Source: OECD (2017[14]), *The Geography of Firm Dynamics: Measuring Business Demography for Regional Development*, https://dx.doi.org/10.1787/9789264286764-en; Ahmad N. (2008[18]), *A Proposed Framework for Business Demography Statistics. In: Congregado E. (eds) Measuring Entrepreneurship. International Studies In Entrepreneurship, vol 16. Springer, Boston, MA.* https://doi.org/10.1007/978-0-387-72288-7_7.

Figure 3.10. The Algarve and Lisbon are the regions with the highest share of scalers in Portugal

Share of employment scalers in all non-micro SMEs by large regions

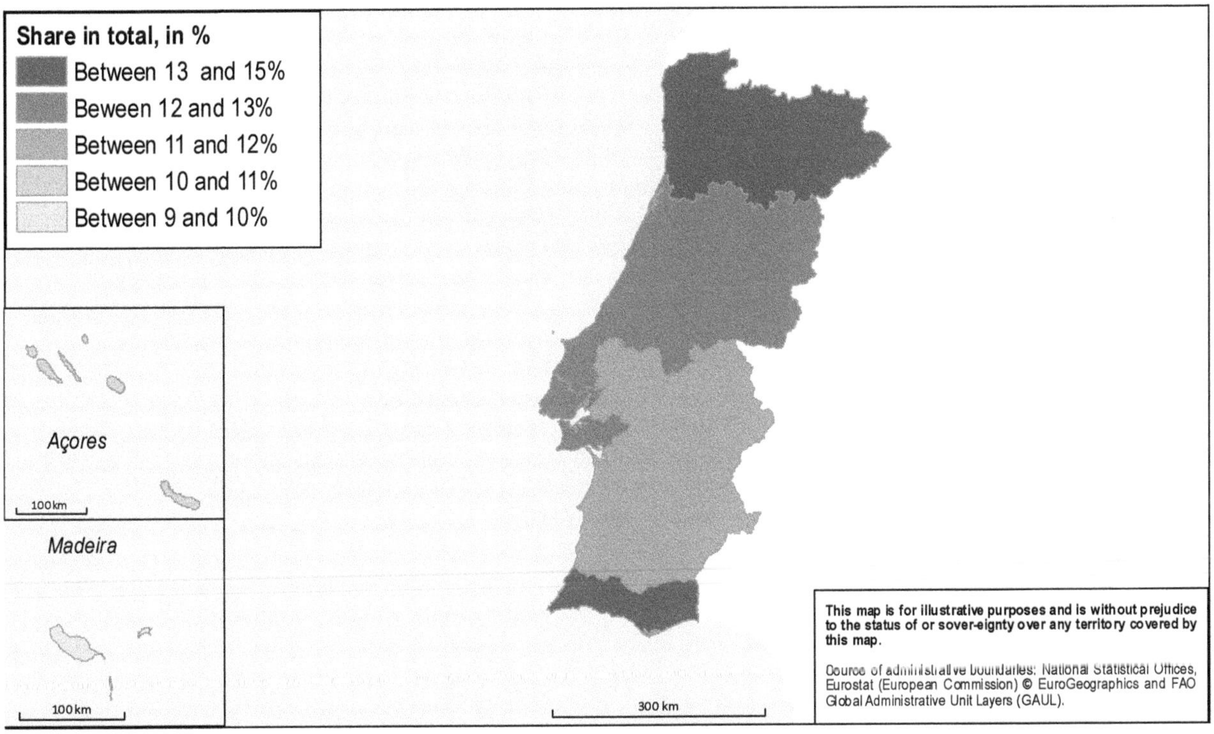

Note: Large regions are TL2 regions – see OECD (2020[19]) for more details. Employment scalers are firms with 10 employees or more that grow in employment by at least 10% per year on average over 3 consecutive years, as defined in Box 1.2. Non-micro SMEs are businesses with total employment of between 10 and 249 employees. The shares are calculated yearly and reported on average across the full period, weighted by the number of firms active in each year. The averages are computed on scalers that end their scaling-up period in 2006 to 2018.
Source: Calculations based on microdata sources. See Annex B for more information.

Figure 3.11. Both wealthy and less-developed regions have a high share of scalers in Spain

Share of employment scalers in all non-micro SMEs by large regions

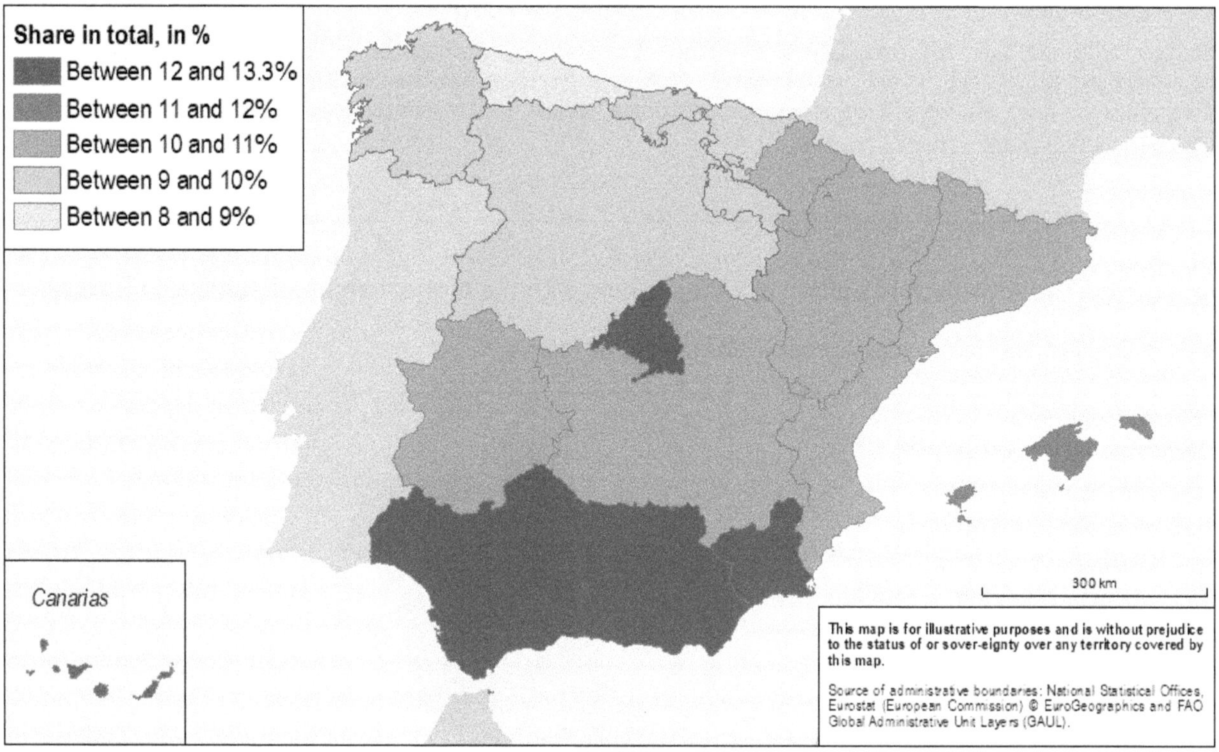

Note: Large regions are TL2 regions – see OECD (2020[19]) for more details. Employment scalers are firms with 10 employees or more that grow in employment by at least 10% per year on average over 3 consecutive years, as defined in Box 1.2. Non-micro SMEs are businesses with total employment of between 10 and 249 employees. The shares are calculated yearly and reported on average across the full period, weighted by the number of firms active in each year. The averages are computed on scalers that end their scaling-up period in 2006 to 2018.
Source: Calculations based on microdata sources. See Annex B for more information.

Figure 3.12. Italian southern regions have a higher share of scalers

Share of employment scalers in all non-micro SMEs by large regions

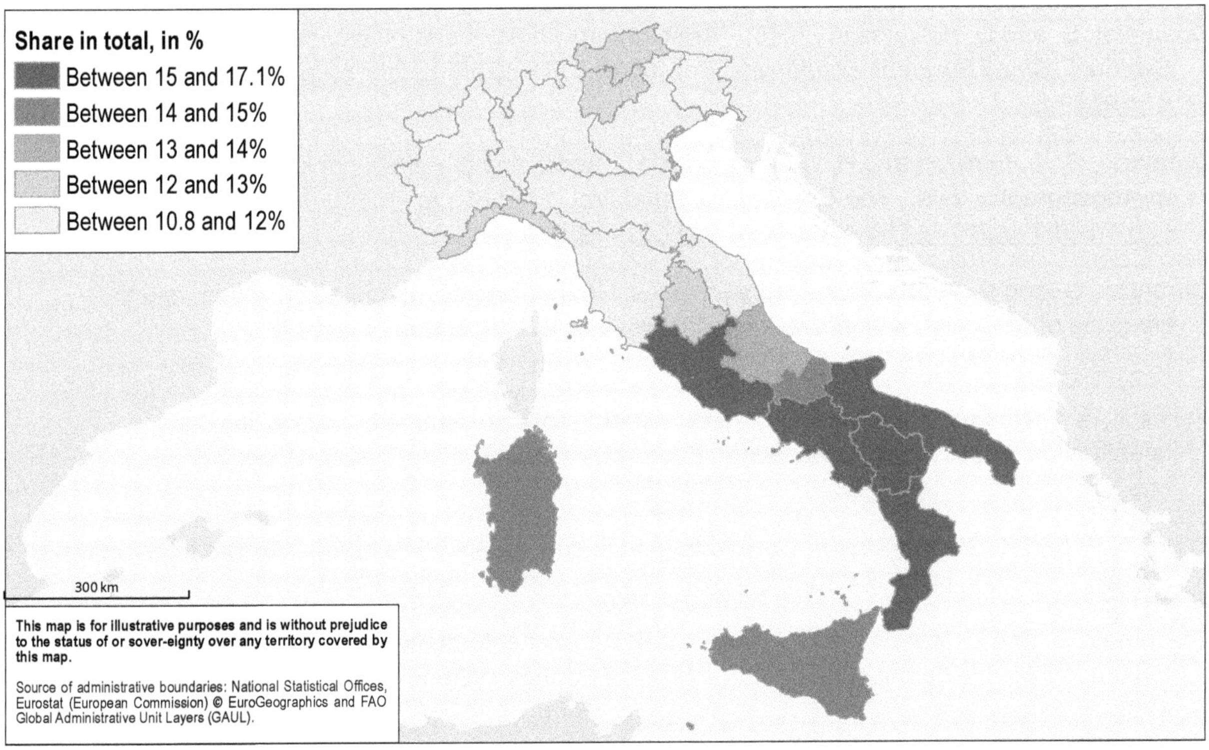

Note: Large regions are TL2 regions – see OECD (2020[19]) for more details. Employment scalers are firms with 10 employees or more that grow in employment by at least 10% per year on average over 3 consecutive years, as defined in Box 1.2. The period of analysis is 2004-18. Non-micro SMEs are businesses with total employment between 10 and 249 employees. The shares are calculated yearly and reported on average across the full period, weighted by the number of firms active in each year. The averages are computed on scalers that end their scaling-up period in 2004 to 2018.
Source: Calculations based on microdata sources. See Annex B for more information.

References

Cabral, L. and J. Mata (2003), "On the evolution of the firm size distribution: Facts and theory", *American Economic Review*, Vol. 93/4, pp. 1075-1090, https://pubs.aeaweb.org/doi/pdfplus/10.1257/000282803769206205 (accessed on 18 July 2019). [22]

Coad, A. and S. Srhoj (2019), "Catching gazelles with a lasso: Big data techniques for the prediction of high-growth firms", *Small Business Economics*, http://dx.doi.org/10.1007/s11187-019-00203-3. [23]

Congregado, E. (ed.) (2008), *A Proposed Framework for Business Demography Statistics*, Springer, https://doi.org/10.1007/978-0-387-72288-7_7. [18]

Criscuolo, C., P. Gal and C. Menon (2014), "The Dynamics of Employment Growth: New Evidence from 18 Countries", *OECD Science, Technology and Industry Policy Papers*, No. 14, OECD Publishing, Paris, https://doi.org/10.1787/5jz417hj6hg6-en. [2]

Daunfeldt, S., N. Elert and D. Johansson (2016), "Are high-growth firms overrepresented in high-tech industries?", *Industrial and Corporate Change*, Vol. 25/1, pp. 1-21, http://dx.doi.org/10.1093/ICC/DTV035. [10]

Daunfeldt, S. and D. Halvarsson (2015), "Are high-growth firms one-hit wonders? Evidence from Sweden", *Small Business Economics*, Vol. 44, pp. 361-383, http://dx.doi.org/10.1007/s11187-014-9599-8. [24]

Duranton, G., L. Gobillon and H. Overman (2011), "Assessing the effects of local taxation using microgeographic data", *The Economic Journal*, Vol. 121/555, pp. 1017-1046, http://dx.doi.org/10.1111/J.1468-0297.2011.02439.X. [16]

Duranton, G. and D. Puga (2001), "Nursery cities: Urban diversity, process innovation, and the life cycle of products", *American Economic Review*, Vol. 91/5, pp. 1454-1477, http://dx.doi.org/10.1257/aer.91.5.1454. [15]

Fellini, I., A. Ferro and G. Fullin (2016), "Recruitment processes and labour mobility: the construction industry in Europe", *Work, Employment and Society*, Vol. 21/2, pp. 277-298, http://dx.doi.org/10.1177/0950017007076635. [12]

Geroski, P. and K. Gugler (2004), "Corporate growth convergence in Europe", *Oxford Economic Papers*, Vol. 56/4, pp. 597-620, http://dx.doi.org/10.1093/oep/gpf055. [21]

Giacomelli, S. and C. Menon (2017), "Does weak contract enforcement affect firm size? Evidence from the neighbour's court", *Journal of Economic Geography*, Vol. 17/6, pp. 1251-1282, http://dx.doi.org/10.1093/JEG/LBW030. [17]

Gibrat, R. (1931), *Les Inégalités économiques*, Recueil Sirey, Paris, https://www.worldcat.org/title/inegalites-economiques/oclc/250098599 (accessed on 19 July 2019). [5]

Giner, J., M. Santa-María and A. Fuster (2017), "High-growth firms: Does location matter?", *International Entrepreneurship and Management* 13, pp. 75–96, http://dx.doi.org/10.1007/s11365-016-0392-9. [25]

Grover Goswami, A., D. Medvedev and E. Olafsen (2019), "High-growth firms: Facts, fiction, and policy options for emerging economies", World Bank, Washington, DC. [3]

Haltiwanger, J. et al. (2017), "High growth young firms: Contribution to job, output and productivity growth", *CARRA Working Paper Series*, https://www.census.gov/content/dam/Census/library/working-papers/2017/adrm/carra-wp-2017-03.pdf (accessed on 18 July 2019). [26]

Haltiwanger, J., R. Jarmin and J. Miranda (2011), "Who creates jobs? Small vs. large vs. young", *NBER Working Paper*, No. 16300, http://econweb.umd.edu/~haltiwan/size_age_paper_R&R_Aug_16_2011.pdf (accessed on 11 October 2019). [1]

Jones, B. (2009), "The burden of knowledge and the "Death of the Renaissance Man": Is innovation getting harder?", *Review of Economic Studies*, Vol. 76/1, pp. 283-317, http://dx.doi.org/10.1111/J.1467-937X.2008.00531.X. [6]

Jovanovic, B. (1982), "Selection and the evolution of industry", *Econometrica*, Vol. 50/3, http://dx.doi.org/10.2307/1912606. [4]

Li, M. et al. (2015), "Location determinants of high-growth firms", *Entrepreneurship & Regional Development*, Vol. 28/1-2, pp. 97-125, http://dx.doi.org/10.1080/08985626.2015.1109003. [27]

Lotti, F. and E. Santarelli (2001), "Is firm growth proportional? An appraisal of firm size distribution", *Economics Bulletin*, Vol. 12/6, pp. 1-7. [20]

Melitz, M. (2003), "The impact of trade on intra-industry reallocations and aggregate industry productivity", *Econometrica*, Vol. 71/6, pp. 1695-1725, http://dx.doi.org/10.1111/1468-0262.00467. [7]

OECD (2021), "Local entrepreneurship ecosystems and emerging industries: Case study of Cambridgeshire and Peterborough, United Kingdom", *OECD Local Economic and Employment Development (LEED) Papers*, No. 2021/01, OECD Publishing, Paris, https://doi.org/10.1787/044ffc1d-en (accessed on 8 October 2021). [13]

OECD (2021), *The Digital Transformation of SMEs*, OECD Studies on SMEs and Entrepreneurship, OECD Publishing, Paris, https://dx.doi.org/10.1787/bdb9256a-en. [9]

OECD (2020), *OECD Regions and Cities at a Glance*, OECD Publishing, Paris, https://dx.doi.org/10.1787/26173212. [19]

OECD (2019), *OECD SME and Entrepreneurship Outlook 2019*, OECD Publishing, Paris, https://dx.doi.org/10.1787/34907e9c-en. [8]

OECD (2018), *Productivity and Jobs in a Globalised World: (How) Can All Regions Benefit?*, OECD Publishing, Paris, https://dx.doi.org/10.1787/9789264293137-en. [11]

OECD (2017), *The Geography of Firm Dynamics: Measuring Business Demography for Regional Development*, OECD Publishing, Paris, https://dx.doi.org/10.1787/9789264286764-en. [14]

OECD.stats (2021), *Regional Economy*, OECD, Paris, https://stats.oecd.org/ (accessed on 8 October 2021). [31]

Santarelli, E., L. Klomp and A. Thurik (2006), "Gibrat's Law: An overview of the empirical literature", in *Entrepreneurship, Growth, and Innovation*, Springer US, http://dx.doi.org/10.1007/0-387-32314-7_3. [28]

Sedláček, P. and V. Sterk (2017), "The growth potential of startups over the business cycle", *American Economic Review*, Vol. 107/10, pp. 3182-3210, http://dx.doi.org/10.1257/aer.20141280. [29]

Sterk, V., S. Petr and B. Pugsley (2021), "The nature of firm growth", *American Economic Review*, Vol. 111/2, pp. 547-79. [30]

Notes

[1] Recent studies that investigate the decline of the high-growth start-ups rate in the US conclude that the characteristics and the environment of firms at inception explain how they react to external conditions and shocks during their life and this accounts for most of the subsequent growth. It follows that the growth potential of a firm is mainly determined by its structural characteristics at birth and posterior internal

transformations only play a negligible role in the growth rate (Sedláček and Sterk, 2017[29]; Sterk, Petr and Pugsley, 2021[30]).

2 See, for example, Daunfeldt and Halvarsson (2015[24]), Grover Goswami, Medvedev and Olafsen (2019[3]), Coad and Srhoj (2019[23]) and Geroski and Gugler (2004[21]).

3 Sixteen percent of old firms scale in turnover, 7% scale in employment. Among young firms, 32% scale in turnover and 20% scale in employment. The probability of scaling among other age groups is between these two extremes.

4 The initial studies focused on the growth of firms being independent of their initial size but several more recent studies contradicted the finding, with most of the studies focusing on individual countries and industries often finding that smaller firms grow faster. For example, Gibrat's Law holds for a sample of firms of greater than minimum efficient size (Santarelli, Klomp and Thurik, 2006[28]). Studies across countries and focused on different industries often find that growth slows in large firms (Cabral and Mata, 2003[22]; Lotti and Santarelli, 2001[20]).

5 This evidence is aligned with some of the "known facts" on scalers discussed in Chapter 1.

6 The finding that the construction sector has a particularly high output share accounted for by scalers also applies to the US (Haltiwanger et al., 2017[26]).

7 Data on the regional breakdown are not available for Finland.

8 A study on Spanish firms show that scalers are more likely to be found in technological clusters and urban areas (Giner, Santa-María and Fuster, 2017[25]). Evidence from US shows that scalers are located in countries with larger average establishment size, higher educational attainment and more natural amenities (Li et al., 2015[27]).

9 Territorial Level 2 (TL2) is a sub-national classification of large regions representing the first administrative tier of subnational government (https://www.oecd.org/regional/regional-policy/regionalstatisticsandindicators.htm).

10 In 2017, the GDP per capita of the Algarve is the second highest after the metropolitan area of Lisbon (OECD.stats, 2021[31]).

11 These values are based on enterprise-level indicators, which can be a source of bias when used to assess the location of the employment generated by existing firms. Large, multi-plant firms (which tend to have headquarters in cities) may operate a substantial number of plants (and employ workers) outside of the region where the headquarters are located. If all workers employed in multi-plant firms are attributed to the headquarters' regions (as is the case with enterprise-level indicators), the real geographical distribution of employment presents a "headquarter bias". In fact, employment indicators based on the enterprise approach do not reflect regional employment but rather the employment controlled by firms with headquarters in a given region (OECD, 2017[14]).

4 How do scalers transform as they grow?

The chapter presents new evidence on the transformation process that distinguishes small- and medium-sized enterprises (SMEs) that scale up from comparable firms that do not scale. The analysis builds on detailed information on individual firms in up to four OECD countries. The chapter presents different transformation models that underpin scaling up and describes the transformation of scalers based on dynamic characteristics such as their innovative activity, integration into global markets, digitalisation or workforce characteristics.

In Brief

SMEs that scale up change more than "just" their size

Different transformation models underpin scaling up, depending on the main factors that trigger scaling. Scaling up is much more than "just" a period of rapid growth: it is the expression of a transformative process that a firm undergoes. Transformation can potentially include aspects such as changes in the managerial structure or ownership, or a firm's engagement in new activities, e.g. research or export. For some firms, scaling is the result of a forward-looking growth strategy grounded on innovation and productivity improvements that involves a deep transformation of the inner structure of the firm. For other firms, the scaling transformation may be driven by a surge in demand or by the replication of existing business processes that leaves the core structure of the firm unaltered. Therefore, the timing and nature of the transformation provide some indications on which scaling models prevail.

The transformation of scalers can be captured in four stylised models. They are stylised as, in reality, firms will rarely follow a single model but a combination of them, which may evolve as they grow. The first model is "disruptive innovators" that invest in technological innovations, typically research and development (R&D)-based, which result in disruptive changes to their product range or the ways they produce. The second model is "gradual innovators" that prepare to scale by investing in human capital and upgrading their production processes with gains in new market shares arising from gradual improvements in the productivity of existing processes rather than from disruptive innovation. The third model is scalers that do "more of the same", i.e. expansion without changes in the composition of the workforce. For example, a manufacturing firm might add a second production facility or a local retailer might add another store. The fourth model is "demand-driven scalers" that face an external and temporary increase in demand that translates into a sales windfall.

The analysis of rich firm-level data provides new evidence on the transformation models of scalers by following firms before, during and after scaling. Understanding the extent of SMEs transformation requires a rich set of data, typically linked to different administrative and survey data sources. For this chapter, detailed information on firms' financial accounts is available for Finland, Italy, Portugal and Spain with additional information on firm workforces only available for Finland and Portugal. The analysis compares scalers with peers over a period of seven years: two years before scaling, three years during the scaling phase and two years after. The dynamic factors that are analysed include innovation and digitalisation, workforce skills and education, access to global markets, productivity and debt. Peers are firms in the same sector, founded around the same time and of similar size, before the scaler enters its high-growth phase.

Several factors are permanently different in scalers – during, before and after scaling – and define the "DNA" of firms with potential and ambition for fast growth. Attempts to predict future scaling, in general, perform poorly, which confirms that every type of SME can grow fast. However, the analysis of the transformation process of Finnish and Portuguese scalers identifies some factors that could potentially change over time but are instead stable over the seven-year period. For instance, scalers employ about 30% to 50% more information technology (IT) specialists than peers – before, during and after scaling. This points to the role that differences in the uptake of digital technologies among SMEs may play in distinguishing scalers from their peers and the maturity of their digitalisation approach as they focus on in-house digitalisation rather than relying on outside services. Another permanent difference is the age of the employees. Scalers' workforce is on average around 1-2 years younger than their peers. The managing director in scalers is also younger.

Scalers widen the differences with non-scaling peers as they grow. During and after scaling, Finnish and Portuguese scaler workforces become more diverse as they employ 10-30% more foreign-born employees than their peers. In Italy, Portugal and Spain, scalers' profitability grows in correspondence with scaling up to become 15-30% higher among employment scalers and 40% to 100% higher in turnover scalers than in peers; turnover scalers are 10-35% more productive than their peers after scaling. Some of the extra profit is used to accumulate cash and other current assets that can be sold quickly, possibly to create a buffer to deal with bad times or to accumulate funds for future investments. Part of the profits is also shared with the employees, as wages are 1-2% higher in scalers than their peers for comparable workers during and after scaling.

Overall, scaling appears to be a strategic choice, as scalers' transformation begins before scaling materialises. The transformation is not confined to the years in which scaling takes place. For many dynamic factors, such as labour productivity, integration in foreign markets or access to credit, the differences compared to non-scaling peers are most evident in the two years that precede scaling and are thus classified as "anticipatory differences". For instance, employment scalers in Finland, Italy, Portugal and Spain are 5-15% more productive than their peers before scaling up. Scalers also appear to prepare their expansion by hiring 15% to 40% more workers specialised in R&D than peers. In addition, scalers are more indebted than peers to support their investments, in the attempt to develop a disruptive innovation or to increase their productivity. In some dimensions such as integration into global markets, before growing scalers are already similar to firms in the larger size class that they achieve after scaling. This points to scaling being predominantly the outcome of a strategic gradual innovation path rather than a random event that makes the scaler a "one-hit wonder".

Introduction

Scaling up is much more than "just" a period of rapid growth. Scaling up is the expression of a transformative process that a firm undertakes. Transformation can include aspects such as changes in the managerial structure or ownership, or a firm's engagement in new activities, e.g. research or export. Importantly, transformation might already start before a firm scales up while some transformative changes are only taking place during the scaling-up phase or afterwards, as a firm consolidates its new scale.

The type of transformative process that scalers undertake depends on the factors that trigger scaling. For some firms, scaling is the result of a forward-looking growth strategy grounded on innovation and productivity improvements that involve a deep transformation of the inner structure of the firm. For other firms, the scaling transformation may be driven by a surge in demand or by the replication of existing business processes that leaves the core structure of the firm unaltered. Conceptually, this can be broken down into four models of scaling up elaborated in the next section: i) scaling through R&D investment and disruptive innovation that change what or how firms produce or operate; ii) scaling through gradual innovation that yields productivity improvements that compress costs and lead to better products or services; iii) scaling by replicating current production processes, i.e. traditional "economies of scale"; and iv) scaling thanks to an increase in demand due to external factors that result in a windfall for the company.

The analysis of the transformation process associated with scaling up compares an extensive set of dynamic factors in scalers and non-scalers. To understand scalers' transformation, detailed data on the inner workings of the firm is required. Leveraging on microdata for four countries, the analysis compares scalers with similar firms, i.e. "peers" that have a similar size, age, operate in the same economic sector and are located in the same region. This comparison allows identifying the distinctive elements of scalers' transformation patterns.

Scalers are assessed over a seven-year period. In addition to the three years of the high-growth phase, scalers characteristics are considered in the two years before and the two years after scaling. For each country, the timespan analysed is the central seven-year interval within the available dataset, i.e. 2010-16 for Finland, 2006-12 for Italy, 2011-17 for Portugal and 2007-13 for Spain. For each year, the values of a broad group of dynamic factors among scalers – such as the share of R&D employees among all employees, the number of exported products or productivity – are compared against the values in similar non-scaler "peers" (i.e. firms of similar size and age in the same country, sector and location that do not scale over the same period). The analysis uses econometric methods to account for potential confounding factors and time trends, as well as to test whether differences between scalers and their peers are statistically significant.

Different transformation models underpin scaling up

Scaling up can be triggered by different factors that lead to four different (stylised) models that capture the transformation of scalers before, during and after scaling up. The four models try to address that in some cases the scaling transformation entails a change in a long-term strategy that results in deep changes in the firm production processes, while in other cases the demand-driven transformation arises from the replication of existing business processes that leaves the core production structure unaltered. The models also explain why the transformation can be incremental, going from strength to strength and eventually building a persistent advantage with respect to peers, or rather result in a more abrupt change that may be temporary (Table 4.1).

Table 4.1. The key elements of the four transformation models

Transformation model	Disruptive or incremental innovation	Corporate strategy	Temporary or persistent change	Demand or supply-driven
Disruptive innovator	Disruptive	Anticipatory	Temporary/Persistent	Supply
Gradual innovator	Incremental	Anticipatory	Persistent	Supply
More-of-the-same scaler	Incremental	Anticipatory	Persistent	Both
Demand-driven scaler	Disruptive	Reactive	Temporary	Demand

The "disruptive innovator" develops new products or processes to gain a competitive advantage. The firm invests in R&D or makes other innovation investments, e.g. in digitalisation, to innovate its products or the way it operates in anticipation of scaling.[1] If successful, the firm can enjoy (temporary) competitive advantages and gain market shares, either because the new products are unique or of better quality compared to the competition, or because the firm can produce at a lower cost. The firm, therefore, is characterised by higher productivity and profitability than peers during scaling. Higher profit may also translate into a wage premium for employees, depending on the functioning of the local labour market. This group of scalers is characterised by permanent differences that are linked to innovation, such as greater workforce diversity and younger workforce and management than in peers.

The "gradual innovator" invests in human and physical capital and in intangible assets to become more productive than its peers. In anticipation of scaling, this strategy requires accessing external capital (e.g. equity or bank credit) for training the workforce, hiring specialised staff, developing intangible assets, adopting new management practices, etc. If the investments are successful, productivity improves, output quality increases or prices decrease, and the firm scales up by gaining additional market shares. The higher productivity in comparison to peers can also lead to a wage premium for the employees. This type of scaler is characterised by persistent differences compared to its peers in human capital (which can be captured by the share of educated workers and IT specialists for example), which is a key driver of productivity advantages. While there are some similarities between this model and the "disruptive innovator", the transformation is a sudden and discrete change that revolutionises the way the firm operates in the case of the "disruptive innovator" and a more incremental process that adds strength to strength in the case of the "gradual scaler".

The "more-of-the-same" scaler achieves a larger size without changing production processes. This is the economist's case of "economies of scale". A manufacturing firm, for example, might build a second production line within the same establishment to double its capacity. There are productivity gains as some assets can serve both facilities. An important feature is a need for significant upfront investment. Scaling can occur along the turnover margin only, for example in the case of a software company for which the initial investment in product development is high and variable production costs are low. In the manufacturing example, scaling in employment or both employment and turnover is the most likely, as the capacity of the new facility would not be fully utilised from the outset and workers will increase as production expands. New firms that enter the market at a lower size than competitors and that need to quickly reach a viable scale to survive also fall into this group. This type of scaler is characterised by a higher investment rate and higher debt than peers in anticipation of scaling, while productivity and profitability tend to align to peers as the firm grows and reaches its efficient scale.

The "demand-driven scaler" enjoys a sudden demand windfall. This scaler is a firm that benefits from an increase in demand for its products or services due to factors that are external to the firm. This can be the case, for example, of a construction company that is operating in an area where the public authorities procure new transport infrastructures or of a company producing face masks in the outbreak of pandemics. To expand production and satisfy increased demand, the firm needs to hire many new workers in a short period of time. The firm may therefore offer higher salaries than peers to attract workers or hire workers that have fewer opportunities in the labour market, such as older or low-educated individuals. For this type of scaler, there are no anticipatory or permanent differences in which it differentiates itself from its peers, as scaling is not anticipated. Factors driving increased demand are often temporary, which also means that scaling is not sustainable and the firm may go back to the initial size. In the analysis, this transformation model can be captured by the following transformational factors: higher debt to finance operations; higher wage premium to attract new workers in a short period of time; an expanded workforce with low-educated and low-skilled workers to support operations; and larger workforce diversity.

Differences between scalers and their peers take the form of anticipatory, transformational and permanent differences depending on whether scalers differ before, during (and after) or always from their peers (Table 4.2):

- **Anticipatory differences**: Scalers differ from their peers in the years just before the high-growth phase and converge toward similar values by the end of the high-growth phase. These factors help define the scale-up strategy of firms. A firm can prepare for achieving a new scale in the future by employing a different workforce, getting indebted or engaging in innovative activity. Other forms of strategy could involve an ambition to enlarge the market by exporting, which can then lead to scaling up.
- **Permanent differences**: These are factors that are permanently different between scalers and their peers, without significant variations during, before or after the scaling-up phase, even if they potentially vary over time. These factors, therefore, point to some *ex ante* characteristics that may be important to explain the ability of a firm to scale.
- **Transformational factors**: These are firm characteristics that vary significantly during scaling and that may continue to be different also at the new scale.

Table 4.2. Scaling up as a transformative process

A stylised taxonomy of different transformation patterns

Transformation model	Measurable dynamic differences from peers		
	Permanent differences	Anticipatory differences	Transformational factors
Disruptive innovator The firm develops technological innovation that translates into a competitive advantage.	• More workforce diversity • Younger workers and management	• Higher share of R&D and IT workforce • Higher debt	• Higher wage premium, productivity and profitability
Gradual innovator The firm invests in human capital and new production processes to become more productive than its peers and gain market shares.	• Higher share of educated workers • Higher share of IT specialists	• Higher debt	• Higher wage premium, productivity and profitability
More-of-the-same scaler The firm scales by producing additional output using the same business model.		• Lower productivity and profitability • Higher debt	• Profitability and productivity start from a lower level and align with peers after scaling
Demand-driven scaler The firm faces an exogenous and temporary increase in demand.			• Higher debt • Higher wage premium • More workforce diversity • More low-educated and low-skilled workers • Higher share of current assets

While the four models are presented separately, in reality, scalers may resemble a combination of different models, which may overlap and coexist in firms. For instance, an initial demand-driven expansion may allow the firm the accumulate the financial resources that are then used to fund a supply-driven growth strategy and the two phases may partially overlap. A gradual innovator that focuses on incremental productivity improvements may also develop some process innovations that are more disruptive in nature. Therefore, the aim is not to assign scalers to a specific "model" group but to link the empirical analysis to the different ways in which scaling can happen in firms. The four models take stock of a large body of literature on firm growth dynamics.[2]

The empirical analysis identifies the anticipatory differences, transformational factors and permanent differences that link to the four scaling models. The analysis considers a broad range of firm time-variant characteristics, comparing scalers with similar firms that share the same predetermined factors (size and age class, sector, location) but that do not scale. Scalers are compared to peers along a seven-year period: two years before scaling, three years during the scaling phase and two years afterwards. For each year, the values of a broad group of dynamic factors – such as a share of R&D employees, number of exported products or productivity – among scalers are compared against the values for similar non-scalers (i.e. firms that have not scaled up over the seven-year period) in the same age, size and sector group. The methodology is explained in detail in Box 4.1. The results of the analysis reflect the scaling pattern that prevails on average in each country and therefore provide information on which scaling models prevail. Future research can look at different groups of scalers (e.g. scalers in different sectors) within countries to understand whether some scaling models are more strongly associated with some types of scalers.

Box 4.1. A dynamic portrait of the transformation factors

The econometric analysis builds upon the following elements:

- **Time period**: Scalers and their peers are tracked for a period of seven years – two before the high-growth phase, the three years of the high-growth phase and two years afterwards. A shorter period than seven years would limit the ability to observe changes happening before or after the high-growth phase. A longer period would reduce the number of firms in the sample because of entry and exit events.
- **Scalers**: The group of scalers is composed of all firms that end their first high-growth period in the fifth year of the seven-year window.
- **Non-scalers**: Scalers are compared with "peers", i.e. firms with at least ten employees in the same size class, age class, sector and location, that are not entering as new firms, closing operations or scaling up over the seven-year period.

Both the group of scalers and non-scalers include both SMEs with 10 to 250 employees and larger firms with more than 250 employees. Since the first group accounts for more than 95% of all firms across the countries analysed, the results are mainly relevant for the SME population.

Visualising scalers' transformation patterns

For each dynamic factor, the results of the analysis are visualised in a chart. Figure 4.1 provides an example for the case of the export probability in Portugal. For each of the seven years, the line in the chart reports the estimate of the difference in the export probability between scalers and comparable non-scalers in the same sector, year, size class, age class and location (TL2 region), measured in percentage points. The grey shaded area visualises the extent of the possible statistical errors around that estimate – e.g. if the shaded area intersects the zero axis, the estimate is not statistically different from zero. The chart shows that, before and in the first part of the high-growth phase (Years 1 to 4), scalers are around 3 percentage points more likely to be exporters than non-scalers. At the end of the high-growth phase (Year 5), the difference becomes statistically insignificant and remains close to 0 in the 2 years following scaling up. The control variables for firm size and age are time-variant, i.e. they are updated each year. For example, if in Year 1 a future scaler has between 10 and 19 employees, the control group is composed of its peers in the same size (and age, sector and location) category. However, when this firm hits the peak of growth and reaches the 20-49 size class in Years 6 and 7, it is compared with firms in this new size (age, industry, location) category.

The example in Figure 4.1 shows that scalers "punch above their weight" before their high-growth phase, as their export propensity is higher than their peers before scaling up takes place and is aligned with the average in the new size class at the end of the high-growth phase.

Tracking absolute changes in scalers

Absolute changes – i.e. not relative to peers – in all of the variables under scrutiny over the seven years are also computed. In this case, the only factors that are also controlled for in the econometric analysis are the age of the company and the year in which the variable is measured. The absolute metrics allow assessing whether a given variable increases or decreases before, during and after scaling. This information proves to be a useful complement to the analysis based on comparison with peers. Indeed, there may be counterintuitive situations in which scalers reduce their difference compared to their peers in their export propensity for example but the factor may increase in absolute value as they grow. This situation can arise either if peers reduce their export propensity or – as in the example of Portugal above – if export propensity among new (larger) peers is lower than among former (smaller) peers.

Figure 4.1. Example of analysis of dynamic factors

Difference in the export probability in percentage points, scalers vs. non-scalers, Portugal

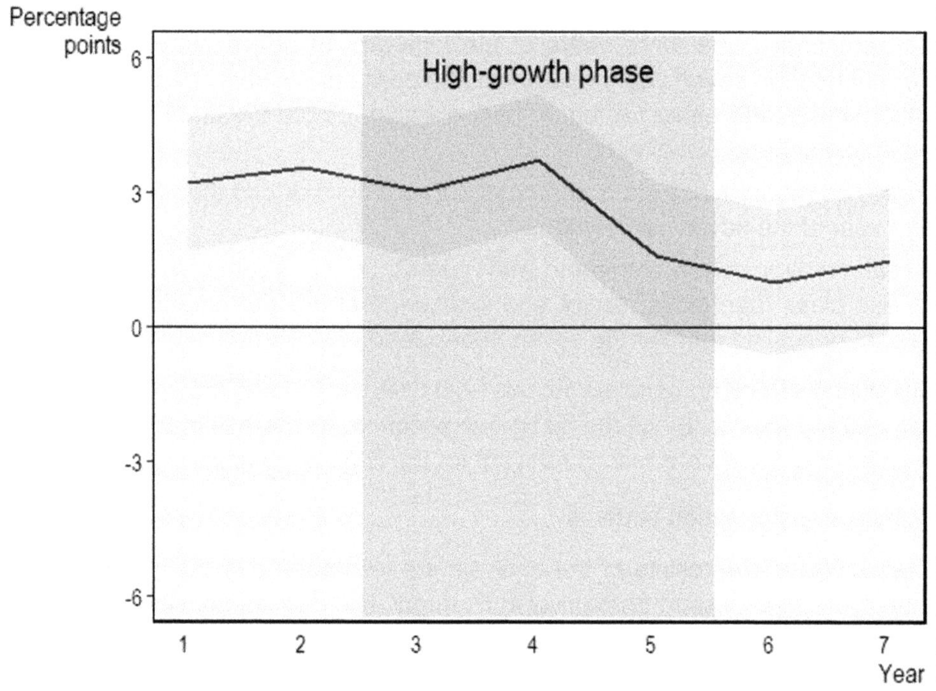

Source: Calculations based on microdata sources from Portugal. See Annex B for more details.

Innovation and digitalisation in scalers

Key findings on innovation and digitalisation

- **Anticipatory differences**: R&D employment grows in anticipation of the scaling-up phase.
  - Scalers employ 15% more R&D staff in Portugal compared to peers.
  - Scalers employ 20-40% more R&D staff in Finland compared to peers.
- **Permanent differences**: The share of IT employees is always higher in scalers – before, during and after the scaling-up phase.
  - Scalers have 2-3 IT specialists for every 100 employees compared to 1 in non-scalers in Portugal.
  - Scalers have 3-4 IT specialists for every 100 employees compared to 2-3 in non-scalers in Finland.

Note: Results are only available for Finland and Portugal due to data constraints.

Innovation is a key driver of firm growth. Process or product innovations improve firm performance by lowering costs, which increases return on investments and value to customers; enhance product quality, which increases competitiveness and value for customers; develop new products, which increases market share; and improve customer service, which increases the value to customers and improves competitiveness (Neely et al., 2001[1]). Organisational innovation, i.e. the implementation of a new organisational method in the firm's business practices, workplace organisation or external relations, can play a key role in complementing product and process innovations (Bresnahan, Brynjolfsson and Hitt, 2002[2]). In this analysis, innovation is measured using workforce data. This approach is possible because of the availability of linked employer-employee datasets that provide detailed occupation classification of all employees working in a given firm, which allows identifying the share of staff with innovation-related functions. The methodology is explained in detail in Box 4.2.

Scalers employ a higher share of R&D staff than their peers. Across countries and for both employment and turnover scalers, the share of R&D personnel is consistently higher than in non-scalers. In Portugal, for instance, the share of R&D staff is around 15% higher in scalers than in their peers, which employ on average around 3% of the workforce in R&D-related positions. The difference is even higher in Finland, where between 5% and 6% of employees work in R&D-related positions in scalers, which is around 20-40% more than in non-scalers. There is some variation, however, in the timing of the increase. For example, turnover scalers in Finland have, on average, always more R&D employees than their peers over the seven years taken into consideration. Turnover scalers in Portugal and employment scalers in both countries are more likely to increase R&D employment in the year before scaling. As scalers reach their new scale, the share of R&D jobs remains higher or reaches a comparable level to the share in non-scalers with similar characteristics (Table A.1).[3]

Box 4.2. Definitions and measurement of innovation indicators

Occupation-based measures of innovation

In this analysis, innovation is measured using workforce data. This approach is possible because of the availability of linked employer-employee datasets that provide detailed occupation classification of all employees working in a given firm. In a knowledge-based economy, implementing innovation requires an educated and skilled workforce. This is not limited to R&D specialists, as the development of new products is often preceded by organisational transformation processes (OECD, 2010[3]). For instance, previous literature argues that marketing capabilities are one of the major determinants of firms' performance, as companies making better use of information show an improved ability to develop an effective response to changes in the marketplace (Cacciolatti and Fearne, 2013[4]).

Transformation is captured by changes in the share of jobs in the total firm's workforce that are classified with the following functions: R&D; HR and training; management; marketing; and IT. The first group – R&D specialists – captures an important input of the innovation process. HR and training functions reflect the firm's efforts in organisational changes and in leveraging its human capital. Management and marketing functions are associated with new business processes and new sale channels. IT specialists are instead an essential component of investments in digitalisation. Further details on the occupations included in each group are reported in the methodological annex (Annex C).

Innovation measurement beyond occupations

Measurement of innovation commonly relies on data on R&D expenditures or patenting activity. This approach however entails a narrow definition of innovation as most R&D expenditures and patents are generated by few (and often the largest) firms in few sectors. Firms can also innovate without reporting R&D spending. For example, around 35% of firms not engaged in R&D in Australia introduced new products on the market between 2006 and 2007, compared to 40% of firms declaring to perform in-house R&D (OECD, 2010[3]). The same applies to patents, with survey data showing that the majority of firms prefer secrecy over patenting (Arundel, 2001[5]). Occupation-based measures thus may provide a more comprehensive overview of innovation activities among SMEs. Some surveys, notably Community Innovation Surveys (CIS) co-ordinated by Eurostat, offer more insights into firms' technological processes in countries that opt to participate. The evaluation of CIS data reveals that around 6% of firms that experience high growth in employment also introduce organisational, marketing, product or process innovation. While informative and useful for many purposes, the surveys cover only a small sample of firms. Given the small incidence of scaling up, the CIS data are of limited use in this analysis.

Source: OECD (2010[3]), *Measuring Innovation: A New Perspective*, https://doi.org/10.1787/9789264059474-en; Cacciolatti, L. and A. Fearne (2013[4]), "Marketing intelligence in SMEs: Implications for the industry and policy makers", http://dx.doi.org/10.1108/02634501311292894; Arundel, A. (2001[5]), "The relative effectiveness of patents and secrecy for appropriation", http://dx.doi.org/10.1016/S0048-7333(00)00100-1.

Finnish and Portuguese scalers display little differences in employment of human resources, management or training specialists compared to peers. The finding suggests that organisational innovation plays a minor role in scaling (at least to the extent that it can be measured with workforce indicators). The share of managers in scalers increases as they scale up but remains aligned to peers in the new size class. In addition, the transformation process of scalers in the organisation of the business process, as measured by the share of workers employed in human resources (HR), marketing or training functions, is not any different from peers. In Portugal, scalers and non-scalers employ similar shares of HR professionals among their workforce; the share of employment in jobs with marketing functions is also similar to non-scalers. In Finland, scalers employ a smaller share of HR professionals or managers before, during and after scaling than peers (Table A A.1).

Digitalisation is an important enabler of innovation and, for many SMEs, innovation has a strong digital component. Digitalisation reduces transaction costs by providing better and quicker access to information and communication between staff, suppliers and networks. It facilitates access to resources, including training, finance (e.g. peer-to-peer lending) and recruitment channels, and enable firms to generate data and analyse their operations in new ways (OECD, 2021[6]). Digitalisation also provides greater access to innovation assets, acting as an enabler of innovation, in particular for product and marketing innovation (Spiezia, 2011[7]; Bertschek, Cerquera and Klein, 2013[8]). Scalers and firms that plan to grow show a considerably larger adoption rate of digital technologies than other enterprises (Benedetti Fasil et al., 2021[9]). This points to the importance of addressing the digital divide among SMEs to create more opportunities for scaling, as discussed in Chapter 1.

Digitalisation is strongly associated with scaling up in Finland and Portugal. Scalers hire more IT specialists than their peers in anticipation of their new scale and the difference persists during scaling. In Portugal, about 1 in 100 workers is an IT specialist in non-scalers, whereas scalers employ 2-3 IT specialists on average. Similarly, the average Finnish scaler employs 3 to 4 IT specialists in every 100 employees, about 1 employee more than comparable non-scalers (this corresponds to a 1 percentage point difference as shown in Figure 4.2). The need for IT specialists remains relevant after reaching the new scale, as Portuguese turnover scalers and Finnish employment scalers employ higher shares of IT specialists over the full seven-year period analysed.

The findings on R&D and digitalisation suggest that many scalers follow the transformation model of the "disruptive innovator" and the "gradual innovator". Scalers embark on an innovation and digitalisation strategy in anticipation of scaling. Many scalers prepare their expansion by investing in innovation inputs, in the attempt to develop a disruptive innovation or to increase their productivity through more incremental improvements of their products or production processes. Furthermore, the stronger digitalisation component is a distinctive feature of scalers that persist before, during and after scaling. This confirms that, for SMEs, the ability to unleash the productivity advantages of digitalisation is a game-changer.

Figure 4.2. Finnish scalers employ a higher share of IT staff than their peers

Difference in the share of IT employees between employment scalers and their peers in Finland, 2010-16

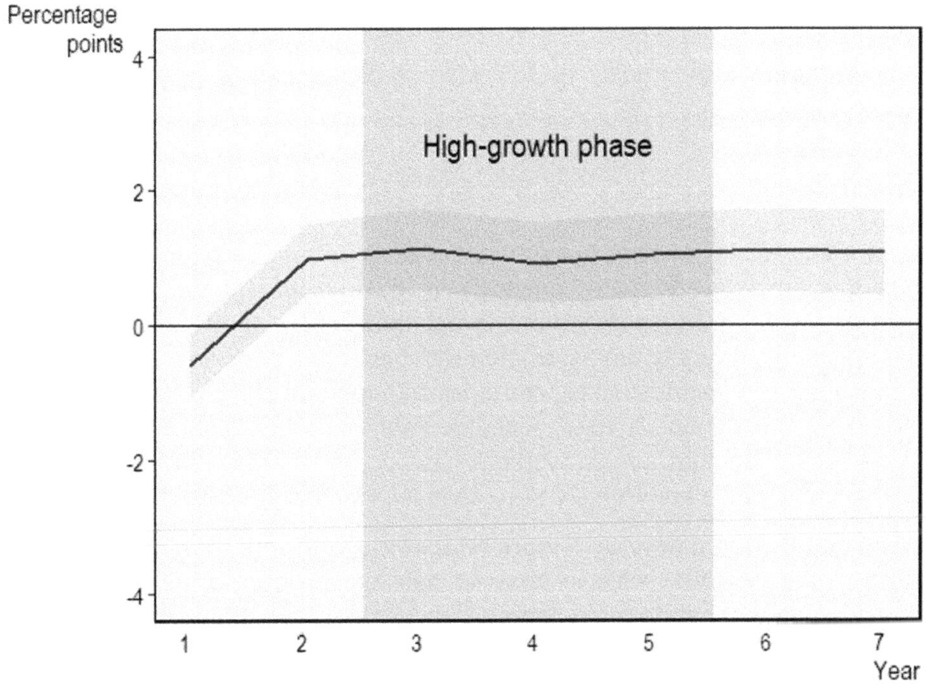

Note: The graphs indicate the difference between scalers and peers in the share of IT employees before (Years 1-2), during (Years 3-5) and after (Years 6-7) the high-growth phase. The years on the x-axis correspond to years 2010 to 2016. The line represents yearly estimated values and the grey bands around the line represent 90% confidence intervals. The difference between scalers and their peers is statistically significant when the confidence interval band does not intersect the horizontal line at zero. Grey vertical bands indicate the period of scaling up (scaling-up phase starts at 3 and ends at 5). Scalers grow in employment or turnover by at least 10% per year over 3 consecutive years on average, as defined in Box 1.2. The results are based on 84 219 observations for Finland. The regressions control for year, age, size bin, sector and region fixed effects. The sample is limited to firms with at least 10 employees in the first year and surviving for the whole period. See Box 4.1 for a detailed description of the methodology.
Source: Estimations based on microdata sources from Finland. See Annex B for more information.

Scalers' workers are younger and more educated than those of their peers

Key findings on human capital and workforce composition

- **Permanent differences**
  - The share of university-educated workers is higher in scalers than in their peers before scaling up and the difference persists during and after scaling up.
    - Finnish scalers employ 15-20% more workers with a master's degree than peers.
    - Portuguese scalers employ 5-10% more workers with a graduate degree and 20-40% more workers with a PhD than peers.
  - Scalers' employees and senior managers are two years younger than those in peer firms.
- **Transformational factors**
  - Wages are 1-2% higher in scalers than in their peers for comparable workers during and after scaling.
  - As scalers grow, they employ 10-30% more foreign-born employees than their peers.

Note: Results are only available for Finland and Portugal due to data constraints.

Human capital is a key driver of firm growth. Studies on data in Belgium, Italy, Portugal and Spain provide evidence that firms that scale in employment have higher human capital (as measured by employees' education level)[4] and successful firms invest more in training (Barringer, Jones and Neubaum, 2005[10]). Gender and ethnic diversity are associated with better firm performance in growth-oriented firms and, if properly managed and valorised, it proves to be an important complementary asset that enhances firm core competencies (McMahon, 2010[11]; Richard, Triana and Li, 2020[12]). For instance, studies on French and Israeli firms show that foreign workers have complementary skills that help firms increase productivity (Mitaritonna, Orefice and Peri, 2017[13]; Gandal, Hanson and Slaughter, 2004[14]).

Scalers in Finland and Portugal employ a more educated workforce than their peers before, during and after scaling. A firm that will scale in turnover has, on average, a 15% to 30% higher share of employees with a graduate or postgraduate degree.[5] In the case of Portugal, this means that about every 6th employee has a graduate degree in a scaler firm, which compares to only every 7th employee in a non-scaler firm. The share of university graduates continues to increase slightly in scalers after they scale up. In Finland, scalers employ 15-20% more university-educated employees before scaling up. For turnover scalers, the difference remains stable at about 15%, corresponding to 1.5 percentage points before scaling and about 1 percentage point during and after scaling (Figure 4.3). For employment scalers, the difference with their peers disappears as they scale. Thus, workers' education is an important factor for scaling and may represent a bottleneck for scalers in places that struggle to develop, attract or retain highly educated workers. The higher share of highly educated workers compared to peers in anticipation of scaling points to the importance of the disruptive and gradual innovator models. These workers may be instrumental to develop disruptive innovations that lead to a competitive advantage or to improve the production processes to achieve higher productivity.

Scalers also retain employees with low education levels as they scale. The share of low-educated workers does not increase in itself but becomes larger than in peers as scalers move to an upper size class and are benchmarked with larger firms. In Finland, the share is aligned with peers before scaling up and becomes larger than in peers by 2% to 4% after scaling. In Portuguese scalers, the share of workers with basic education (up to 9 years of schooling) is lower than in peers before scaling by 1% to 2% and becomes comparable to the new peers as they scale. Retaining employees may be a strategy adopted by scalers to preserve the company's tacit knowledge and know-how, and to facilitate the integration of a large number of new employees.

Scalers employ a younger workforce and have younger managers. The average age of employees in both employment and turnover scalers in Finland and Portugal (Figure 4.4) is about one to two years younger than in non-scaler firms. This holds for the entire period of seven years under scrutiny. Already before scaling, scalers start with a younger workforce than non-scalers. As they scale, scalers consolidate the age gap. In-depth analysis of Portuguese data shows that this is driven by additional hiring of middle-aged (sometimes referred to as "prime-age") workers that are between 30-49 years old, rather than hiring of "young" workers below the age of 30.[6] Scalers, therefore, look for workers with some experience, who are still younger than the average worker in a non-scaler. Middle-aged employees may be more attracted by higher wages and learning and career opportunities than older ones, and this may explain their preference for more dynamic companies. Younger workers may be also more suited to training on the job and learning specific skills. The most senior manager in scalers is also younger than in peers: in both Finland and Portugal, the most senior manager (proxied by the most paid worker in a management position) is two years younger in scalers than in their peers, on average across firms. This difference with peers persists before, during and after scaling.

Figure 4.3. Scalers employ more highly educated workers than peers

Difference in the share of employees with graduate degrees in Finnish turnover scalers and their peers, 2010-16

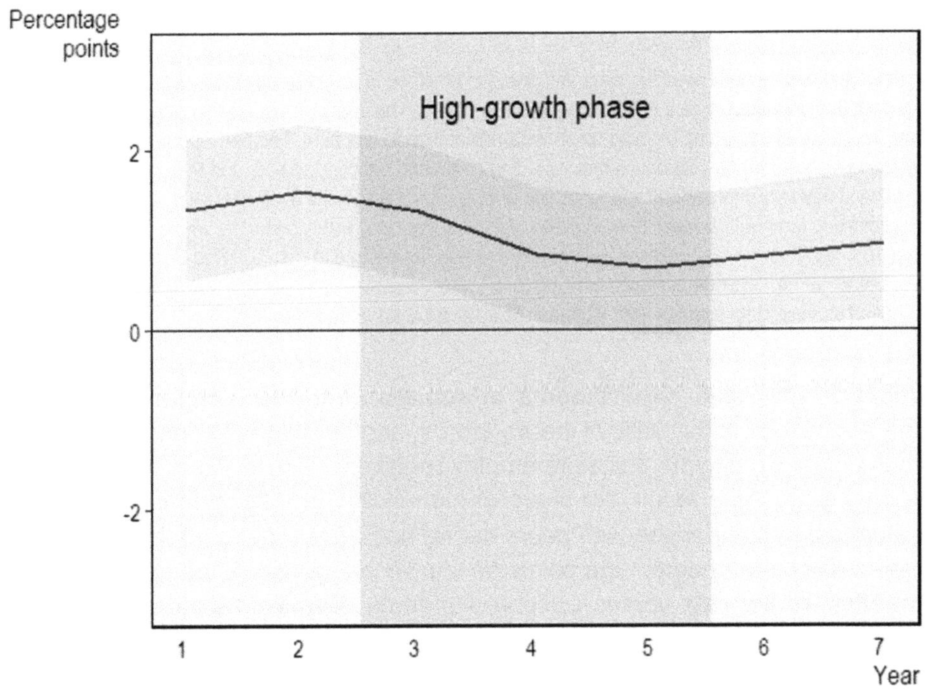

Note: The graphs indicate the difference between scalers and peers in shares of employees with a graduate degree before (Years 1-2), during (Years 3-5) and after (Years 6-7) the high-growth phase. The years on the x-axis correspond to years 2010 to 2016. Grey vertical bands indicate the period of scaling up (scaling-up phase starts at 3 and ends at 5). The line represents yearly estimated values and the grey bands around the line represent 90% confidence intervals. The difference between scalers and their peers is statistically significant when the confidence interval band does not intersect the horizontal line at zero. Scalers grow in employment or turnover by at least 10% per year over 3 consecutive years on average, as defined in Box 1.2. Results based on 68 590 observations for turnover scalers. The regressions control for year, age, size bin, sector and region fixed effects. The sample is limited to firms with at least 10 employees in the first year and surviving for the whole period. See Box 4.1 for a detailed description of the methodology

Source: Estimations based on microdata sources from Finland. See Annex B for more information.

Figure 4.4. Scalers' workforce is younger than that of their peers

Difference in the average age of employees between turnover scalers and their peers in Portugal, 2011-17

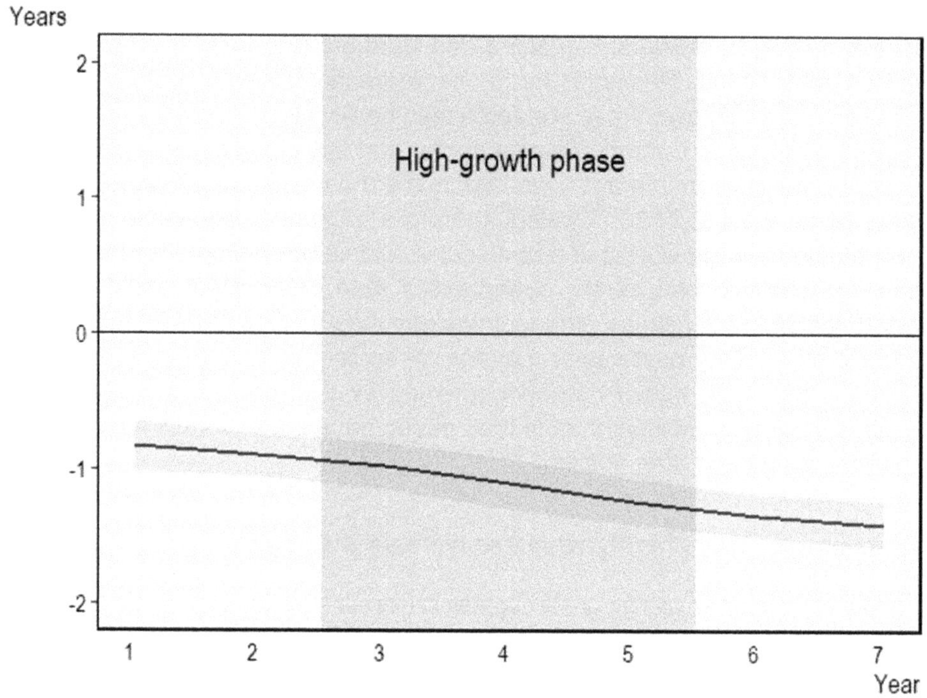

Note: The graphs indicate the difference between scalers and peers in employees' average age in scalers as compared to non-scalers before (Years 1-2), during (Years 3-5) and after (Years 6-7) the high-growth phase. The years on the x-axis correspond to years 2011 to 2017. Grey vertical bands indicate the period of scaling up (scaling-up phase starts at 3 and ends at 5). The line represents yearly estimated values and the grey bands around the line represent 90% confidence intervals. The difference between scalers and their peers is statistically significant when the confidence interval band does not intersect the horizontal line at zero. The regressions control for year, age, size bin, sector and region fixed effects. The sample is limited to firms with at least 10 employees in the first year and surviving for the whole period. Scalers grow in employment or turnover by at least 10% per year over 3 consecutive years on average, as defined in Box 1.2. See Box 4.1 for a detailed description of the methodology. Results based on 190 335 observations.
Source: Estimations based on microdata sources from Portugal. See Annex B for more information.

Workforce education and skill requirements in scalers changes compared to peers. Educational attainment is one way to look at the skills of the workforce; another way is to consider the roles that workers fill, i.e. their occupations. Employment scalers employ relatively more workers in low- and medium-skilled occupations as they grow. As a result, the share of high-skilled employment is smaller by 5% in Finland and by 10% in Portugal in comparison with peers during and after scaling (in the example of Finland, this drop is equivalent to fall by 2-3 percentage points as shown in Figure 4.5, left panel). This may come from the composition effect of the new versus existing workforce. New workers might be younger and more educated and they may accept low-skill occupations in exchange for opportunities for learning and a fast career progression in the longer term. It can also mean that scalers prefer hiring employees in low-skill occupations and training them. Low-skill occupations in scalers may therefore attract highly educated workers looking for career opportunities. This points to a disconnect between education and skills that is observed in the data for Portugal: workers in low-skill occupations are not necessarily low-educated. The relative increase in low- and medium-skill occupations as scalers enter the expansion phase may also reflect a shift from R&D to production, which is aligned with the disruptive innovator model.

Figure 4.5. Scalers hire low- and medium-skilled workforce as they transform

Difference in the share of workers in high-skilled or low-skilled occupations between employment scalers and their peers in Finland, 2010-16

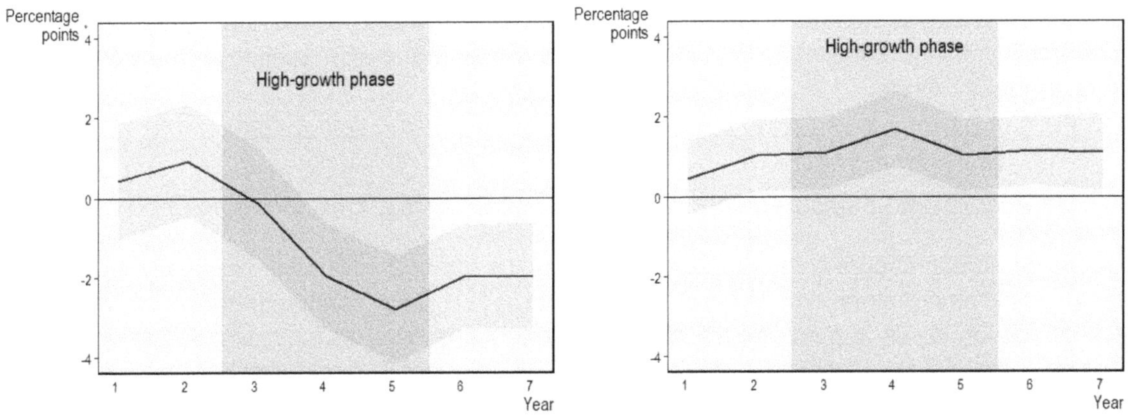

Note: The graphs indicate the difference between scalers and peers in shares of high- and low-skilled employment before (Years 1-2), during (Years 3-5) and after (Years 6-7) the high-growth phase. The years on the x-axis correspond to years 2010 to 2016. The vertical axes report differences in percentage points. Grey vertical bands indicate the period of scaling up (scaling-up phase starts at 3 and ends at 5). The line represents yearly estimated values and the grey bands around the line represent 90% confidence intervals. The difference between scalers and their peers is statistically significant when the confidence interval band does not intersect the horizontal line at zero. The results are based on 84 167 observations for both charts. Scalers grow in employment or turnover by at least 10% per year over 3 consecutive years on average, as defined in Box 1.2. See Box 4.1 for a detailed description of the methodology.
Source: Estimations based on microdata sources from Finland. See Annex B for more information.

Scalers hire foreign-born employees as they scale. The difference between scalers and peers in the share of foreign-born employees increases by up to 1 percentage point during their high-growth phase. Given the small baseline share of foreign-born employees – e.g. about 5% in Portuguese firms – the increase is substantial. Foreign-born employment remains higher in scalers than in peers after the scaling period. For example, Finnish employment scalers employ 2-3 percentage points more foreign-born workers than peers after scaling, which corresponds to a 30% higher share (Figure 4.6). Foreign-born employees can represent an asset to the firm. They might increase productivity with their complementary skills, bring specialised knowledge such as information about foreign markets, help expand the firm's network or contribute to workforce diversity spill-overs by, for example, lowering management costs.[7]

Scalers employ fewer women than their peers. In Portugal, the share of female workers in non-scalers is around 45% and is about 5 percentage points lower in scalers. The gender imbalance further increases during the transformation period by around 1 percentage point. Finnish turnover scalers have always a lower share of female employment – by about 10% - than non-scaler SMEs.

Scalers are likely to be less selective in hiring as they need additional workers quickly, which can create opportunities for disadvantaged workers. The lower selectivity of scalers, dictated by the need to hire many workers in a short period of time or to fill in positions that require a specific set of skills, translates into hiring opportunities for workers that may face discrimination or stigma in the labour market, such as foreign-born individuals or long-term unemployed.[8]

Scalers pay a wage premium as they transform. The wages of workers with similar characteristics (e.g. level of education or working in the same occupation) often differ across firms. Aggregating these differences for all workers in a firm gives the firm average wage premium (Box 4.3). Before their high-growth phase, scalers pay similar wages to their peers. Transformation brings a temporary wage premium in employment scalers in Finland. In Portugal, employment scalers' wage premium is not different from non-scalers as they scale but is still higher than before scaling, meaning that scalers increased their wages to match their new peers and competitors in the labour market. For turnover scalers, the wage premium lasts beyond the period of transformation, as they continue paying wages higher by 1% in Portugal to 2% in Finland for the same type of workers than comparable firms (Figure 4.7). A wage premium might attract workers and help fill the staffing needs in a short period of time, which is particularly important for demand-driven scalers that need to expand production quickly. However, a wage premium may also indicate higher labour productivity. Its increase in scalers relative to peers during and after scaling is thus consistent with the gradual innovator model.

Box 4.3. Definitions and measurements of human capital and workforce composition indicators

Information on human capital at the firm level leverages the strength of linked microdata on employees and their employers (linked employee-employer data). The data contain detailed information on workers' education levels and other personal characteristics, as well as their occupation and pay. To capture scalers' transformation with respect to the human capital of its workforce, several indicators are derived from the data.

Education

Education level reports the highest attained education of an employee, categorised according to the European Qualifications Framework (EQF) classification; the indicators used are the percentage of employees with less than undergraduate (low-educated), undergraduate (middle-educated) and postgraduate education (high-educated) respectively.

Occupations and skill requirements

Skill levels are obtained from job classification by the International Standard Classification of Occupations (ISCO 2008) and occupations are classified as high-skilled, medium-skilled and low-skilled. For example, managers and science and engineering professionals are considered as high-skilled occupations and sales workers and clerical support workers as medium-skilled occupations (ILO, 2012[15]).

Senior manager

The senior manager is identified as the person with a managing position corresponding to the 1-digit sub-group "Managers" of ISCO 2008 and paid the highest hourly gross wage (if there are several managers). The senior manager's characteristics of age, gender and educational attainment, depending on their availability, then serve as a proxy for leadership characteristics. If there are no workers classified in management occupation, the most senior manager is the worker with the highest wage.

Wage premium

The wage premium is defined as the average difference in hourly wage for comparable workers in the same sector. It is calculated as the average firm-year residual in regression at the worker-year level of the hourly wage on workers' observable characteristics (skills, education, age, age squared, work experience) and 2-digit industry dummies. The indicator measures the extent to which a firm pays its workers more or less than other firms in the same sector in a given year.

Workforce characteristics

Workforce characteristics include the average age of the workforce, the share of foreign-born employees and gender balance.

The age of the workforce is defined as the average age (in years) of all employees in the firm.

The share of foreign-born employees is defined as the share of employees with a country of birth other than the country of analysis in total employment.

The gender imbalance is calculated as the share of male workers in total employment.

Source: ILO (2012[15]), *International Standard Classification of Occupations 2008 (ISCO-08): Structure, Group Definitions and Correspondence Tables*, http://www.ilo.org/global/publications/ilo-bookstore/order-online/books/WCMS_172572/lang--en/index.htm (accessed on 9 June 2021).

Figure 4.6. Scalers' increase their share of foreign-born workers as they scale

Difference in the share of foreign-born employment in employment scalers and their peers in Finland, 2011-16

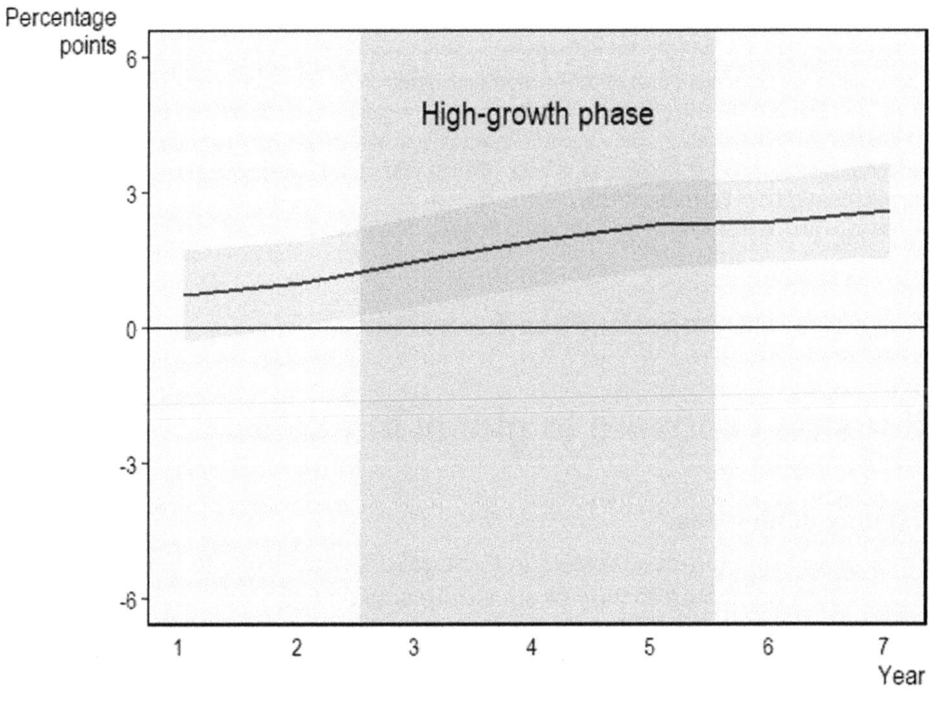

Note: The graphs indicate the difference between scalers and peers in the share of foreign employees share before (Years 1-2), during (Years 3-5) and after (Years 6-7) the high-growth phase. The years on the x-axis correspond to years 2010 to 2016. Grey vertical bands indicate the period of scaling up (scaling-up phase starts at 3 and ends at 5). The line represents yearly estimated values and the grey bands around the line represent 90% confidence intervals. The difference between scalers and their peers is statistically significant when the confidence interval band does not intersect the horizontal line at zero. Results based on 84 219 observations. The regressions control for the year in which the variable is measured and for firm age and size class, sector and region. The sample is limited to firms with at least 10 employees in the first year and surviving for the whole period. Scalers grow in employment or turnover by at least 10% per year over 3 consecutive years on average, as defined in Box 1.2. See Box 4.1 for a detailed description of the methodology.
Source: Estimations based on microdata sources from Finland. See Annex B for more information.

Figure 4.7. The wage premium paid by turnover scalers lasts beyond the high-growth phase

Difference in the wage premium between turnover scalers and their peers

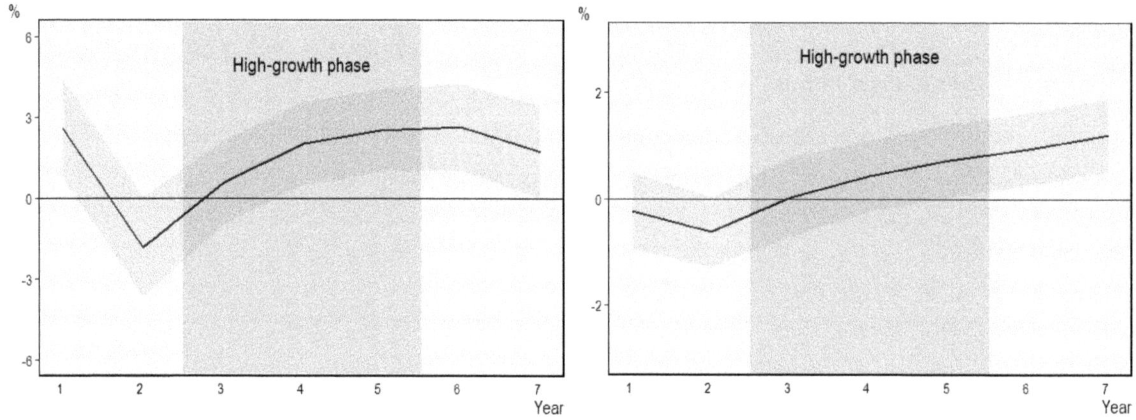

Note: The graphs indicate the difference between scalers and peers in wage premium before (Years 1-2), during (Years 3-5) and after (Years 6-7) the high-growth phase. The years on the x-axis correspond to years 2010 to 2016 in Finland and 2011 to 2017 in Portugal. Grey vertical bands indicate the period of scaling up (scaling-up phase starts at 3 and ends at 5). The line represents yearly estimated values and the grey bands around the line represent 90% confidence intervals. The difference between scalers and their peers is statistically significant when the confidence interval band does not intersect the horizontal line at zero. The results are based on 84 167 observations for both charts. The results are based on 68 181 observations in Finland and 189 545 observations in Portugal. The regressions control for the year in which the variable is measured and for firm age and size class, sector and region. The sample is limited to firms with at least 10 employees in the first year and surviving for the whole period. Scalers grow in employment or turnover by at least 10% per year over 3 consecutive years on average, as defined in Box 1.2. See Box 4.1 for a detailed description of the methodology.

Source: Estimations based on microdata sources from Finland and Portugal. See Annex B for more information.

Global markets provide opportunities for scaling

Key findings on exposure to global markets

- **Anticipatory differences**:
  - Employment and turnover scalers in Portugal are more likely to export and import by about 25% to 60% compared to their peers before scaling up.
  - In Finland, the probability of trading grows by around 3 percentage points in anticipation of scaling in turnover scalers compared to peers; trade intensity (as measured by the number of export countries and exported products) also grows by around 5%.
- **Transformational factors**:
  - In Finland, the probability of trading decreases by around 3 percentage points in employment scalers as they grow; the trade intensity also decreases by around 5%.

Note: Results are only available for Finland and Portugal due to data constraints.

Selling products (or services) to foreign markets can be an important way to scale up for SMEs in the tradable sector. Going global can increase the potential for firms to scale up through several mechanisms. Beyond having the opportunity to sell their products or services to more consumers, they can also "learn from exporting" – i.e. improve product quality and adopt higher-quality standards – and optimise their sourcing strategies by choosing higher-quality inputs. Some evidence documents that access to global markets is associated with scaling up. Manufacturers in the People's Republic of China (China hereafter) that scale are at least occasional exporters (Moschella, Tamagni and Yu, 2019[16]). Similarly, the value of exports predicts scaling up in turnover in Croatia and Slovenia (Coad and Srhoj, 2019[17]). A sudden surge in export – e.g. because some trade barriers are removed – can underpin a demand-driven scaling model. At the same time, accessing global markets is an innovative marketing strategy that requires dedicated investments and can thus be part of a gradual innovator growth pattern.

Scalers increase their global market presence as they scale. The analysis of firm-level trade data (Box 4.4) shows that 20% of scalers in Portugal and 15% of scalers in Finland export before they start scaling up. By the end of the high-growth phase, 26% of scalers are exporters in Portugal and about 20% in Finland. Given that both countries are open economies with relatively small internal markets, it is not surprising that fast growth in size is intertwined with integration in foreign markets.

Box 4.4. Definitions and measurement of global markets indicators

Foreign trade data are maintained by customs agencies and their structure is harmonised across European countries. The data includes yearly information on volumes and values of external trade for each firm, classified by product and by origin or destination country. The traded products are defined using the Combined Nomenclature (CN) classification or the Harmonised System (HS) classification. In this report, only trade in goods is analysed as data are more readily accessible, although statistics on trade in services are increasingly becoming available.

The analysis relies on the consolidated six-digit (HS6) level of products and only considers imports or exports of a given product for a given firm if the trade is valued over EUR 1 000 in a given year.

Using the value of the HS6 product level identifier of exports and imports per product and country, the following indicators are used:

1. Trade participation
    a. Export status.
    b. Import status.
2. Trade intensity
    a. Number of export destination countries (products can vary across destinations).
    b. Number of products exported (count of different HS6 codes).
    c. Number of source countries (products can vary across destinations).
    d. Number of imported products (the same product can be imported from multiple source countries).

The indicators are aggregated on the level of the firm as an indicator of import or export status or count of products and destinations.[9]

Scalers "punch above their weight" by exporting as much as larger firms. Trade participation indicators show that future scalers in Finland and Portugal overperform in export and import participation in anticipation of scaling, with their propensity to trade being similar to firms of larger size to whom they eventually catch up after scaling. Turnover scalers in Portugal continue overperforming in export and import participation also after their transformation (Figure 4.8). Trade intensity indicators show the same pattern. Portuguese employment scalers export to about 5% more destinations and their portfolio of exported products is larger by a similar margin. However, by the end of the scaling, they resemble firms of their size (Figure 4.9). Employment scalers in Finland tend to have an even narrower portfolio of exported products after scaling compared to firms in the new size category, which explains the decreasing trend (compared to peers) during the transformation (Figure 4.10). The reduction in the number of exported products may reflect a strategy aimed at focusing on a limited number of core successful products as scalers consolidate, after a period of experimentation of different products in several foreign markets.

Figure 4.8. Turnover scalers are more likely to be engaged in trade than non-scalers

Difference in the probability of being an exporter between turnover scalers and their peers in Portugal, 2011-17

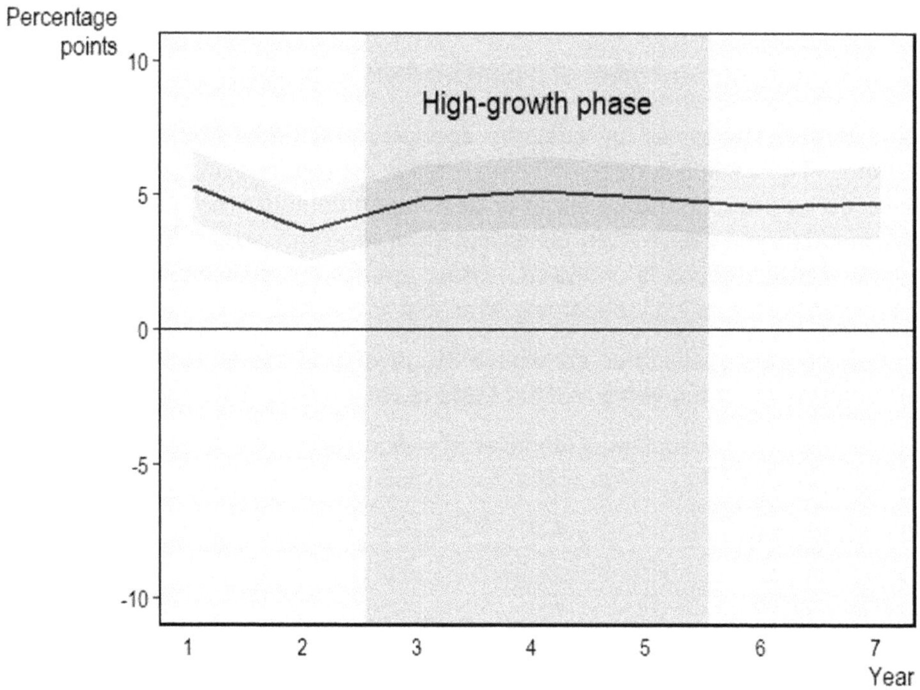

Note: The graphs indicate the difference between scalers and peers in the export status before (Years 1-2), during (Years 3-5) and after (Years 6-7) the high-growth phase. The years on the x-axis correspond to years 2011 to 2017. Grey vertical bands indicate the period of scaling up (scaling-up phase starts at 3 and ends at 5). The line represents yearly estimated values and the grey bands around the line represent 90% confidence intervals. The difference between scalers and their peers is statistically significant when the confidence interval band does not intersect the horizontal line at zero. Results are based on 190 339 observations. The regressions control for the year in which the variable is measured and for firm age and size class, sector and region. The sample is limited to firms with at least 10 employees in the first year and surviving for the whole period. Scalers grow in employment or turnover by at least 10% per year over 3 consecutive years on average, as defined in Box 1.2. See Box 4.1 for a detailed description of the methodology.
Source: Estimations based on microdata sources from Portugal. See Annex B for more information.

The timing of the increased exposure to the global market, as compared to peers, suggests that access to global markets is part of a scaling strategy. Scalers do not appear to grow because of a sudden increase in foreign demand, i.e. scaling does not seem to be a random lucky episode but rather a strategic choice to experiment with more products and destinations. This evidence is therefore more aligned to the transformation model of the gradual innovator that prepares its growth with targeted investments, rather than the demand-driven model in which growth is driven by factors that are external to the firm. The results also suggest that scale-up policies could aim to facilitate the integration into global markets, e.g. by providing related training or advisory services to the firm's management.[10]

Figure 4.9. Portuguese scalers "punch above their weight" by exporting as much as larger firms

Difference in the number of exported products and destinations between employment scalers and their peers in Portugal, 2011-17

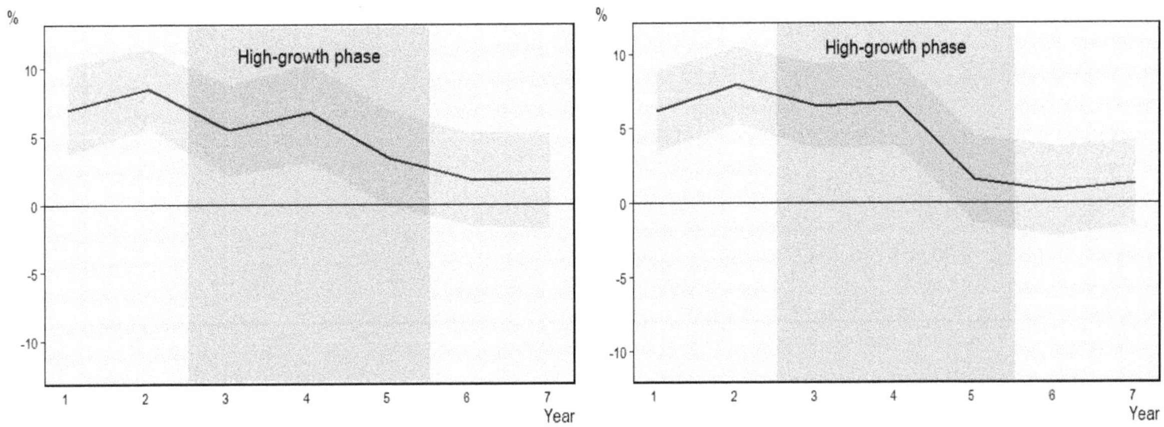

Note: The graphs indicate the difference between scalers and peers in the number of exported products and the number of destination countries before (Years 1-2), during (Years 3-5) and after (Years 6-7) the high-growth phase. The years on the x-axis correspond to years 2011 to 2017. Grey vertical bands indicate the period of scaling up (scaling-up phase starts at 3 and ends at 5). Scalers grow in employment or turnover by at least 10% per year over 3 consecutive years on average, as defined in Box 1.2. The line represents yearly estimated values and the grey bands around the line represent 90% confidence intervals. The difference between scalers and their peers is statistically significant when the confidence interval band does not intersect the horizontal line at zero. Results are based on 221 420 observations for Portugal. The regressions control for the year in which the variable is measured and for firm age and size class, sector and region. The sample is limited to firms with at least 10 employees in the first year and surviving for the whole period. See Box 4.1 for a detailed description of the methodology.
Source: Estimations based on microdata sources from Portugal. See Annex B for more information.

Figure 4.10. Finnish employment scalers export fewer products than peers

Difference in the number of exported products between employment scalers and their peers in Finland, 2010-16

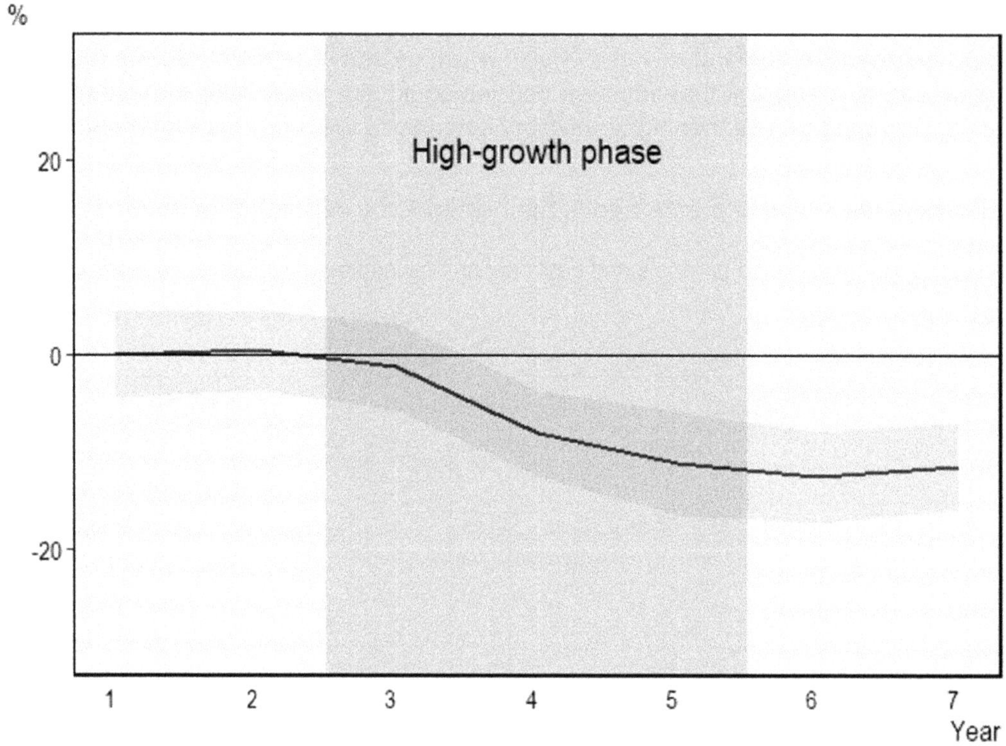

Note: The graphs indicate the difference between scalers and peers in the number of exported products before (Years 1-2), during (Years 3-5) and after (Years 6-7) the high-growth phase. The years on the x-axis correspond to years 2011 to 2017. Grey vertical bands indicate the period of scaling up (scaling-up phase starts at 3 and ends at 5). Scalers grow in employment or turnover by at least 10% per year over 3 consecutive years on average, as defined in Box 1.2. The line represents yearly estimated values and the grey bands around the line represent 90% confidence intervals. The difference between scalers and their peers is statistically significant when the confidence interval band does not intersect the horizontal line at zero. Results are based on 87 094 observations. The regressions control for the year in which the variable is measured and for firm age and size class, sector and region. The sample is limited to firms with at least 10 employees in the first year and surviving for the whole period. See Box 4.1 for a detailed description of the methodology.
Source: Estimations based on microdata sources from Portugal. See Annex B for more information.

Scalers rely on external finance to prepare to grow

Key findings on access to finance

Finance indicators are available for Italy, Portugal and Spain.

- **Anticipatory differences**:
  - Bank loans increase in anticipation of scaling in employment and turnover scalers (in employment or turnover) in Italy, Portugal and Spain.
  - The loan to turnover ratio is higher by 10% to 70% compared to peers in both types of scalers in Italy and Spain and in turnover scalers in Portugal.
- **Transformational factors**:
  - The percentage of current assets in total assets increases during the high-growth period by 2-3 percentage points in turnover scalers compared to peers across countries.

Note: Results are only available for Italy, Portugal and Spain due to data constraints.

Firms that plan to grow make different financing choices than firms with no growth ambition. For SMEs, challenges in access to external finance and an overreliance on internal funds are often major constraints for growth (OECD, 2020[18]). Scalers tend to be more indebted than peers, i.e. they managed to raise external finance. Scalers also pay higher interests per unit of sales – which points to a higher risk rating – and have a larger debt-to-asset ratio than other firms (Bianchini, Bottazzi and Tamagni, 2017[19]). High-risk ratings may arise from investments in innovative activities that may not be fully collateralised and are thus in line with the disruptive scaler model. A large amount of debt to support investments in productivity improvements is also consistent with the gradual innovator model. Bank loans, however, may not be the most suitable form of financing for young, risky and fast-growing firms, with limited collateral and uncertain revenues in the short term. Equity financing would be a more suitable instrument for these companies but market failures make it hard for SMEs to access them (Aernoudt, 2017[20]; Rodrigues, Tavares and de Barros, 2021[21]). Equity financing can include venture capital (VC), initial public offering (IPO), angel investments, private debt or other forms of asset-based lending.[11] While data on equity finance is not currently available for this analysis, their inclusion represents an important direction for future work.

Bank debt supports SMEs in preparing to scale up. The debt ratio (as measured by bank loans as a percentage of turnover (see Box 4.5 for details on definitions and measurement) increases in anticipation of scaling up in both employment and turnover scalers. For example, in Spain, the average scaler increases its debt ratio by 50 percentage points, which corresponds to a 35% higher share than similar firms (Figure 4.11). Borrowing spikes just before the high-growth period in both turnover and employment scalers in Italy and Spain and turnover scalers in Portugal. The debt ratio then tends to fall as the scalers grow, suggesting that the availability of finance is an enabling factor for exceptional growth.[12] The fall in the debt ratio at the end of the transformation also suggests that the new size gives more room for scalers to self-finance their operations and makes them less dependent on bank finance compared to peers in the new size class.

Box 4.5. Definitions and measurement of finance indicators

Finance indicators are extracted from firms' balance sheets. The following two indicators are included in the analysis:

- **Loans** include short- and long-term bank debt and other loans that are listed in the balance sheet. Loans are measured as a ratio of loans over turnover and approximate the propensity of scalers to borrow.
- **Current assets** include cash, inventory and other assets that can be sold quickly, typically during the same financial year. The variable is expressed as a ratio to total assets and proxy for firms' propensity to immobilise capital for long-term investments or rather to keep it in liquid form to deal with future volatility.

Figure 4.11. Scalers finance their growth by borrowing before scaling up

Difference in bank loan ratio between turnover scalers and their peers in Spain

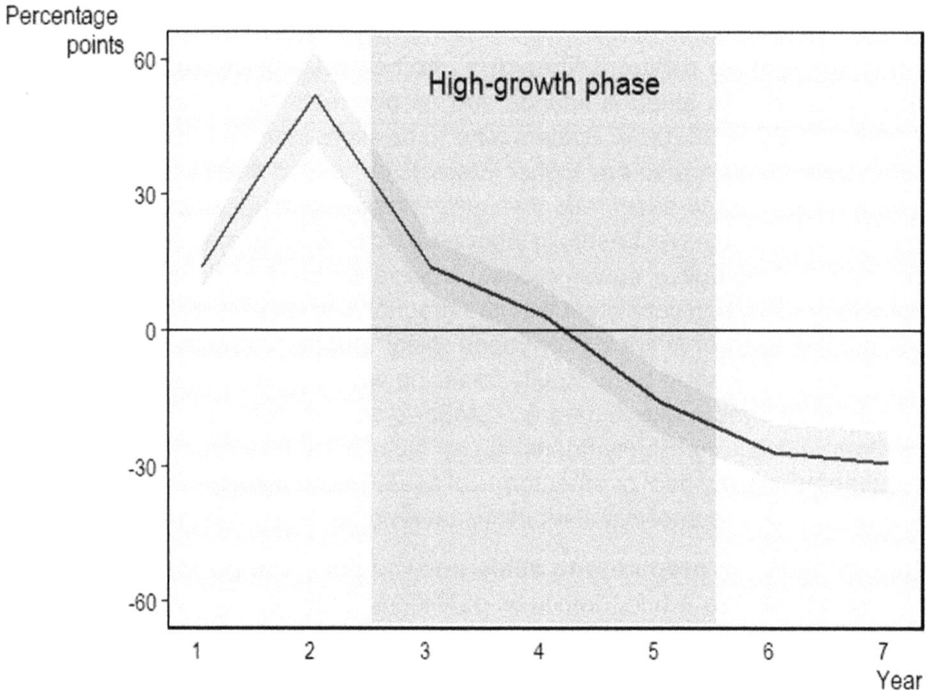

Note: The graphs indicate the difference between scalers and peers in loans (as a share of turnover) before (Years 1-2), during (Years 3-5) and after (Years 6-7) the high-growth phase. The years on the x-axis correspond to years 2007 to 2013. Grey vertical bands indicate the period of scaling up (scaling-up phase starts at 3 and ends at 5). Scalers grow in employment or turnover by at least 10% per year over 3 consecutive years on average, as defined in Box 1.2. The line represents yearly estimated values and the grey bands around the line represent 90% confidence intervals. The difference between scalers and their peers is statistically significant when the confidence interval band does not intersect the horizontal line at zero. Results based on 457 104 observations. The regressions control for the year in which the variable is measured and for firm age and size class, sector and region. The sample is limited to firms with at least 10 employees in the first year and surviving for the whole period. See Box 4.1 for a detailed description of the methodology.
Source: Estimations based on microdata sources from Spain. See Annex B for more information.

Turnover scalers accumulate a current asset buffer. During scaling, turnover scalers in Italy, Portugal and Spain increase the share of current assets in total assets by 2-3 percentage points compared to peers. Italian employment scalers show a similar pattern. Current assets include cash, inventory and other assets that can be converted into cash quickly. The increase in current assets among turnover scalers reflects a choice that can arise from a larger need for liquidity or expected future volatility in profits. For some turnover scalers – especially those for which the fast growth is demand-driven – the success may come suddenly and unexpectedly and thus the fast growth may indicate that a specular downturn may also be hard to predict and prepare for. Therefore, turnover scalers may opt to hold on to more liquidity and refrain from immediate long-term investment choices. External volatility in market conditions thus plays an important role for turnover scalers. In this respect, a policy and regulatory environment that is stable and predictable can help reduce some of the volatility and uncertainty to which SMEs are exposed. The refrain might also simply come from a lack of strategy for further investment. Unlike turnover scalers, employment scalers do not differ in their current asset buffer from peers. Employment scalers are likely to face less demand volatility as changes in the workforce are long-term decisions. It follows that they are less in need to accumulate current assets, which explains why their long-term investment pattern is similar to non-scalers (see Annex A, Table A A.4).

Productivity precedes scaling up, profitability follows

Key findings on productivity and profitability

- **Anticipatory differences**:
  - Employment scalers in Finland, Italy, Portugal and Spain are 5-15% more productive than their peers before scaling up.
- **Transformation factors**:
  - Turnover scalers across the 4 countries are 10-35% more productive than their peers after scaling.
  - In scalers in Finland, Italy and Spain, profitability grows during scaling up to become 15-30% higher for employment scalers and 40-100% higher for turnover scalers than in peers by the end of the scaling period.

Note: Due to data constraints, labour productivity indicators are available for Finland, Italy, Portugal and Spain. Profitability indicators are available for Finland, Italy and Spain.

Employment scalers are more productive as they enter their high-growth phase, to then align with peers as they grow. Across the four countries for which data are available (Finland, Italy, Portugal and Spain), the level of labour productivity (Box 4.6) is up to 10% higher in scalers than in non-scalers in the 2 years before scaling and in the first 2 years of the scaling period. Toward the end of the high-growth period, productivity levels align to those of non-scalers (Figure 4.12, left panel), indicating that output grows at a slower pace than employment. For employment scalers in Finland and Italy, the productivity after scaling is lower than in peers.[13]

Turnover scalers prepare for a new scale by hiring new personnel. The expansion of the workforce results in a drop in productivity in the year before scaling (Figure 4.12, right panel). During the subsequent period of high growth in turnover, employment grows on average at a slower pace. This makes scalers more productive than comparable non-scalers. The new productivity level is sustained beyond the high-growth phase as it is still higher two periods after achieving the new scale.

Box 4.6. Definitions and measurement of productivity and profitability indicators

Productivity and profitability measures rely on the information provided by balance sheets.

- **Labour productivity** is measured by the number of units of output per employee. The output is measured with turnover or value-added.
- **Profitability** is measured by the ratio of gross profit over turnover. Gross profit is calculated as the difference between turnover (or sales) and the costs associated with making and selling products or providing services.

Figure 4.12. Scalers are more productive than their peers

Difference in labour productivity between employment (left) and turnover (right) scalers and their peers in Portugal

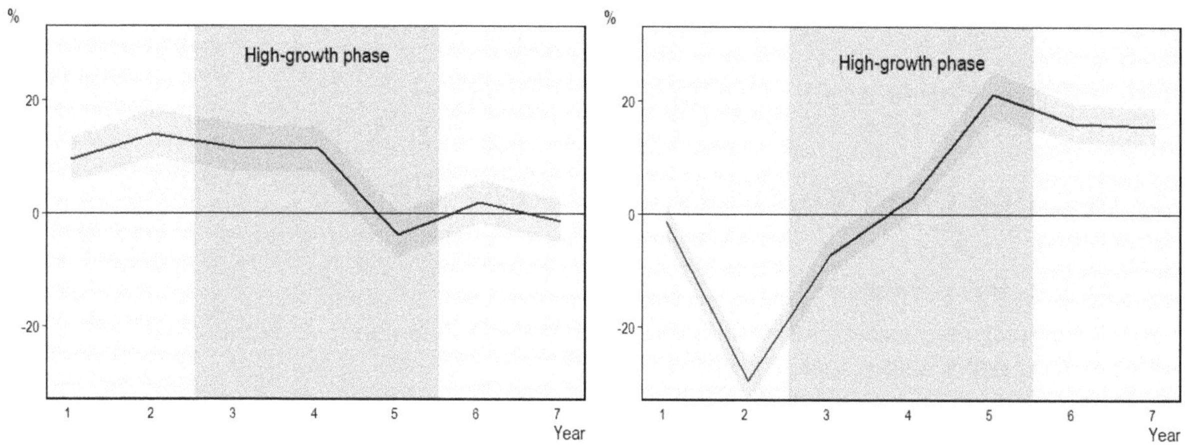

Note: The graphs indicate the difference between scalers and peers in productivity (measured as a log value of turnover per unit of employment) before (Years 1-2), during (Years 3-5) and after (Years 6-7) the high-growth phase. The years on the x-axis correspond to years 2007 to 2013. Grey vertical bands indicate the period of scaling up (scaling-up phase starts at 3 and ends at 5). The line represents yearly estimated values and the grey bands around the line represent 90% confidence intervals. The difference between scalers and their peers is statistically significant when the confidence interval band does not intersect the horizontal line at zero. Scalers grow in employment or turnover by at least 10% per year over 3 consecutive years on average, as defined in Box 1.2. Results based on 215 588 observations for employment scalers and 184 353 observations for turnover scalers. The regressions control for the year in which the variable is measured and for firm age and size class, sector and region. The sample is limited to firms with at least 10 employees in the first year and surviving for the whole period. See Box 4.1 for a detailed description of the methodology.

Source: Estimations based on microdata sources from Portugal. See Annex B for more information.

Scalers become more profitable as they grow – both in absolute terms and compared to peers. By the end of scaling up, turnover scalers become 1-4 percentage points more profitable than peers, which corresponds to a 40-100% difference, given that profitability (measured as profits as a share of total turnover – see Box 4.6), on average, is typically less than 5%. Before scaling, scalers are slightly less profitable or comparably profitable to peers, except for Spanish employment scalers, which tend to be more profitable than peers even before scaling. During scaling, the profitability of scalers grows by up to 4 percentage points, which explains the positive difference compared to peers. The profitability is a sustained change, as it tends to last after the new scale is achieved (Figure 4.13, see also Annex A, Table A A.6 for a summary by country).

Figure 4.13. Turnover scalers show steady growth in profitability

Difference in profitability between scalers and their peers in Spain.

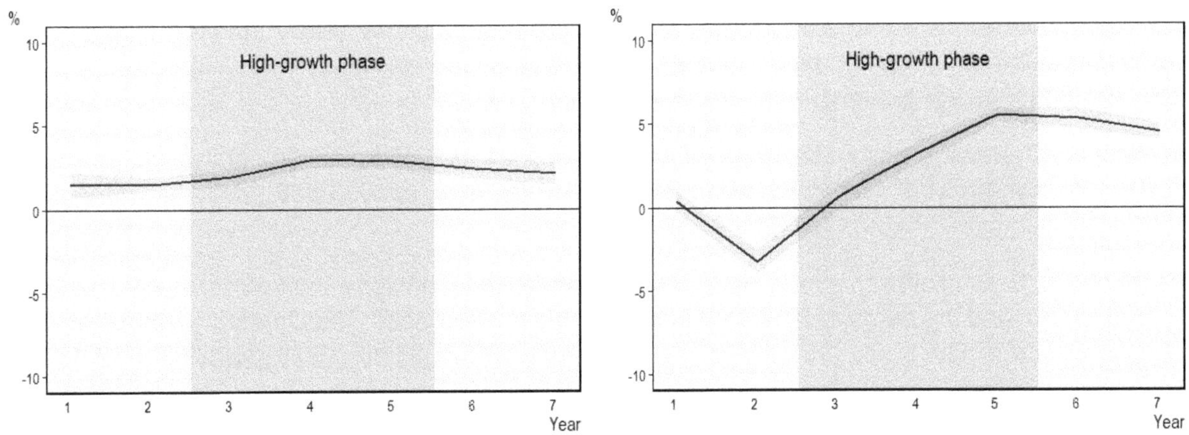

Note: The graphs indicate the difference between scalers and peers in gross profits as a proportion of turnover before (Years 1-2), during (Years 3-5) and after (Years 6-7) the high-growth phase. The years on the x-axis correspond to years 2007 to 2013. Grey vertical bands indicate the period of scaling up (scaling-up phase starts at 3 and ends at 5). The line represents yearly estimated values and the grey bands around the line represent 90% confidence intervals. The difference between scalers and their peers is statistically significant when the confidence interval band does not intersect the horizontal line at zero. Scalers grow in employment or turnover by at least 10% per year over 3 consecutive years on average, as defined in Box 1.2. Results are based on 457 561 observations for turnover and 494 309 observations for employment scalers in Spain. The regressions control for the year in which the variable is measured and for firm age and size class, sector, and region. The sample is limited to firms with at least 10 employees in the first year and surviving for the whole period. See Box 4.1 for a detailed description of the methodology.
Source: Estimations based on microdata sources from Spain. See Annex B for more information.

References

Aernoudt, R. (2017), "Executive forum: The scale-up gap and how to address it", *Venture Capital*, Vol. 19/4, pp. 361-372, http://dx.doi.org/10.1080/13691066.2017.1348724. [20]

Andrews, M., T. Schank and R. Upward (2017), "Do foreign workers reduce trade barriers? Microeconomic evidence", *World Economy*, Vol. 40/9, pp. 1750-1774, http://dx.doi.org/10.1111/TWEC.12486. [38]

Arrighetti, A. and A. Lasagni (2013), "Assessing the determinants of high-growth manufacturing firms in Italy", *International Journal of the Economics of Business*, Vol. 20/2, pp. 245-267, http://dx.doi.org/10.1080/13571516.2013.783456. [30]

Arundel, A. (2001), "The relative effectiveness of patents and secrecy for appropriation", *Research Policy*, Vol. 30/4, pp. 611-624, http://dx.doi.org/10.1016/S0048-7333(00)00100-1. [5]

Barringer, B., F. Jones and D. Neubaum (2005), "A quantitative content analysis of the characteristics of rapid-growth firms and their founders", *Journal of Business Venturing*, Vol. 20/5, pp. 663-687, http://dx.doi.org/10.1016/j.jbusvent.2004.03.004. [10]

Benedetti Fasil, C. et al. (2021), *High Growth Enterprises in the COVID-19 Crisis Context*, Publications Office of the European Union, https://publications.jrc.ec.europa.eu/repository/handle/JRC124469 (accessed on 17 June 2021). [9]

Bertschek, I., D. Cerquera and G. Klein (2013), "More bits – more bucks? Measuring the impact of broadband internet on firm performance", *Information Economics and Policy*, Vol. 25/3, pp. 190-203, http://dx.doi.org/10.1016/j.infoecopol.2012.11.002. [8]

Bianchini, S., G. Bottazzi and F. Tamagni (2017), "What does (not) characterize persistent corporate high-growth?", *Small Business Economics*, Vol. 48/3, pp. 633-656, http://dx.doi.org/10.1007/s11187-016-9790-1. [19]

Bresnahan, T., E. Brynjolfsson and L. Hitt (2002), "Information technology, workplace organization, and the demand for skilled labor: Firm-level evidence", *The Quarterly Journal of Economics*, Vol. 117/1, pp. 339-376, http://dx.doi.org/10.1162/003355302753399526. [2]

Cacciolatti, L. and A. Fearne (2013), "Marketing intelligence in SMEs: Implications for the industry and policy makers", *Marketing Intelligence & Planning*, Vol. 31/1, pp. 4-26, http://dx.doi.org/10.1108/02634501311292894. [4]

Coad, A. (2010), "Exploring the processes of firm growth: Evidence from a vector auto-regression", *Industrial and Corporate Change*, Vol. 19/6, pp. 1677-1703, http://dx.doi.org/10.1093/icc/dtq018. [23]

Coad, A. (2007), *Firm Growth : a Survey*, https://halshs.archives-ouvertes.fr/halshs-00155762 (accessed on 19 July 2019). [35]

Coad, A. et al. (2014), "Whom do high-growth firms hire?", *Industrial and Corporate Change*, Vol. 23/1, http://dx.doi.org/10.1093/icc/dtt051. [36]

Coad, A. and S. Srhoj (2019), "Catching gazelles with a lasso: Big data techniques for the prediction of high-growth firms", *Small Business Economics*, http://dx.doi.org/10.1007/s11187-019-00203-3. [17]

Daunfeldt, S. and H. Westerberg (2019), "High-growth firms and the labor market entry of first generation immigrants", *HFI Working Papers*, Institute of Retail Economics (Handelns Forskningsinstitut). [27]

Du, J. and Y. Temouri (2015), "High-growth firms and productivity: Evidence from the United Kingdom", *Small Business Economics*, Vol. 44/1, pp. 123-143, http://dx.doi.org/10.1007/s11187-014-9584-2. [24]

Gandal, N., G. Hanson and M. Slaughter (2004), "Technology, trade, and adjustment to immigration in Israel", *European Economic Review*, Vol. 48/2, pp. 403-428, http://dx.doi.org/10.1016/S0014-2921(02)00265-9. [14]

Geroski, P. (1999), "The growth of firms in theory and in practice", *CEPR Discussion Papers*, No. 2092. [31]

Goedhuys, M. and L. Sleuwaegen (2015), "High-growth versus declining firms: The differential impact of human capital and R&D", http://dx.doi.org/10.1080/13504851.2015.1076139. [28]

Hiller, S. (2013), “Does Immigrant Employment Matter for Exports? Evidence From Denmark”, *Review of World Economics*, Vol. 149/2, pp. 369-394. [37]

ILO (2012), *International Standard Classification of Occupations 2008 (ISCO-08): Structure, Group Definitions and Correspondence Tables*, International Labour Organization, http://www.ilo.org/global/publications/ilo-bookstore/order-online/books/WCMS_172572/lang--en/index.htm (accessed on 9 June 2021). [15]

Jovanovic, B. (1982), “Selection and the evolution of industry”, *Econometrica*, Vol. 50/3, http://dx.doi.org/10.2307/1912606. [32]

Lopez-Garcia, P. and S. Puente (2012), “What makes a high-growth firm? A dynamic probit analysis using Spanish firm-level data”, *Small Business Economics*, Vol. 39/4, pp. 1029-1041, http://dx.doi.org/10.1007/s11187-011-9321-z. [29]

Manaresi, F. et al. (2021), “Export management and labor demand. Evidence from a policy experiment”, Mimeo. [26]

McMahon, A. (2010), “Does workplace diversity matter? A survey of empirical studies on diversity and firm performance, 2000-09”, *Journal of Diversity Management*, Vol. 5/2, http://dx.doi.org/10.19030/JDM.V5I2.808. [11]

Mitaritonna, C., G. Orefice and G. Peri (2017), “Immigrants and firms’ outcomes: Evidence from France”, *European Economic Review*, Vol. 96, pp. 62-82, http://dx.doi.org/10.1016/j.euroecorev.2017.05.001. [13]

Moschella, D., F. Tamagni and X. Yu (2019), “Persistent high-growth firms in China’s manufacturing”, *Small Business Economics*, Vol. 52/3, pp. 573-594, http://dx.doi.org/10.1007/s11187-017-9973-4. [16]

Neely, A. et al. (2001), “A framework for analysing business performance, firm innovation and related contextual factors: Perceptions of managers and policy makers in two European regions”, *Integrated Manufacturing Systems*, Vol. 12/2, pp. 114-124, http://dx.doi.org/10.1108/09576060110384307. [1]

OECD (2021), *The Digital Transformation of SMEs*, OECD Studies on SMEs and Entrepreneurship, OECD Publishing, Paris, https://dx.doi.org/10.1787/bdb9256a-en. [6]

OECD (2020), *Financing SMEs and Entrepreneurs 2020: An OECD Scoreboard*, OECD Publishing, Paris, https://dx.doi.org/10.1787/061fe03d-en. [18]

OECD (2010), *Measuring Innovation: A New Perspective*, OECD Publishing, Paris, https://doi.org/10.1787/9789264059474-en. [3]

OECD/Eurostat (2018), *Oslo Manual 2018: Guidelines for Collecting, Reporting and Using Data on Innovation, 4th Edition*, The Measurement of Scientific, Technological and Innovation Activities, OECD Publishing, Paris/Eurostat, Luxembourg, https://dx.doi.org/10.1787/9789264304604-en. [22]

Penrose, E. (1955), “Limits to the growth and size of firms”, *American Economic Review*, Vol. 45/2, pp. 531-543, https://www.jstor.org/stable/1823582?seq=1#metadata_info_tab_contents (accessed on 1 September 2021). [33]

Publishing, E. (ed.) (2009), *The Growth of Firms: A Survey of Theories and Empirical Evidence*. [34]

Raes, S. (2021), "Understanding SME heterogeneity: Towards policy relevant typologies for SMEs and entrepreneurship: An OECD Strategy for SMEs and Entrepreneurship", *OECD SME and Entrepreneurship Papers*, No. 28, OECD Publishing, Paris, https://doi.org/10.1787/c7074049-en. [25]

Richard, O., M. Triana and M. Li (2020), "The effects of racial diversity congruence between upper management and lower management on firm productivity", *Academy of Management Journal*, http://dx.doi.org/10.5465/amj.2019.0468. [12]

Rodrigues, F., N. Tavares and G. de Barros (2021), "Drivers of exceptional job creation – A dynamic probit approach using portuguese firm-level data", *Portuguese Economic Journal*, Vol. 20/1, pp. 45-69. [21]

Spiezia, V. (2011), "Are ICT Users More Innovative?: An Analysis of ICT-Enabled Innovation in OECD Firms", *OECD Journal: Economic Studies*, Vol. 2011/1, https://dx.doi.org/10.1787/eco_studies-2011-5kg2d2hkn6vg. [7]

Notes

[1] The Oslo Manual, a joint OECD and Eurostat publication that provides recognised guidelines for collecting and interpreting technological innovation data, defines two major types of innovation that a firm can introduce: innovations that change the firm's products (product innovations) and innovations that change the firm's business processes (business process innovations) (OECD/Eurostat, 2018[22]).

[2] See, for example, Coad (2009[34]; 2007[35]), Geroski (1999[31]), Jovanovic (1982[32]) and Penrose (1955[33]). Raes (2021[25]) also provides a comprehensive review of SME taxonomies that have been developed in the economic and business literature.

[3] It is worth noting that these findings apply to the average scaler. However, the share of R&D employees shows large variation across sectors and types of scalers. For instance, in Portugal, about 60% of employment scalers in the period 2015-17 do not have R&D staff at the end of the scaling period, while in around 10% of scalers more than 1 out of 10 employees is working in R&D. The difference between scalers and peers for the latter group of R&D-intensive scalers are therefore likely to be larger than for the average scalers.

[4] See Goedhuys and Sleuwaegen (2015[28]) for Belgium; Lopez-Garcia and Puente (2012[29]) for Spain; Arrighetti and Lasagni (2013[30]) for Italy; and Rodrigues, Tavares and de Barros (2021[21]) for Portugal.

[5] Until 2005, the Portuguese university education awarded a degree after four- to six-year programmes. Implementing the Bologna Process, the system changed into two-cycle university studies: a three-year first cycle that leads to bachelor's degree, followed by two-year cycle that awards a master's degree. Most of the university-educated employees that are considered for this study received their degree prior to the system change. As no equivalent to bachelor's degree exists prior 2005, the measure of university-educated in this study considers all university degrees up to the master's degree-level combined. As the doctorate degrees remain unaffected by this change, they are examined in further detail. In contrast, the Finnish higher education offered by the universities corresponds to the Bologna system. The split of a master's programme into bachelor's and master's degrees concerned only engineering degrees. Hence, the education measures in this study differentiate between undergraduate (bachelor's) degree and graduate (master's) degree and above.

[6] Non-scalers, instead, hire disproportionately from the below 30-employee group but new hires account for a much smaller share of their entire workforce. Thus, the effect on the average age of the whole workforce is negligible.

[7] Research shows that foreign workers have complementary skills that help firms increase productivity (Mitaritonna, Orefice and Peri, 2017[13]; Gandal, Hanson and Slaughter, 2004[14]). Foreign workers are hired by firms that prepare to export due to their market-specific knowledge (Hiller, 2013[37]; Andrews, Schank and Upward, 2017[38]). Racially diverse upper and lower management increases productivity by lowering co-ordination costs (Richard, Triana and Li, 2020[12]).

[8] Studies on Swedish firms have shown that scalers are thus more likely to hire workers that are unemployed for short or long periods and also hire immigrants, young workers and less educated individuals (Daunfeldt and Westerberg, 2019[27]; Coad et al., 2014[36]).

[9] SMEs, especially the smaller ones, may not have the internal capacity to operate in foreign markets and may therefore rely on external service providers to import or export. Firm-level foreign trade indicators for SMEs may suffer from a bias originating from the presence of "aggregators", i.e. intermediary firms that channel the imported and exported goods and services of the producing firm. The share of exporting and importing firms may therefore be underestimated, as a firm that produces goods that are sold in a foreign market may not report any direct export flow in the customs data. However, there is no reason to assume that the bias may be systematically different in scalers and in their peers.

[10] The Italian government recent implemented a "vouchers for internationalisation" policy that aims at directly increasing export capacity by expanding the managerial skills of firms through a subsidized consultancy service led by a "temporary export manager" (Manaresi et al., 2021[26]).

[11] Although research on equity financing and scaling up is rare because of the lack of comprehensive data, some definitions of scaling up rely on thresholds of equity-based capital. For example, for Mind the Bridge, a global innovation advisory organisation with headquarters in the US, a scaler is a firm that raised at least USD 1 million of funding in its first 10 years.

[12] An absolute decline in the debt ratio is to be expected if firms borrow in anticipation of scaling as turnover increases during scaling up.

[13] Previous research shows that labour productivity, profitability and investment intensity are higher in firms that will scale up in the next period in either employment or turnover (Moschella, Tamagni and Yu, 2019[16]; Coad, 2010[23]). Firms that start as highly productive ones also tend to turn into high-growth firms in their life cycle (Arrighetti and Lasagni, 2013[30]). Similarly, firms with larger productivity growth are likely to become high-growth turnover firms (Du and Temouri, 2015[24]).

Annex A. Additional charts and tables

Sustainability of turnover scalers in employment growth

Scaling-up is a sustainable transformation for 40% to 70% of employment scalers, which remain at their new scale or continue to grow after the first high-growth episode. In addition, 14% to 32% of these employment scalers continue scaling up in turnover in the following 3-year period. The pattern of sustainability repeats for turnover scalers. On average across 4 countries, 59% of turnover scalers consolidate the new scale or continue growing. However, it is slightly less common for turnover scalers to turn into employment scalers than for employment scalers to continue scaling up in turnover. Between 10% and 21% of turnover scalers scale in employment in the 3 years after they scaled up (Figure A A.1). The lower probability of future employment growth for turnover scalers shows that it is more difficult to scale in employment and only a few firms undergo this transition. Employment growth can also be a predecessor of turnover growth. Firms that plan their business expansion might first prepare for the increase in demand by hiring the needed employment and, in the next phase, expand the output.

Figure A A.1. Turnover scalers are less likely to continue scaling up in employment

Growth dynamics of turnover scalers in the three years after scaling

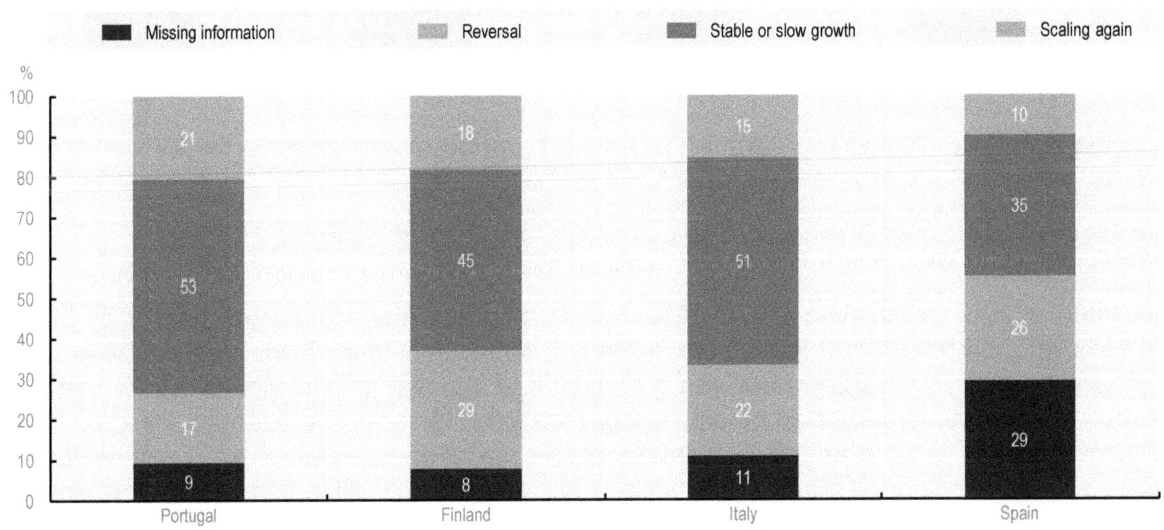

Note: Turnover scalers grow in employment by at least 10% per year over 3 consecutive years on average, as defined in Box 1.2. The sample includes scalers that end their first 3-year scaling period between 2011 and 2015 in Finland, 2004 to 2015 in Italy, 2013 to 2014 in Portugal and 2006 to 2015 in Spain. The sample is limited to the non-financial business economy. Owing to methodological differences, figures may differ from official statistics.
Source: Calculations based on microdata sources from four countries. See Annex B for more information.

Redistribution of turnover scalers by age group

The characteristics of the firm, including size and age, play a similar role in predicting scaling up in turnover scalers as in employment scalers. For example, the probability of being a scaler decreases with a firm's age. However, one notable difference is that there is a higher proportion of old firms among turnover scalers than among employment scalers (Figure A A.2). One-quarter of turnover scalers are small- and medium-sized enterprises (SMEs) established 21 years ago, while their share among employment scalers is 20%. At the same time, the group of young firms is smaller among turnover scalers. One-quarter of turnover scalers are young firms, compared to 28% of employment scalers.

Figure A A.2. Young firms constitute a smaller share of turnover scalers

Share of turnover scalers in all scalers by age category

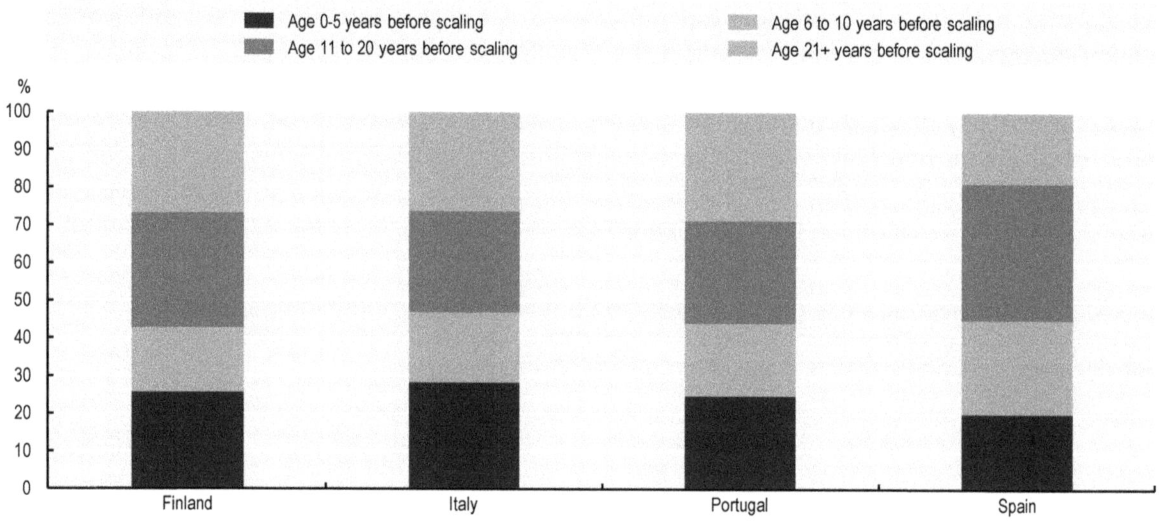

Note: Turnover scalers grow in employment by at least 10% per year over 3 consecutive years on average, as defined in Box 1.2. The sample includes scalers that end their first 3-year scaling period between 2011 and 2015 in Finland, 2004 to 2015 in Italy, 2013 to 2014 in Portugal and 2006 to 2015 in Spain. The sample is limited to the non-financial business economy.
Source: Calculations based on microdata sources from four countries. See Annex B for more information.

Employment scalers contribute to 47% to 69% of gross job creation and turnover scalers to 51 to 71% of gross turnover growth. Turnover scalers are also major contributors to gross job creation (38-65%). To a lesser extent, employment scalers are also contributors to turnover growth. Between 27% and 47% of gross turnover growth is generated by employment scalers (Figure A A.3). Although the contribution of employment scalers to turnover growth is smaller in size than the equivalent share of contribution to job creation by turnover scalers, it remains substantial when taking into consideration that employment scalers are 50% to 80% less numerous than turnover scalers. An average employment scaler, therefore, contributes a similar share to turnover growth to the average turnover scaler.

Figure A A.3. Employment scalers account for one-third of gross turnover growth

Gross turnover creation and destruction by young and mature employment scalers and other non-micro SMEs, 2015-17

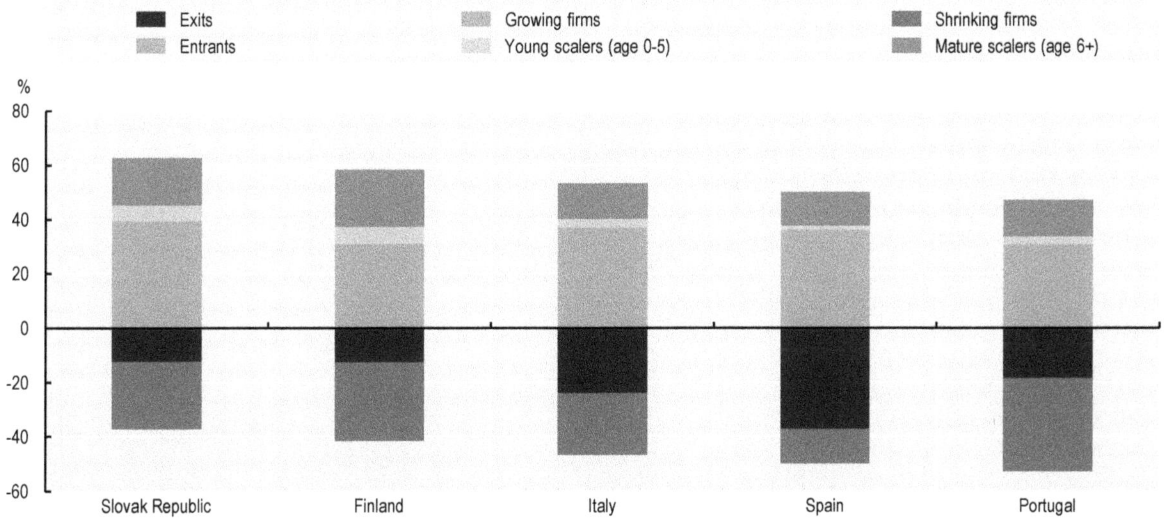

Note: Gross turnover creation is calculated as the total turnover added by all non-micro SMEs growing in turnover over the triennium. The contribution by each group of firms is reported as a percentage of the sum of gross turnover growth and gross turnover destruction in absolute value, which implies that, for each country, the positive and negative segments of the sum of the bars is 100 in absolute values. Scalers grow in employment or turnover by at least 10% per year over 3 consecutive years on average, as defined in Box 1.2. The sample includes firms with at least 10 and at most 249 employees. The sample is limited to the non-financial business economy. Owing to methodological differences, figures may differ from official statistics.
Source: Calculations based on microdata sources from five countries. See Annex B for more information.

Measuring and visualising differences in structural factors between scalers and non-scalers with econometric analysis

Structural factors are firm characteristics that change only rarely over time, such as size group, industry, and location of a firm, or they change in an expected, incremental way, such as age. The probability of scaling up for firms within the same groups of structural factors is estimated in two different ways. The first simpler approach consists of calculating the share of scalers within each group, e.g. the share of scalers among firms with 10 to 49 employees. However, this metric may be prone to a composition bias. For example, firms in information technology are more likely to scale but they also tend to be smaller; the higher incidence of scalers among small firms can be only a sector-driven outcome.

The firm-level data allow estimating the relative probability of scaling up controlling simultaneously for structural factors and this way reducing the potential composition bias.[1] The outcomes of the estimations generally confirm the results obtained from calculated shares within each group. For example, the propensity to be a scaler falls with the firm age. Firms in older age groups have a 7 to 16 percentage points lower probability to scale up than the youngest firms in Finland (Figure A A.4). This effect is an average difference across firms within the same size class and the same industry class, which means that the age impact is free of the potential influence of other structural factors.

Figure A A.4. Estimated propensity to scale up by firm age

Percentage difference of probability of being a turnover scaler in Finland as compared to young firms

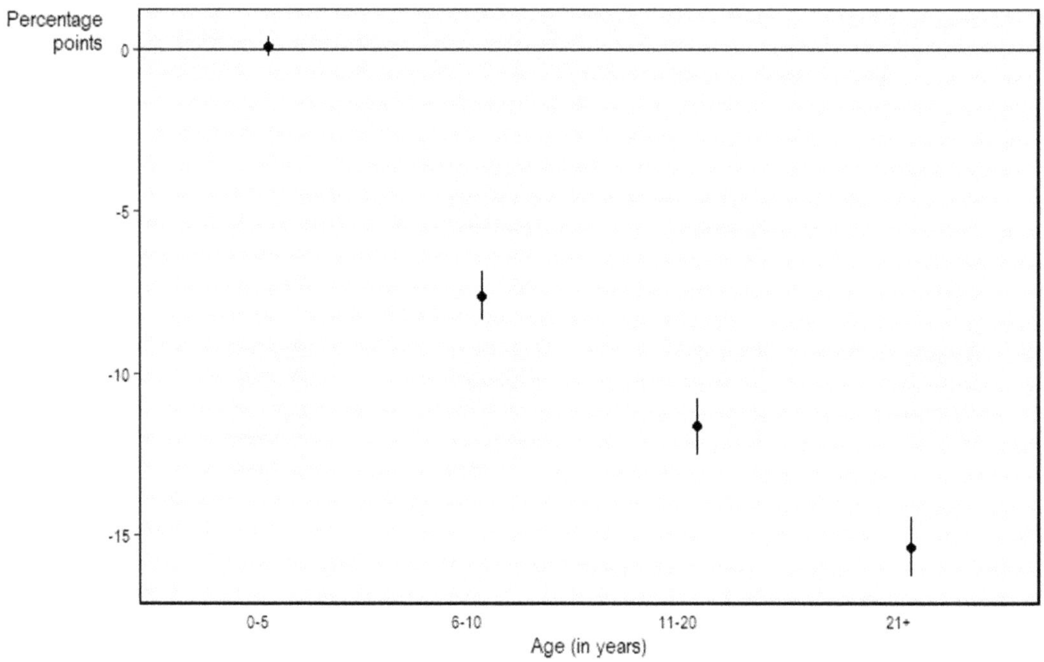

Note: Scalers grow in turnover by at least 10% per year over 3 consecutive years on average, as defined in Box 1.2. The graph indicates the magnitude of the probability to be a scaler compared to the baseline probability of scaling up among young firms. Points represent the estimated values and the vertical lines 90% confidence intervals. If the confidence interval crosses the zero line, the results are statistically insignificant. The vertical axis reports percentage differences in the probability of being a scaler between the given age group and young firms. The negative value implies lower levels as compared to the baseline. The regressions control for a year, size bin, sector and region fixed effects. The sample is limited to firms with at least 10 employees in the first year and surviving for the whole period. The sample includes observations from 2008 and 2018 in Finland.
Source: Calculations based on microdata sources from Finland. See Annex B for more information.

In some countries such as Italy and Spain, the probability of being a scaler among firms in different size classes is between 10-13% and smaller firms have a slightly larger probability to scale up. However, when age and sector variables are included in the evaluation, the marginal probability for firms of being scalers might increase with firm size. For example, in Italy, firms with at least 50 and at most 99 employees have a 1 percentage point higher probability of being a scaler and medium-sized firms with at least 100 and at most 249 employees scale half of a percentage point more than the smallest firms with 10 to 19 employees (Figure A A.5). In the results using simple averages by size class, the composition of age and sector has increased the overall probability of becoming scalers for small firms. Removing these composition effects shows that small size is a poor predictor of scaling up.

Figure A A.5. Propensity to scale up by firm size

Percentage difference in probability to be an employment scaler in Italy as compared to the firms with 10 to 19 employees.

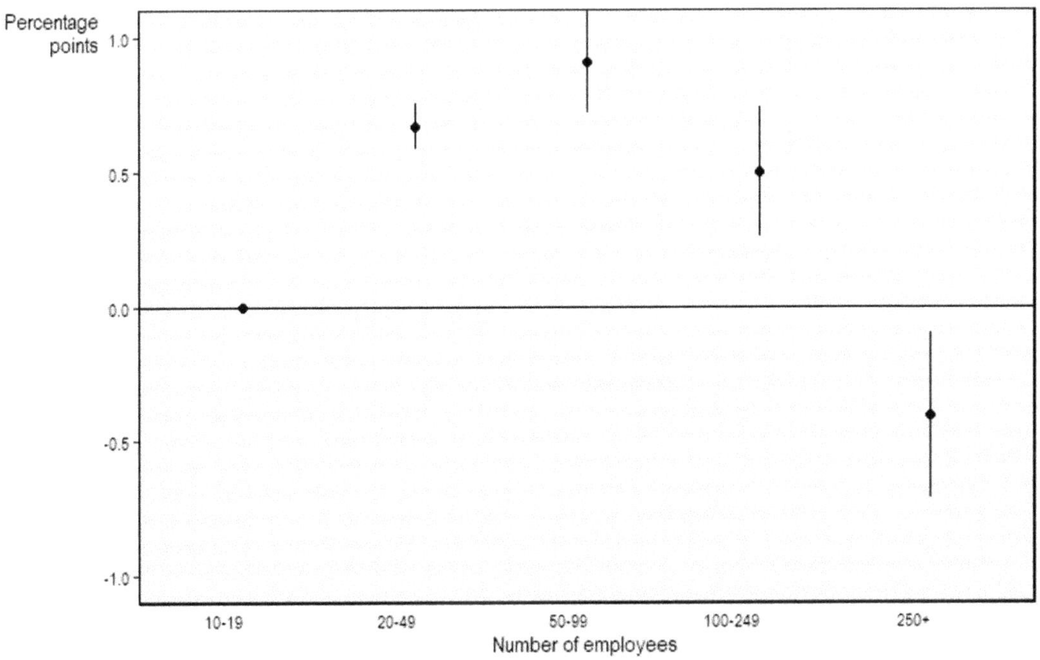

Note: Scalers grow in employment by at least 10% per year over 3 consecutive years on average, as defined in Box 1.2. The graph indicates the magnitude of the probability of being a scaler compared to the baseline probability of scaling-up among firms with 10 to 19 employees. Points represent the estimated values and the vertical lines 90% confidence intervals. If the confidence interval crosses the zero line, the results are statistically insignificant. The vertical axis reports percentage differences in the probability of being a scaler between the firms in a given size group and firms with 10 to 19 employees. The positive value shows that the factor is higher than among the baseline, the negative sign implies lower levels as compared to the baseline. The regressions control for a year, age bin, sector and region fixed effects. The sample is limited to firms with at least 10 employees in the first year and surviving for the whole period. The sample includes observations from 2001 to 2018 in Italy.
Source: Calculations based on microdata sources from Italy. See Annex B for more information.

Country-specific analysis of dynamic factors from regression analysis

The analysis described in Chapter 4 considers a broad range of firm time-variant characteristics, comparing scalers with similar firms that share the same predetermined factors (size and age class, sector, location) but that do not scale. The tables listed in this section summarise these time-variant characteristics for each country where the analysis was possible and for both types of scalers. The results are organised into tables by topic as follows: innovation in Table A A.1. , human capital in Table A A.2, global markets in Table A A.3, financial indicators in Table A A.4, productivity and profitability in Table A A.5, and workforce characteristics in Table A A.6.

Table A A.1. Scalers differ from non-scalers in higher research and development (R&D) and information technology (IT) employment intensity

Innovative dynamic factors in scalers compared to non-scalers

Dynamic factors	Finland	Portugal
	Employment scalers	
Always different	Human resources (HR) employment (-)	
	IT employment (+)	
Anticipatory	R&D employment (+)	R&D employment (+)
		IT employment (+)
Transformational		
Never different	Marketing employment	Marketing employment
	Management employment	Management employment
		HR employment
	Turnover scalers	
Always different	R&D employment (+)	IT employment (+)
	Management employment (-)	
Anticipatory	IT employment (+)	R&D employment (+)
Transformational		
Never different	Marketing employment	Marketing employment
	HR employment	Management employment
		HR employment

Note: The table summarises the results on dynamic factors related to R&D, digitalisation, marketing, management and human resource employment. The results are obtained from regression analyses and describe the differences of scalers and non-scalers before the period of high growth (anticipatory phase), during the period of high growth and after high growth (transformational phase). The positive sign (+) shows that the outcome in the given factor is higher in scalers; the negative sign (-) shows lower levels in scalers as compared to non-scalers. If the difference is evident during all or most years of the analysis, the dynamic factor is classified as "always different". If no statistical difference is recorded during the seven-year period, the factor is classified as "never different". The analysis compares scalers and non-scalers of the same size group, age group, sector and location within the same year (Box 4.1). Scalers grow in employment or turnover by at least 10% per year over 3 consecutive years on average, as defined in Box 1.2. The sample includes observations from 2010 to 2016 in Finland and 2011 to 2017 in Portugal.
Source: Calculations based on microdata sources from Finland and Portugal. See Annex B for more information.

Table A A.2. Summary of human capital dynamic factors

Human capital dynamic factors in scalers compared to non-scalers

Dynamic factors	Finland	Portugal
	Employment scalers	
Always different	Promotion of senior manager (+)	Primary education (-)
Anticipatory	University education: graduate degree (+)	University education (+)
Transformational	Low-skilled and medium-skilled (+)	Low- and medium-skilled (+)
	Low-educated (+)	High-school education (-)
	High-skilled employees (-)	High-skilled employees (-)
	University education: undergraduate degree (-)	PhD (+)
	Wage premium (+)	Promotion of senior manager (+)
Never different	Primary education	Wage premium
	Turnover scalers	
Always different	University education: graduate degree (+)	PhD (+)
	Promotion of senior manager (+)	
Anticipatory	Medium-skilled (-)	University education (+)
	High school education (-)	
	High-skilled employment (+)	

Dynamic factors	Finland	Portugal
Transformational	Medium-skilled (+ in the short run)	Medium-skilled (+)
	University education: undergraduate degrees (-)	High-skilled (-)
	Wage premium (+)	Wage premium (+)
		Promotion of senior manager (+)
Never different	Primary education	Low-educated (high school and less)
	Low-skilled	Low-skilled

Note: The table summarises the results on dynamic factors related to human capital. The results are obtained from regression analyses and describe the differences of scalers and non-scalers before the period of high growth (anticipatory phase), during the period of high growth and after high growth (transformational phase). The positive sign (+) shows that the factor is higher in scalers; the negative sign (-) shows that the factor is lower in scalers as compared to non-scalers. If the difference is evident during all or most years of the analysis, the dynamic factor is classified as "always different". If no statistical difference is recorded during the period of seven years, the factor is classified as "never different". The analysis compares scalers and non-scalers of the same size group, age group, sector and location within the same year (Box 4.1). Scalers grow in employment or turnover by at least 10% per year over 3 consecutive years on average, as defined in Box 1.2. The sample includes observations from 2010 to 2016 in Finland and 2011 to 2017 in Portugal.
Source: Calculations based on microdata sources from Finland and Portugal. See Annex B for more information.

Table A A.3. Summary of access to global markets by scalers

Globalisation factors in scalers compared to non-scalers

Dynamic factors	Finland	Portugal
	Employment scalers	
Always different		
Anticipatory		Exporter (+)
		Importer (+)
		Destination and source countries (+)
		Exported and imported products (+)
Transformational	Exporter (-)	
	Destination countries (-)	
	Source countries (-)	
	Exported products (-)	
	Imported products (-)	
Never different	Import status	
	Turnover scalers	
Always different		Exporter (+)
		Importer (+)
		Destination and source countries (+)
		Exported and imported products (+)
Anticipatory	Exporter (+)	
	Importer (+)	
	Destination and source countries (+)	
Transformational		
Never different	Number of products	

Note: The table summarises the results on dynamic factors related to access to global markets. The results are obtained from regression analyses and describe the differences of scalers and non-scalers before the period of high growth (anticipatory phase), during the period of high growth and after high growth (transformational phase). The positive sign (+) shows that the factor is higher in scalers; the negative sign (-) shows that the factor is lower in scalers as compared to non-scalers. If the difference is evident during all or most years of the analysis, the dynamic factor is classified as "always different". If no statistical difference is recorded during the period of seven years, the factor is classified as "never different". The analysis compares scalers and non-scalers of the same size group, age group, sector and location within the same year (Box 4.1). Scalers grow in employment or turnover by at least 10% per year over 3 consecutive years on average, as defined in Box 1.2. The sample includes observations from 2010 to 2016 in Finland and 2011 to 2017 in Portugal.
Source: Calculations based on microdata sources from Finland and Portugal. See Annex B for more information.

Table A A.4. Summary of financial factors

Finance factors in scalers compared to non-scalers

Dynamic factors	Portugal	Italy	Spain
		Employment scalers	
Always different			Cash flow (+)
Anticipatory		Loans (+)	Loans (+)
		Cash flow (-)	
Transformational	Loans (-)		
	Cash flow (-)		
		Current assets (+)	
Never different	Current assets		Current assets
		Turnover scalers	
Always different			
Anticipatory	Loans (+)	Loans (+)	Loans (+)
	Cash flow (+)	Cash flow (-)	
			Current assets (-)
Transformational			Cash flow (+)
	Current assets (+)	Current assets (+)	Current assets (+)
Never different			

Note: The table summarises the results on dynamic factors related to finance. The results are obtained from regression analyses and describe the differences of scalers and non-scalers before the period of high growth (anticipatory phase), during the period of high growth and after high growth (transformational phase). The positive sign (+) shows that the factor is higher in scalers; the negative sign (-) shows that the factor is lower in scalers as compared to non-scalers. If the difference is evident during all or most years of the analysis, the dynamic factor is classified as "always different". If no statistical difference is recorded during the period of seven years, the factor is classified as "never different". The analysis compares scalers and non-scalers of the same size group, age group, sector and location within the same year (Box 4.1). Scalers grow in employment or turnover by at least 10% per year over 3 consecutive years on average, as defined in Box 1.2. The sample includes observations from 2006 to 2012 in Italy, 2011 to 2017 in Portugal, and 2007 to 2013 in Spain.
Source: Calculations based on microdata sources from three countries. See Annex B for more information.

Table A A.5. Summary of results for productivity

Productivity in scalers compared to non-scalers

Dynamic factors	Finland	Portugal	Italy	Spain
		Employment scalers		
Always different				Profitability (+)
Anticipatory	Productivity (+)	Productivity (+)	Productivity (+)	Productivity (+)
			Profitability (-)	
Transformational	Productivity (-)			
	Profitability (+)	Profitability (+)	Profitability (+)	
Never different				
		Turnover scalers		
Always different				
Anticipatory	Productivity (-)	Productivity (-)	Productivity (-)	
	Profitability (-)		Profitability (-)	Profitability (-)
Transformational	Productivity (+)	Productivity (+)	Productivity (+)	Productivity (+)
	Profitability (+)		Profitability (+)	Profitability (+)
Never different				

Note: The table summarises the results on dynamic factors related to the productivity and profitability of firms. The results are obtained from regression analyses and describe the differences of scalers and non-scalers before the period of high growth (anticipatory phase), during the period of high growth and after high growth (transformational phase). The positive sign (+) shows that the factor is higher in scalers; the negative sign (-) shows that the factor is lower in scalers as compared to non-scalers. If the difference is evident during all or most years of the analysis, the dynamic factor is classified as "always different". If no statistical difference is recorded during the period of seven years, the factor is classified as "never different". The analysis compares scalers and non-scalers of the same size group, age group, sector and location within the same year (Box 4.1). Scalers grow in employment or turnover by at least 10% per year over 3 consecutive years on average, as defined in Box 1.2. The sample includes observations from 2010 to 2016 in Finland, 2006 to 2012 in Italy, 2011 to 2017 in Portugal, and 2007 to 2013 in Spain.
Source: Calculations based on microdata sources from four countries. See Annex B for more information.

Table A A.6. Scalers employ a younger workforce, more foreign workers and in some cases fewer women

Workforce diversity factors in the 2011-14 scalers compared to non-scalers

Dynamic factors	Finland	Portugal
	Employment and turnover scalers	
Always different	Employees' average age (-)	
	Age of top manager (-)	
Transformational	Foreign employment (+)	
	Employment scalers	
Always different		
Anticipatory		
Transformational		Female employment (-)
Never different	Female employment	
	Gender of the top manager	Gender of the top manager
	Gender wage gap	Gender wage gap
	Turnover scalers	
Always different	Female employment (-)	
	Top manager man (+)	
Anticipatory		
Transformational		Female employment (-)
Never different		Gender of the top manager
	Gender wage gap	Gender wage gap

Note: The table summarises the results on dynamic factors related to workforce diversity. The results are obtained from regression analyses and describe the differences of scalers and non-scalers before the period of high growth (anticipatory phase), during the period of high growth and after high growth (transformational phase). The positive sign (+) shows that the factor is higher in scalers; the negative sign (-) shows that the factor is lower in scalers as compared to non-scalers. If the difference is evident during all or most years of the analysis, the dynamic factor is classified as "always different". If no statistical difference is recorded during the period of seven years, the factor is classified as "never different". The analysis compares scalers and non-scalers of the same size group, age group, sector and location within the same year (Box 4.1). Scalers grow in employment or turnover by at least 10% per year over 3 consecutive years on average, as defined in Box 1.2. The sample includes observations from 2010 to 2016 in Finland and 2011 to 2017 in Portugal.
Source: Calculations based on microdata sources from Finland and Portugal. See Annex B for more information.

Annex B. National firm-level data sources

Finland

The outcomes from Finland were generated thanks to the co-operation with Statistics Finland.

The data is available for the years 2008 to 2018. The final dataset covers the business world in Finland.

The final dataset used for the analysis is compiled of the following sources that contain corresponding information:

- The *Statistical Business Register* includes the following variables used in the scale-up analysis: firm-level identifier, start date, end date, the field of activity, legal form.
- *Structural Business Statistics* includes information on turnover, value-added, EBITDA[2], purchases, total employment costs, number of full-time equivalent (FTE) positions.
- *International Trade in Goods Statistics* reports information on exports and imports for each trading firm by product and country. Data for International Trade in Goods Statistics are collected by Finnish Customs
- *FOLK* is a linked employer-employee register with information on wage, education, occupation, employee age, gender, nationality, last promotion, etc.

The Statistical Business Register is at the core of microdata linking. Data are aggregated on the level of the firm with corresponding shares from the employee- or product-level datasets and linked based on firm-level identifiers available in all data sources.

Employment is measured as headcount at the end of the reference year.

Italy

The analysis for Italy was made possible thanks to the collaboration with researchers from the Bank of Italy.

The sample used includes all corporations observed in the Company Accounts Data System (CADS)[3] database for at least one year between 2001 and 2018. For the period under analysis, the universe of incorporated firms (around 650 000 entities) is covered, which account for about 70% of the total revenues of the private non-financial sector. The data are carefully analysed as this database is used extensively by banks for credit decisions.

CADS contains detailed balance sheet information but the number of employees is reported only for a small number of companies. CADS is therefore complemented with Italian Social Security Institute (*Istituto Nazionale per la Previdenza Sociale*, INPS) data, which report the number of employees for the world of Italian firms, calculated as an average headcount per year.[4]

Portugal

Portuguese data is available for research in-house and is compiled and redistributed by the National Statistical Institute Portugal (*Instituto Nacional de Estatistica*, INE).

The data covers the universe of public-owned and private firms operating between 2010 and 2018. The final database is composed of the following inputs:

- *Quadros de Pessoal* (Personnel Records) contain information on all firms in Portugal excluding self-employed workers. The database provides the annual accounts of all enterprises incorporated under Portuguese law that are legally required to file their annual accounts with the Ministry of Employment of Portugal. These annual accounts typically contain the main figures on turnover, number of employees, date of establishment of an entity, as well as industry and location of a firm.
- The same database, *Quadros de Pessoal*, contains all employees working in firms with at least one employee. The dataset covers all employees in all establishments of a firm and is reported in October of each year. The employee-level variables include wages (normal and overtime pay on an hourly basis), occupation classification, education level and individual characteristics such as age, gender and nationality of a worker.
- Financial data are extracted from the *Integrated Business Accounting System* (IBAS), which comprises information reported by firms, from tax authorities and business register data. The data thus covers the population of companies. Information for firms that do not report in time is replaced by information from the business registry.
- Information on trade, based on customs data, covers firms engaged in exports or imports activities within or outside of the European Union and is defined at a firm-product-destination level. The following information is reported: number of exported and imported products defined with the 8-digit Combined Nomenclature (CN) classification, code of destination or source country, the volume of transactions and nature of flows (exports or imports).

Each firm is identified by a unique identification number, which allows tracing the firm in the cross-section and panel data.

Employment is measured as headcount in the firm in October of each year.

Slovak Republic

The output for the Slovak Republic is an outcome of co-operation with the Institute of Financial Policy (IFP), a branch of the Ministry of Finance of the Slovak Republic. The IFP provided part of the dataset for the OECD's inhouse research. For confidential data, the IFP co-operated with the OECD to produce the final output.

The IFP collects historical data on firms from several sources such as the Statistical Office, the Social Insurance Agency and the registry of financial statements and compiles the individual sources into one database. The final dataset covers a full business population of approximately 200 000 firms. The firms with different accounting standards such as the self-employed are excluded from the dataset.

The database starts in 2004 but the most reliable data are available starting from 2013. Financial statement reporting was voluntary for firms up until 2014, hence the 2004-12 dataset does not contain a full sample of firms and/or variables containing only a subset of firms. Therefore, the scale-up analysis focuses on the period 2013-18. Due to this limitation, it is not possible to compare non-scalers with scalers before, during and after scaling for the Slovak Republic. Data on firm employment from the Social Insurance Agency are available only from 2014 onwards.

The following sources of data are used:

1. The Statistical Office business register dataset, which provides information on the sector, location, ownership, employment size category, incorporation date and termination date.
2. Firms' financial statements, which report information from their yearly balance sheet, including value-added, profits, assets, loans and current/non-current liabilities.
3. Records from the Social Insurance Agency on the firm's total number of employees, the wage structure within the firm and the number of foreign-born employees.

Datasets are merged using a unique firm identification number.

The measure of employment reflects the headcount of full-time personnel in the firm.

Spain

The data for Spain is provided by researchers at the Bank of Spain. It covers the firms over the period 2003 to 2018.

The micro-level firm dataset used for this report is built using the data from financial statements that all firms in Spain are required by law to submit annually to the Commercial Registry (*Registro Mercantil*). Firms are obliged by law to provide accurate information on their financial situation, making the financial statements a reliable source of accurate information. The Commercial Registry regularly transfers to the Bank of Spain digitalised raw data on the financial statements submitted by firms. The Statistical Department of the Bank of Spain then processes and cleans this raw data according to exhaustive statistical and accounting criteria, resulting in the *Central de Balances Integrada* (CBI) dataset. This database is only available for inhouse economists and external researchers working in collaboration with the bank's staff on selected investigation projects.

Despite the continuous efforts to improve the coverage of the dataset, it does not cover private sector firms as it excludes companies that submit information late (after the regular submission deadline) or via paper format. One of the efforts to expand the coverage includes the acquisition of the SABI database.[5] The SABI database also uses the financial statements submitted by firms to the Commercial Registry but its main potential advantage lies in covering large- and medium-sized firms that submit their statements either late or on paper.

Employment data for Spain measure full-time equivalent (FTE) employment over the given year.

Annex C. Methodological notes

Data harmonisation

Comparability of results across different countries is achieved by reproducing the same cleaning procedures and estimation techniques as used on the raw data. The statistical package produced by the OECD includes the following data cleaning instructions, applied to all country source data:

- Firms in sectors (1-digit NACE 2[6]) A, B, O, T, U are dropped.
- All negative values of variables that cannot plausibly be negative (employment, turnover, export revenues, labour costs, fixed costs, operating costs, material costs, depreciation, interest costs, research and development (R&D) expenditures, intangible fixed assets, tangible fixed assets, fixed assets, current assets, total assets, loans) are considered missing.
- Observations with rare values of the variable *year* are dropped (e.g. observations that refer to the future).
- The birth year value is considered missing if it is a later year than the latest year covered by the dataset.
- The accounting indicators based on ratios (e.g. value-added over turnover, intangible assets over tangible assets) are winsorized at 1% level (i.e. values below the first and above the 99th percentile of the distribution are replaced with the value of the 2nd and 98th percentile respectively).

The sector groups

Firms are classified within the industry-standard classification system (NACE 2 rev.2 sector classification). The regression analyses rely on the 4-digit classification. Sectoral analysis aggregates the NACE sections into six groups depending on the intensity of high-technology and knowledge (Table A C.1).

Table A C.1. Sectoral groups with corresponding NACE sector divisions

Aggregated sector groups	NACE Rev. 2 Divisions	Sector names
Low-tech and medium-low-technology manufacturing	10-12	Manufacture of food products, beverages and tobacco products
	13-15	Manufacture of textiles, apparel, leather and related products
	16-18	Manufacture of wood and paper products, and printing
	19	Manufacture of coke and refined petroleum products
	22, 23	Manufacture of rubber and plastics products, and other non-metallic mineral products
	24, 25	Manufacture of basic metals and fabricated metal products, except machinery and equipment
	31-33	Other manufacturing, and repair and installation of machinery and equipment
Medium-high and high-technology manufacturing	20	Manufacture of chemicals and chemical products
	21	Manufacture of pharmaceuticals, medicinal chemicals and botanical products
	26	Manufacture of computer, electronic and optical products
	27	Manufacture of electrical equipment

Aggregated sector groups	NACE Rev. 2 Divisions	Sector names
	28	Manufacture of machinery and equipment
	29, 30	Manufacture of transport equipment
Knowledge-intensive services (KIS)	50-51	Water transport; Air transport
	58-63	Information and communication
	64-66	Financial and insurance activities
	69-75	Professional, scientific and technical activities
	78, 80	Employment activities; Security and investigation activities
Less knowledge-intensive services	45-47	Wholesale and retail trade and repair of motor vehicles and motorcycles
	49	Land transport and transport via pipelines
	52-53	Warehousing and support activities for transportation; Postal and courier activities
	55-56	Accommodation and food service activities
	68	Real estate activities
	77	Rental and leasing activities
	79	Travel agency, tour operator, reservation service and related activities
	81-82	Services to buildings and landscape activities; Office administrative, office support and other business support activities
Education, social care and health services	85-88	Education; Human health and social work activities
Construction	41-43	Construction

Note: The manufacturing sectors are aggregated using Eurostat's high-technology classification of manufacturing industries (https://ec.europa.eu/eurostat/statistics-explained/index.php?title=Glossary:High-tech_classification_of_manufacturing_industries). The service sectors are aggregated using Eurostat's definition of knowledge-intensive and less knowledge-intensive services.
Source: NACE division codes are extracted from https://ec.europa.eu/competition/mergers/cases/index/nace_all.html.

Identification of innovative activities in firms

The job functions that are used to approximate innovative activity in firms are classified depending on the keywords in the job function description. Types of classifications can vary across countries. For Finland and Portugal, job functions are classified using the International Standard Classification of Occupations (ISCO-08) classification.

The ISCO-08 classification provides a description of job functions with four different levels of detail for each job: major groups, sub-major groups, minor groups and unit groups. Each level includes a list of tasks typically required for the job.

The jobs that fall under the group "HR job functions" need to mention one or more of the following keywords: "human resource", "career", "training" and "staff development".

These keywords correspond to ISCO occupation unit groups as follows:

- 1212 Human Resource Managers.
- 2423 Personnel and Careers Professionals.
- 2424 Training and Staff Development Professionals.
- 4416 Personnel Clerks.

Management can be tracked by identification of job function groups, which have "management", "organisation" or "planning" in their title.

Management is represented by the following ISCO occupations:

- 1213 Policy and Planning Managers.
- 2421 Management and Organisation Analyst.
- 2422 Management Policy Specialist.

The digital technology job functions are all jobs that mention "information technology", "multimedia", "software", "programmers", "database", "network" and "system" in their title or job functions.

These generate the following list of ISCO occupations:

- 1330 Information and Communications Technology Services Managers.
- 2356 Information Technology Trainers.
- Sub-major group 25:
  - 251 Software and Applications Developers and Analysts (2511 System Analysts, 5512 Software Developers, 2513 Web and Multimedia Developers, 2514 Applications Programmers, 2519 Software and Application Developers and Analysts).
  - 252 Database and Network Professionals (2521 Database Designers and Administrators, 2522 Systems Administrators, 2523 Computer Network Professionals, 2529 Database and Network Professionals).
  - Minor group 351 Information and Communications Technology Operations and User Support Technicians (3511 Information and Communications Technology Operations Technicians, 3512 Information and Communications Technology User Support Technicians, 3513 Computer Network and Systems Technicians, 3514 Web Technicians).

Research job functions are the jobs that mention "research" in the title of their profession (excluding 4227 Survey and Market Research Interviewers) and as well as "research" among the first tasks in the description of the occupation.

These are the following job functions by ISCO-08 classification:

- 1223 Research and Development Managers.
- 21 Science and Engineering Professionals.
- 2310 University and Higher Education Teachers.
- 2351 Education Methods Specialists.
- 2631 Economists.
- 2632 Sociologists, Anthropologists and Related Professionals.
- 2633 Philosophers, Historians and Political Scientists.
- 2634 Psychologists.

Marketing job functions typically have "marketing", "advertising" or "public relations" in their job title. This includes the following jobs:

- 1221 Sales and Marketing Managers.
- 1222 Advertising and Public Relations Managers.
- 2431 Advertising and Marketing Specialist.
- 2432 Public Relations Specialist.

Each employee in the administrative dataset is assigned a value of one if their job belongs to one of the five groups of job functions, zero otherwise. The employee dataset is then aggregated on the firm level, such that it contains the firm identifier, year (if applicable) and a number of contracts/persons that worked in each of the five innovative job groups. Such an aggregated employment dataset is linked to balance sheet data for scaling-up analysis.

For other types of classification, cross-validation of identified job categories needs to ensure that analysis considers only relevant employees. Labelling of the job functions involves a correct and sensible translation of the keywords used in the data. Besides identifying the desired groups of job functions, other jobs with the same keywords may appear in a selection without characterising the targeted job category. For example, "management" can appear in titles or descriptions of non-managerial job functions.

Classification of workers by skill and education level

Education

The educational attainment of employees is categorised according to the European Qualifications Framework (EQF) classification. Employees are grouped in categories according to their highest-achieved education level as follows: i) less than high school education; ii) high school diploma; iii) undergraduate degree; and iv) at least a graduate university degree. In the case of countries where the education classification is different, the closest possible classification to the four categories is applied.

Skills

Employees are classified by the skill content of their occupations. Following the International Standard Classification of Occupations (ISCO-08), occupations are classified as high-skilled, medium-skilled and low-skilled (ILO, 2012[1]). Occupation refers to the kind of work performed in a job. The concept of occupation is defined as a "set of jobs whose main tasks and duties are characterised by a high degree of similarity". Skill is defined as the ability to carry out the tasks and duties of a given job and is a function of the complexity and range of tasks and duties to be performed in an occupation. Skill level is measured operationally by considering one or more of:

- The nature of the work performed in an occupation in relation to the characteristic tasks and duties defined for each ISCO-08 skill level.
- The level of formal education defined in terms of the International Standard Classification of Education (ISCED) (UNESCO, 1997[2]) required for competent performance of the tasks and duties involved.
- The amount of informal on-the-job training and/or previous experience in a related occupation required for competent performance of these tasks and duties.

Table A C.2. Classification of occupations based on skill requirements

Broad skill level	ISCO-08
Skill levels 3 and 4 (high)	1. Managers
	2. Professionals
	3. Technicians and associate professionals
Skill level 2 (medium)	4. Clerical support workers
	5. Service and sales workers
	6. Skilled agricultural, forestry and fishery workers

Broad skill level	ISCO-08
	7. Craft and related trades workers
	8. Plant and machine operators, and assemblers
Skill level 1 (low)	9. Elementary occupations
Armed forces	0. Armed forces occupations
Not elsewhere classified	X. Not elsewhere classified

Calculation of firm wage premium and the firm gender gap

The wage premium and gender wage gap of high-growth firms compared to non-high-growth firms are based on differences in residual wages. The estimation procedure follows three steps:

1. A Mincer wage regression is estimated, where log hourly wages are regressed on a set of worker characteristics, namely $tenure$ and $tenure^2$, age and age^2, $education$, $occupation$ and $sector$, using data from all workers in all firms. Based on the estimated coefficients from this regression, wage residuals for each individual are estimated by subtracting estimated from actual log wages. This provides estimates of the wage component of individual workers that is not explained by individual characteristics. This procedure controls for potential differences in the workforce composition with respect to individual characteristics across genders or scalers and non-scalers.
2. Two types of mean residual wages are computed for each individual firm. The first type assesses the average wage premium and is computed for all workers in a firm. The second type is computed separately for all male and female workers in a firm to assess the gender wage gap. The average gender wage gap in a firm is then computed by calculating the difference between the average residual earnings of male and female workers in a given firm.
3. Average residual wages and average residual gender wage gaps compare the wage differences between scalers and non-scalers.

References

ILO (2012), "International Standard Classification of Occupations 2008 (ISCO-08): Structure, group definitions and correspondence tables", http://www.ilo.org/global/publications/ilo-bookstore/order-online/books/WCMS_172572/lang--en/index.htm (accessed on 9 June 2021). [1]

UNESCO (1997), *International Standard Classification of Education - ISCED 1997*, http://uis.unesco.org/sites/default/files/documents/international-standard-classification-of-education-1997-en_0.pdf. [2]

Notes

[1] The probability is estimated with a linear probability model (LPM) at the firm level. The dependent variable is a binary indicator equal to one if the firm is in the final year of a three-year scaling-up period and equal to zero otherwise. The dependent variables are size class, age class and 2-digit sector categorical variables. The model also includes year fixed effects.

[2] Earnings before interest, taxes, depreciation.

[3] CADS is a proprietary database administered by CERVED Group Ltd. for credit risk evaluation. It collects detailed balance sheet and income statement information of non-financial corporations since 1982 and it is the largest sample of Italian firms for which financial data are observed.

[4] Neither INPS data nor the labour cost from CADS include independent and agency workers. Information on them cannot be retrieved from either of the two datasets. Although this is a strong limitation, integrating these workers would require estimating statistical imputation rules on a third dataset, and dataset of all active firms, access to which is currently restricted.

[5] The SABI (Iberian Balance-Sheet Analysis System) is owned by the market research company Informa-Bureau van Dijk (http://www.informa.es/en) and constitutes the Spanish input to the Amadeus and Orbis datasets.

[6] Nomenclature of Economic Activities in the European stastical classification of economic activities.

www.ingramcontent.com/pod-product-compliance
Ingram Content Group UK Ltd.
Pitfield, Milton Keynes, MK11 3LW, UK
UKHW051506290926
15471UKWH00008B/1452

9 789264 933453